Dress-alikes—the author, her mother, her doll

Studies in Popular Culture
M. Thomas Inge, General Editor

Shaping Our Mothers' World

American Women's Magazines

by Nancy A. Walker

University Press of Mississippi / Jackson

www.upress.state.ms.us

08 07 06 05 04 03 02 01 00   4 3 2 1
⊗

Library of Congress Cataloging-in-Publication Data

Walker, Nancy A., 1942–
    Shaping our mothers' world : American women's magazines / Nancy Walker.
        p.   cm. — (Studies in popular culture)
    Includes bibliographical references and index.
    ISBN 1-57806-294-2 (cloth : alk. paper) — ISBN 1-57806-295-0 (pbk. : alk. paper)
        1. Women's periodicals, American—History—20th century.   I. Studies in popular
culture (Jackson, Miss.)

    PN4879.W35   2000
    051'.082'09044—dc21   00-027341

British Library Cataloging-in-Publication Data available

CONTENTS

INTRODUCTION

This study examines American women's magazines of the 1940s and 1950s as participants in the shift in cultural values that redefined American domestic life during and after World War II. In the course of this book, I will investigate the magazines' multiple roles—as businesses; as advisers on readers' personal, social, and family lives; as expressions of editorial philosophies; and as sources of entertainment and information. I will also be concerned with the ways in which these periodicals interacted with other elements of American culture, including politics, the economy, technology, demographics, and fields such as psychology and social science. While American culture at midcentury was in many ways remade in the wake of a depression and a world war, and the magazines reflect these changes, certain themes that assumed prominence in magazines in the 1940s and 1950s, such as the woman as household consumer, were the culmination of trends begun decades before, so I will periodically return to these earlier decades to trace these developments. To bracket off the magazines at midcentury entirely from earlier cultural developments that informed the contents would be to deny the process of evolution in which artifacts of popular culture inevitably participate. Moreover, to trace the pre-1940 concept of the woman as household consumer, as I do in chapter 4, is to point up more sharply the contrast between the earlier emphasis on income levels and consumer goods and the postwar association between the purchase of products and the well-being of the family and the nation.

One point that will become clear is that at no time during their histories have women's magazines delivered perfectly consistent, monolithic messages to their readers. Indeed, precisely in the contradictory messages that the magazines frequently conveyed is it possible to see the domestic as a contested and negotiated concept rather than a proscribed and stable one. Not only have periodicals as different as, for example, *Good Housekeeping* and *Harper's Bazaar* made widely divergent assumptions about their readers' needs, tastes, and values, but even within the same magazine—indeed, even within single issues of the same magazine—various elements of the magazines' content have provided conflicting images and advice. To cite just one example here, the April 1934 *Woman's Home Companion* featured a report from a reader describing how she and her unemployed husband were making ends meet during the Depression by selling homemade meat pies to the workers at a nearby aircraft plant; a page later appears the floor plan of a house that includes a maid's room. While these contradictory messages appear to result from the editors' desire to appeal to a diverse readership during a period of economic hardship, the conflicting messages of the next two decades seem instead to originate in genuine cultural ambivalence about the shape of the domestic world that the magazines were helping to create.

The concept of the *domestic* is as vexed and elusive as many other ideologies associated with the World War II and postwar periods. As I use the term in this study, and as I believe it was understood by both the magazines and the larger culture at the time, the *domestic* means more than housekeeping tasks and the physical structure of the home, although these were important, especially to the large-circulation magazines that had historically addressed the household. The *domestic* also includes family and social relationships, child-rearing practices, personal well-being, purchasing habits, recreation, schools and neighborhoods, gardening, civic involvement, food preferences, health, and personal appearance. The emphasis given to these aspects of the domestic varied, of course, from one magazine to another, usually suggested by the periodical title. Thus *Vogue* primarily addressed fashion and upper-class social interaction, whereas *Good Housekeeping* focused on the practicalities of middle-class homemaking; *Mademoiselle*, with its audience of college-age young women, was concerned with education, appearance, and social life; and *Ladies' Home Journal* presented perhaps the most diverse and comprehensive conception of domestic life. As the postwar years went on and the Cold War increasingly linked home and family to national security, many magazines' definitions of the domestic widened in scope, taking in mental health and a perceived crisis in American education as well as an escalation of middle-class material consumption. During a time of intense nationalism, *domestic* also connoted that which was not foreign, from political ideologies to foods.

I argue in the chapters that follow that women's magazines in the period from 1940 to 1960 conveyed not a unitary but instead a multivocal concept of the domestic world during a period when that concept was being contested and expanded. The magazines at times celebrated woman's primary role as homemaker and at other times subverted that ideology. As businesses concerned with circulation figures and profits, they could not afford to alienate large groups of readers or advertisers; at the same time, their editors could not ignore the often dramatic changes brought about by war, increased affluence, alterations in employment patterns, and concern for national security during the early years of the Cold War. At the same time that the magazines—especially the service magazines such as *Good Housekeeping*—honored their traditional role of providing advice on accomplishing specific tasks within the home, their pages included debates on the nature and significance of the homemaker's role that reveal the cultural fluidity of such concepts as *home* and *domestic* at midcentury. And there is considerable evidence that the readers of these magazines did not absorb their messages uncritically but instead participated in the formulation of values that would be ascribed to a considerably expanded and ever-changing domestic world in which all Americans were perceived to have a stake.

American women's magazines have been a focus of study since Betty Friedan indicted them for contributing to the "feminine mystique" in her well-known 1963 book by that title. Many observers have followed Friedan's lead in regarding periodicals ranging from *Ladies' Home Journal* to *Seventeen* to *Vogue* as antithetical to women's autonomy and individual development because of the publications' emphasis on domestic responsibilities, physical appearance, and acquisition of consumer goods. Jennifer Scanlon, for example, in *Inarticulate Longings*, a study of *Ladies' Home Journal* between 1910 and 1930, argues that the magazine channeled women's desires for such things as economic independence, sensuality, and self-worth into longings for material goods: "The *Ladies' Home Journal*'s domestic ideology essentially urged its readership to expand their role as consumers rather than as producers, to accept the corporate capitalist model and their home-based role in it" (7). Using a different methodology and focusing on a different period, Ellen McCracken arrives at similar conclusions. In *Decoding Women's Magazines: From* Mademoiselle *to* Ms., McCracken analyzes the visual and verbal systems of women's magazines of the early 1980s, positing that "the visual, verbal, and sometimes olfactory signifiers in these magazines offer women multiple layers of signifieds; along with the pleasure come messages that encourage insecurities, heighten gender stereotypes, and urge reifying definitions of the self through consumer goods" (8–9).

While it is certainly true that, like all periodicals heavily dependent on advertising revenue, women's magazines have for more than a century served in part as showcases for products ranging from toothpaste to toasters, to view such periodicals as portable department stores sandwiched between glossy covers, having the power to divert the reader's desires from personal ambition to the purchase of a stove or a dress, is simultaneously to underestimate the reader's capacity to resist consumer messages and to overestimate the editors' desire to constrain women's aspirations. More importantly, however, an analysis that focuses primarily on the magazines' role in domestic consumption ignores these periodicals' complex interaction with the larger culture's values. Rather than attempting consciously to project a model of female behavior that conforms to what Friedan called the "feminine mystique," the magazines—in both editorial and advertising content—result from a series of negotiations with other cultural forces, including economic conditions, developments in science and technology, definitions of social class, changes in employment patterns and family configurations, and even federal government policies. In fact, the magazines' interactions with other facets of American culture, not the specificity of their primarily female readership, makes them revealing as cultural artifacts.

I do not intend in this study to defend women's magazines against their critics. There is no question that the magazines have been among the cultural institutions that promote consumer spending—sometimes deliberately, such as during the transition from a wartime to a peacetime economy following World War II. Nor can it reasonably be claimed that they have represented fully the diversity of American women's backgrounds, experiences, and values. Writing about the *Ladies' Home Journal* in the early twentieth century, Scanlon asserts that this and other magazines "obscured fundamental differences among women in every issue, creating in the consuming woman an amalgam defined and limited by race, class, and ethnicity but promoted now as 'average' " (6–7). While such a statement is challenged by, among other evidence, the series of cover illustrations featuring women of various ethnic backgrounds that Neysa McMein created for *McCall's* in the 1920s, the large-circulation service magazines deliberately, unapologetically, and early on defined their audience as primarily middle class, at least in part because that group was an ideal of mainstream political rhetoric and immigrant aspiration. And the magazines were certainly not alone in identifying "middle class" with "Caucasian" during the first half of the century. When the magazines' contents are examined in the context of the historical processes in which they participated, they emerge as dynamic elements of American popular culture, responding to and interacting with events and ideologies that had wide cultural currency.

Implicit in the various critiques of women's magazines is the argument that by featuring articles and material goods for the maintenance of the home and the family, the magazines encouraged a separate women's "sphere" not unlike that idealized in nineteenth-century rhetoric. However, not only have the magazines frequently addressed issues beyond the private sphere, but there is also ample evidence that particularly during the primary period of this study, concern with home, family, and all that is commonly associated with the domestic was by no means the sole province of women but instead permeated American culture. For some cultural historians, such as David Abrahamson, the primary impetus for this development in national values was economic. Abrahamson cites statistics showing that increased affluence, particularly in the postwar years, altered both spending habits and values. Between 1945 and 1960, the nation's gross national product increased by 250 percent, consumption of personal services grew by 300 percent, and new construction—much of it suburban homes—leaped by 900 percent. Further, whereas just before the Depression only 31 percent of Americans enjoyed a middle-class standard of living, in the mid-1950s that number had climbed to 60 percent (Abrahamson 10). The change, Abrahamson proposes, went beyond economics to attitudes and priorities: "Fueled by this extraordinary economic expansion, much of American society was transformed, and in the process the fabric of social reality was rewoven. In the tangible terms of the era, it is likely that most Americans believed that changes for the better had occurred. For many, virtually every aspect of material aspiration and social prospect was improved. Driven by the newly created wealth, marked societal change occurred in a number of interrelated dimensions. Matters of class and consumption, education, residence, and recreation were all affected" (10). Instead, that is, of merely spending more money on domestic consumer goods, Americans reshaped their values to accord with a new vision of cultural possibilities.

Lary May posits an even more sweeping shift in values in the immediate postwar period. In his introduction to *Recasting America*, May outlines a transformation from a national ethos characterized by conflict and by social movements that "validated an ideology of republican citizenship often in conflict with monopoly capital" to a culture in which "politicians and businessmen spoke with one voice in praise of the modern corporation and an affluent society where conflicts over scarce resources were a thing of the past" (2–5). May, like Abrahamson, links this shift to a heightened emphasis on domestic life. The "ideology of consensus," as May terms it, coincided with "an unprecedented domestic revival," and the "vision of abundant home life also provided a focal point for an unprecedented quest for personal fulfillment and consumption" (5). And, like others who have recently revised our conceptions of the 1940s and 1950s, May recognizes that corollary to this consensus culture were anxieties that cut in two directions at once: fears about failing to fit the corporate, middle-class mold and alienation from such norms as evidenced in, among other phenomena, film noir and the poetry of the Beats.

In capturing and conveying such shifts in consciousness and values, the women's magazines of midcentury, far from isolating women in an enclosed domestic arena, involved their readers in the culture as a whole, implicitly— and often explicitly—drawing connections between the home and the nation, the domestic and the global. Further, while most cultural historians locate shifts in national values and priorities in the immediate postwar years, it can be argued that women's magazines reveal such changes beginning in the immediate prewar period. Perhaps most notable in this regard is the "How America Lives" series begun in the *Ladies' Home Journal* in February 1940, which I will discuss in more detail in chapter 4. By seeking to introduce American families of different regions and economic levels to one another in the pages of the magazine, the *Journal* editors drew explicit connections between family and nation and between the domestic and democracy itself. In addition, during World War II, as I will explore in chapter 3, the women's magazines consistently linked the home and women's responsibilities within it to the war effort and the preservation of American values—not only in planting the well-known victory gardens but also in using dress patterns that required less cloth, cooking with nonrationed foods, and avoiding black-market products. While magazine editors as well as advertisers revealed deep ambivalence about women working in munitions factories, the magazines nonetheless viewed readers as active participants in the national struggle and presented the war itself as having entered the home.

Chapter 1 posits that the midcentury women's magazines participated in several ways in the shift from popular to mass culture that Michael Kammen analyzes in *American Culture, American Tastes*. Whereas in earlier decades the magazines had tended to emphasize individual choice and aspiration, by the 1940s the focus had shifted to a sense of collectivity and common purpose that can be seen to parallel the ultimate uniformity afforded by fast-food restaurants and television. If the magazines fostered certain kinds of conformity to a broadly conceived domestic ideal, they did so no more and no less than other aspects of the culture, such as designers of suburban homes, the growth of corporate culture, and calls for national unity against the threat of Hitler and then communism. Whereas in earlier decades of the century the magazines and those who chose to advertise products in their pages emphasized individual social mobility and personal choice, by the middle of the century they reflected the national emphasis on core middle-class values in which the home and its various activities loomed large. Just as important, however, is the fact that the magazines did not deliver a simple consensus message about either the domestic arena or woman's place within it, as Friedan proposed in 1963. The domestic remained contested ground: the woman who mopped the kitchen floor wearing high heels was also a participant in the political process; readers were already protesting that fashion models were unrealistically thin, and magazine fiction sometimes hinted at marital infidelity.

Chapter 2 examines American women's magazines in several contexts. One of them is as the target of criticism preceding *The Feminine Mystique*. Testifying to the perceived cultural power of the magazines are attacks on their messages that appeared in other magazines during the 1940s and 1950s. When we then look at what a variety of twentieth-century editors of women's magazines have written about their goals and priorities, however, it becomes clear that they regarded their readers with respect even when viewing their roles as restricted and that the editors were conscious of running businesses that had to negotiate among competing interests, including advertisers, the needs of the contemporary family, and trends in popular culture, technology, and politics. In a historical context, the midcentury magazines represented a culmination of more than a hundred years of publications that advised women on everything from etiquette to dressmaking. By the 1940s, the range of subjects the magazines addressed had expanded to include virtually everything that affected the middle-class home.

Chapter 3 deals with the magazines' depiction of the domestic during World War II. The war made dramatic changes in women's work patterns, with millions joining the paid labor force for the first time, often performing industrial jobs that had previously been the province of men. In their lives at home, most women coped with the rationing of food and fuel and shortages of products and appliances. While the women's magazines saw it as their duty to assist with women's challenges as homemakers during the war years, the publications were decidedly ambivalent about women's paid employment, frequently pointing out the dangers of neglected children and the strain of unaccustomed tasks. At least in part as a result of pressure from government agencies, however, the magazines consistently supported the war effort, particularly women's domestic contributions to it: planting victory gardens, volunteering in hospitals, and writing cheerful letters to servicemen. The resultant portrait of the American homemaker during the war is a curious amalgam of the public and the private, as women were continually praised as patriots for work accomplished in their kitchens and living rooms.

Chapter 4 addresses the class and racial implications of the magazines' content, especially in the postwar period. The relative affluence of the period encouraged millions of Americans to dream of—and, to some extent, realize—improvements in their material status. Consumption of both familiar and new products for the household increased at a dramatic rate during the late 1940s, and the magazines were an important source of information about such products and instructions for their use. The suburban home with its complement of appliances was presented as the ideal, representing freedom and democracy in the face of Cold War threats—a bulwark against external enemies and, implicitly, internal disruptions created by the civil rights movement, the communist witch-hunts of McCarthyism, and the Kinsey reports on American sexual behavior. While evidence of such internal upheavals did make their way into the magazines, the domestic arena was visually occupied almost solely by Caucasian Americans. The blatant racism that had been part of both the advertising and, to a lesser extent, the editorial content of the magazines before and during World War II largely disappeared in the postwar years, but the ideal presented by the magazines, like other social institutions of the era, for the most part regarded African Americans and other racial groups as "other."

Chapter 5 examines the role of the "expert" in domestic life. If the late nineteenth century had seen the rise of "scientific" housekeeping, focused primarily on the accomplishment of specific tasks such as cooking and cleaning, the magazines' advice in the mid–twentieth century dealt at least as much with the emotional well-being of home and family. Psychologists, marriage counselors, sociologists, and doctors offered assistance on everything from raising children to improving marital happiness to diagnosing medical problems. The implications of this plethora of expert advice were twofold: readers were responsible for not only the daily maintenance of the household but also for its members' emotional and psychological well-being, and they needed a great deal of assistance in performing such a wide variety of tasks. Instructions for the more routine aspects of homemaking, however, not only failed to disappear but instead became in some ways more demanding. With the help of reliable stoves, electric mixers and blenders, and a host of other "labor-saving" devices, there seemed no reason why the home could not offer more elaborate meals, more order and cleanliness, more harmonious decor, and, by implication, a stronger national fabric.

The final chapter concentrates on the latter years of the period, in particular the changes in defining the domestic that can be seen as prelude to the renewed women's movement of the 1960s and 1970s. While the women's magazines offered a version of the domestic that would have worked against certain avenues to women's personal fulfillment, there are also signs of changes that would lead to inevitable alterations in family structure, social aspirations, and the function of the home within society. As shopping malls, interstate highways, fast-food restaurants, and motels spoke of a more decentralized family life, and as television urged levels of consumption that increased the number of dual-career marriages, the magazines, while not retreating from the celebration of the domestic, were forced to recognize that women wanted a different kind of voice in the culture.

Central to this study are the magazines most heavily invested in women as homemakers: *Ladies' Home Journal, Good Housekeeping, McCall's,* and *Woman's Home Companion.* As the oldest of the women's magazines with the largest circulations at midcentury, they had weathered decades of social change and were read by millions of women. The other magazines from which I have drawn material appealed to more selected audiences. *Vogue* and *Harper's Bazaar* targeted affluent readers interested in the latest fashions; *Mademoiselle* shared a focus on fashion but was intended for college-age women, whereas *Seventeen* was virtually a manual of how to be a successful teenage girl. *Glamour's* readership was young women between eighteen and thirty-four, and *Redbook* was nearing the end of its transition from a fiction periodical to a women's magazine; by the early 1950s it advertised itself as "The Magazine for Young Adults," although the product advertising would have appealed primarily to female readers. *Cosmopolitan* was also evolving during this period from its nineteenth-century origins as an intellectual monthly to its 1960s orientation as a magazine for young career women. *Better Homes and Gardens*, which began publication in 1922, was intended for both male and female readers, but its emphasis on domestic spaces contributed to the midcentury dialogue about women and homemaking.[1] All of these magazines advised readers on multiple aspects of their lives, no matter what their primary emphasis. *Vogue*, for example, included features on travel and food as well as fashion, and *Glamour* published a regular cooking article, which culminated in *The Glamour Magazine After Five Cookbook*, published in 1952. Even though the magazine was intended for what was then called the "working girl," it acknowledged that the woman with a full-time job still faced "the insurmountable problem of preparing an original meal for her husband or companion" (Pepper n.p.). In short, even the more specialized magazines addressed a broad spectrum of women's experiences.

Ironically, the fact that women's magazines presented domestic life as complex and multifaceted both made these periodicals central to the midcentury valorizing of home, family, and the middle class and inspired contemporary accusations that they condescended to readers, who were presumed to need a wide array of instruction. While articles on fashion, childhood diseases, and kitchen appliances could suggest that domestic life was broad enough to include personal appearance, medicine, and technology, such a range of subjects could also be interpreted to mean that the women who were the magazines' primary readers were singlehandedly responsible for everything that affected domestic life or that they were not perceived as capable of deciding how to dress or of choosing their own electric mixers. Those who criticized the magazines in informal essays at midcentury, as well as those who have done so more recently from a scholarly perspective, have viewed these publications as prescriptive texts that set standards for household work and behavior. While such a view is partially justified, not least by the magazines' continuity with nineteenth-century etiquette manuals and conduct books, it is equally valid to see the journals as texts that reflected and described cultural changes occurring quite outside their editorial control.

It would be disingenuous for me to pretend that my interest in the women's magazines of this period is purely scholarly. In a 1952 snapshot, I stand beside my mother in front of a 1950 Buick. My mother and I and the doll I am holding in my right hand wear matching aprons. The apron patterns had appeared, I am sure, in *McCall's*, and they would have presented only a mild challenge to my mother's skill with needle and sewing machine. In many ways my childhood must have been shaped by *Ladies' Home Journal* and *McCall's*, as my teenage years were later informed by *Seventeen* and *Mademoiselle*. When I began doing research on women's magazines in the mid-1990s, then, I encountered a world that seemed remote and familiar at the same time. Long since taught to be critical of media messages, I nonetheless felt the power of this particular medium to project an orderly, stable world of tuna casseroles and matching aprons. But almost as quickly I saw the disorder and doubt that also characterized the middle decades of the century. Countless articles on achieving marital harmony spoke to widespread disharmony; amid all the high-heeled women using vacuum cleaners, Eleanor Roosevelt answered questions from the White House; fashion layouts in *Vogue* presented a world hardly imagined in my barely middle class upbringing, which, in those long-ago days in the South, could nonetheless include a once-a-week black housekeeper whose true existence was nowhere to be found in *Good Housekeeping*. This book has been both a personal and a professional journey, and I hope that the former has invested the latter with a sense of purpose and energy.

Shaping Our Mothers' World

CHAPTER 1

Magazines and Culture in Transition

From Popular to Mass

The World War II and postwar decades fall, significantly, in the period that Michael Kammen has identified as transitional between the era of popular culture and the era of mass culture, a transition that Kammen dates from the mid-1930s to the mid-1960s. Of the two major criteria that Kammen uses to distinguish between popular and mass culture, the one he regards as less important has to do with scale—for example, "thousands of people at an amusement park as opposed to many tens of millions worldwide watching the Super Bowl in January." More significant is the individual's relation to the cultural phenomenon; Kammen regards popular culture *"more often than not . . .* as participatory and interactive, whereas mass culture . . . induced passivity and the privatization of culture" (21–22). Kammen believes the years of World War II to be crucial to the eventual development of a true mass culture. With incomes rising for many Americans but consumer goods such as cars and clothing in short supply, people spent disposable income on entertainment such as films, nightclubs, and books, notably murder mysteries and self-help volumes. Not only did consumption increase, it became more standardized: for example, whereas in 1939 there were 3,900 supermarkets in the United States, by 1944 there were more than 16,000 (59–60). In the same year, the launching of *Seventeen* magazine recognized the existence of a teenaged subculture with interests and spending habits in common (62). In addition, Kammen posits that during the same midcentury period, cultural authority, as represented by intellectual elites such as critics and museums, began to give way to cultural power, dependent not on knowledge but on the "production, promotion, and dissemination of cultural artifacts" (137). Those entities chiefly responsible for the rise of cultural power included "national media . . . , Hollywood, public relations and advertising agencies, large corporations, and even government" (138).

Although it would not be accurate to claim that midcentury women's magazines were a manifestation of mass culture—certainly not in the way that television became by the 1960s—they do reflect in significant ways the cultural transitions that Kammen describes. First, they can be said to straddle popular and mass culture as Kammen distinguishes them. While the act of reading a magazine that millions of others are also reading may be described as passive, the magazines concurrently encouraged certain forms of action— for example, baking a cake, choosing a new brand of soap, voting in elections—and even interactivity in the form of letters to the editor and reader polls on various issues. Second, the magazines participated in the shift from cultural authority to cultural power that Kammen delineates. While one of the functions of women's magazines has always been to provide instruction—indeed, the magazines' role as teachers of everything from how to dust to how to improve a marriage has been a frequent target of critics—the nature of the lessons, who taught them, and who the students were assumed to be underwent dramatic and telling changes between the 1920s and 1930s and the 1950s. In the 1920s, for example, the *Ladies' Home Journal* published a series of articles on the "Makers of American Literature" by William Lyon Phelps, an English professor at Yale, which featured such writers as Ralph Waldo Emerson and Walt Whitman. The February 1932 issue of *Woman's Home Companion* included an article on the major issues in that year's presidential campaign as seen by such commentators as Jane Addams, the president of Mt. Holyoke College, and a former vice president of the Women's Democratic National Committee. By the 1950s, however, such literary and political authority was overshadowed by articles on marriage by staff psychologists and recipes for trendy dinner parties by staff home economists. Even though, as I will discuss in chapter 5, the pages of postwar magazines were filled with advice from "experts," they tended to represent various bureaucratic "institutes" instead of the cultural authority of previous decades.

Rather than presenting an image of a middle-class domestic culture of consensus, the women's magazines of the decades between the world wars tended to stress individual social aspiration and self-development. During the 1920s, *Ladies' Home Journal* routinely featured Parisian fashions, and the April 1923 issue also featured an article on making classic French sauces. The same issue included a lengthy article about America's most exclusive social circles that openly acknowledged America's distinct class system. Although the author lamented the fact that wealth, not merely family background, could admit families to the upper echelons, she was candid about the existence of a social hierarchy: "Politically, America advances the theory that all men are born free and equal. Practically, the nation admits no such thing. If there were this equality there would be no more or less exclusive social circles, hemmed about with aspirants." Moreover, she traced American high society to European aristocracies and credited this social level with the best that American culture had to offer: "The American social system is an offshoot from European aristocracy. Its beginnings were planted in this country by representatives of ancient nobilities who came and settled here. . . . Society . . . represents the cream of the nation's culture." Less than twenty years later, in the December 1940 segment of its "How America Lives" series, the *Journal* announced a radically different stance: at the beginning of the profile of one of America's wealthiest families, the editors stressed the ideal of equality that the author of the 1923 article had dismissed as mere rhetoric: "America is proud to have no aristocracy."

On the issue of women working outside the home, the magazines of the 1920s and 1930s were far less ambivalent than they would be two decades later, when the domestic ideal had become pervasive. In the April 1923 *Journal*, the editor, Barton W. Currie, wrote glowingly of a U.S. Department of Labor–sponsored conference on working women: "It is a pretty fine thing to contemplate," Currie wrote, "this upbuilding of a feminine democracy where all women wish to be workers together." The March 1930 *Journal* featured an article on "Women in Business" that encouraged women to assess carefully their skills and interests to select the most suitable professions. The author did not limit herself to stereotypically feminine careers but included sculpture and painting (citing Mary Cassatt and Georgia O'Keeffe as role models), architecture, law, science, and medicine. In the March 1933 *Delineator*,[1] novelist Frances Parkinson Keyes contributed an admiring profile of Mary T. Norton, member of the House of Representatives from New Jersey and the first woman to chair a congressional committee. Three years earlier, in the January 1930 *Delineator,* Keyes had written about balancing her career as a writer with her duties as the mother of three sons and the wife of a U.S. Senator. In sharp contrast to articles about the difficulties of juggling two sets of responsibilities that appeared in later decades, Keyes did not engage in agonized soul-searching about the validity of her career aspirations but merely described the allocation of her time and priorities. And in the period immediately following the female suffrage amendment, an editorial in the September 1923 *Ladies' Home Journal* expressed outrage at male efforts to keep women out of politics lest they disturb "the good old comfortable and profitable methods of party management and lawmaking."

No doubt facilitating such encouragement of women's participation in business and politics during this period was a general sense that labor-saving technology had advanced to the point at which domestic chores were no longer particularly burdensome. In "The Old Order Changeth," in the August 1930 *Delineator,* home economist Grace L. Pennock hailed the frequent arrival of "some new household product that indicates progress, saves time and effort in the routine of housework, and serves to point out how rapidly our standards of living are changing." In sharp contrast to the post–World War II period, in which new devices were touted as encouragement for women to meet ever higher standards of cooking and cleaning, Pennock stresses the time-saving features of electric refrigerators, irons, and kitchen cabinets. The June 1929 *Ladies' Home Journal* proclaimed "The New Era in Housework" in a lighthearted article about the application of scientific methodology to the management of the household, bringing Americans closer to "the workless home of the millennium." Even though the author believed his wife still had to spend too much time on housework, he acknowledged happily that "she is able, between rising and bedtime, to get in several hours of creative work, companionship, and reading." For some, of course, advancements in household technology were cause for alarm because, without much housework to do, women's sense of homemaking as a "profession" would be diminished. The author of "What Next in Homemaking?" viewed woman's role in this "new order" as "precarious": "the housewifely duties are rapidly disappearing and seem destined to be reduced even further if they do not disappear altogether, since it seems likely that she cannot for long successfully compete with large industrial plants." Whereas in the postwar years those who wrote in the magazines about the dignity and professionalism of homemaking did so with a kind of fanatical certainty, the author of "What Next in Homemaking?" assumed that the title question was real and closed by inviting readers to share their own needs and visions with the *Journal:* "We wish that every one of you would make this an occasion for introducing yourself to us, debating points on which you do not agree, making suggestions that we have overlooked. . . . [W]ill you at any rate tell me what you think a home ought to do for young and old in our present-day world?"

Advertisements in the pre-1940 magazines similarly tended to emphasize readers' individual agency and mobility. While ads for face creams, baby foods, and household cleansers certainly appealed to women's anxieties about looking attractive and taking care of their families, numerous products and services were overtly marketed to people who made their own choices. An advertisement for Piggly Wiggly stores in the June 1929 *Ladies' Home Journal*, for example, included the text, "At last women are free to make *their own decisions* when they buy foods. . . . Here women choose for themselves—help themselves" (italics in original). Leonard refrigerators, in the April 1934 *Woman's Home Companion*, pictured a woman striding along confidently above text that reads, "This Lady has good reason to be satisfied—as any woman has, who chooses as she did." Whereas in the 1940s and 1950s advertisements for household products tended to picture women using them, in the earlier decades the focus was on the product itself rather than on the domestic setting. Campbell's soup, which was to become a major icon of convenience foods by midcentury, is represented in the April 1934 *Woman's Home Companion* by a drawing of a steaming bowl of it rather than by an aproned woman standing at the stove or serving her family, and a ball of crochet thread occupies most of a page in the December 1922 *McCall's* instead of picturing a woman using it. Most telling of all, perhaps, is that in the earlier decades women were foregrounded as drivers and purchasers of automobiles. An Oldsmobile ad in the April 1934 *Companion* shows a woman behind the wheel of a four-door sedan as the neighbors look on admiringly, and the text of a Buick advertisement in the September 1923 *Journal* reads in part, "Women who love a fine motor car will find in this Buick seven-passenger Sedan the power, safety, comfort and beauty they so deeply desire." By midcentury, automobile advertising was virtually absent from women's magazines. Even as the development of the suburbs made the car an increasingly important element of American family life, conventional wisdom held that men made these domestic purchasing decisions.

The fact that advertising images and text are the elements of a magazine over which the editors have the least control makes such changes particularly compelling and underscores the extent to which women's magazines serve as reflectors of cultural change rather than deliberate agents defining women's role. Michael Kammen quotes a 1946 observer who perceived the significance of this part of magazine content: "These humbler adjuncts to literature [advertisements] may prove more valuable to the future historian than the editorial contents [of large magazines]. In them we may trace our sociological history, the rise and fall of fads and crazes, changing interests and tastes, in foods, clothes, amusements and vices, a panorama of life as it was lived, more informing than old diaries or crumbling tombstones" (198). Just as advertising can be a source of understanding of cultural history, it was also an important force in the transition to mass culture that was taking place at midcentury. The emerging mass culture of media and entertainment that Kammen analyzes in *American Culture, American Tastes* has a counterpart in the domestic world that the women's magazines played a part in creating in the 1940s and 1950s. As Campbell's soup, Bisquick, Knox Gelatine, and Spam became ubiquitous, influencing both cooking methods and the American diet, so electric mixers and refrigerators reflected tastes and shopping habits; the increased centrality of the home both encouraged and was encouraged by easily replicated designs for suburban houses and mass-marketed materials with which to build and furnish them. People finally able to enjoy home ownership and a measure of economic security regarded the resulting tendency to conformity, severely criticized by sociologists at the time as well as more recently, as achievement of the American Dream.

Complicating the "Feminine Mystique"

In her highly influential 1963 book, *The Feminine Mystique*, Betty Friedan focused readers' attention on the women's magazines that found their way into millions of American homes each month. Previously a freelance writer for some of these magazines, by 1963 Friedan was convinced that these periodicals had a pernicious effect on the women who read them by encouraging them to confine their goals to perfecting the roles of wife and mother and abandoning the image of the self-sufficient "New Woman" who had won the right to vote in 1920 and set her sights on education and a career. Listing the contents of the July 1960 issue of *McCall's*, Friedan took issue with the portrait of womanhood that she found there: "The image of woman that emerges from this big, pretty magazine is young and frivolous, almost child-like; fluffy and feminine; passive; gaily content in a world of bedroom and kitchen, sex, babies, and home. The magazine surely does not leave out sex; the only passion, the only pursuit, the only goal a woman is permitted is the pursuit of a man. It is crammed full of food, clothing, cosmetics, furniture, and the physical bodies of young women, but where is the world of thought and ideas, the life of the mind and spirit? In the magazine image, women do no work except housework and work to keep their bodies beautiful and to get and keep a man" (36). Friedan pointed out that at the time this *McCall's* issue was published, Fidel Castro led a revolution in Cuba, astronauts were being trained for space flight, debates rocked the world of the visual arts, and the civil rights movement was in full swing—yet none of these events were reflected in a magazine read by more than 5 million women, nearly half of whom had attended college. Friedan's analysis of the four leading women's magazines—*McCall's, Good Housekeeping, Ladies' Home Journal,* and (until its demise in 1957) *Woman's Home Companion*—concentrated in large part on the fiction the magazines published, noting that in the late 1930s the heroines made independent choices about their futures as airplane pilots, geologists, and businesswomen, even within the context of the romance formula. But by 1949, Friedan observed with alarm, the protagonists' "limitless world [had] shrunk to the cozy walls of the home" (44), and women who began stories with careers renounced them in favor of motherhood.

In trying to account for the changes that she found so dismaying, Friedan cited statements by magazine editors about what their readers wanted to read and were capable of understanding: "They're not interested in the broad public issues of the day," remarked one editor. "They are not interested in national or international affairs." Another editor lamented the fact that he could not publish a story about school desegregation: "You just can't link it to woman's world" (37). Friedan's own experience as a writer for the magazines had, she noted, convinced her of the pervasive nature of these attitudes. When, for example, she wanted to write an article about an artist, editorial constraints forced her to emphasize the woman's household responsibilities rather than her professional life: "I wrote about her cooking and marketing and falling in love with her husband, and painting a crib for her baby. I had to leave out the hours she spent painting pictures, her serious work—and the way she felt about it" (53). Even actresses, profiles of whom the magazines often featured, had to be presented as "a sexual object, a babyface bride, or a housewife" (53), and a 1949 *Ladies' Home Journal* article about Edna St. Vincent Millay emphasized the poet's ability to cook. The closest Friedan could come to an explanation for the magazines' increasing glorification of domestic life in the 1940s came from an older female editor, who pointed out that whereas before World War II most editors and writers were women, after the war most of them were men, and many of them had come "back from the war . . . dreaming about home, and a cozy domestic life" (54).

This editor's comment, while it presents an overly simplistic rationale for the changes that Friedan perceived in such magazines as *McCall's,* resonates with the assessments of the postwar period by recent cultural historians. If, in fact, men who yearned for an idealized domestic life occupied influential positions with women's magazines after the war (although a great many staff writers remained women) and wished the magazines to represent this ideal, it does not follow that they intended to reinstate a nineteenth-century separate-spheres ideology; rather, such a comment suggests that both men and women participated in what Lary May terms "an unprecedented domestic revival" (5) that had ramifications far beyond the kitchen and bedroom. Instead, that is, of imposing foxhole dreams on female readers, magazine editors—most of whom, it should be noted, had historically been men—were participating in a cultural shift that made home and family metaphors for America's identity and security.

In short, when seeking an explanation for what seemed to her a potentially destructive trend in women's magazines of the 1940s and 1950s—a trend toward a far narrower definition of women's role than had been the case in earlier decades—Friedan tended to look within the magazine industry itself rather than at the larger culture of which it was a part. Put another way, she viewed the changes she perceived in the postwar women's magazines as a betrayal of women's potential taking place within a cultural vacuum in which male editors pressed their restrictive opinions of women's needs and interests on unsuspecting readers, causing them to adhere to a "feminine mystique." In fact, as subsequent chapters of this study will demonstrate, dramatic changes in the American economy, in American political rhetoric, in technology and industry, and in advertising practices and patterns of consumption interacted in complex ways with the magazines Friedan surveyed. Further, the four major magazines had been self-identified for many years as service magazines for homemakers; all these publications had been founded in the late nineteenth century to provide household advice for a largely rural and small-town readership. In limiting her critique to the service magazines and in failing to observe the diversity of emphases among and within the magazines marketed to women by 1960, Friedan inevitably presented an analysis that is at best partial. By the mid–twentieth century, the women's magazine market had become segmented in terms of age, social class, and interests. A magazine such as *Mademoiselle*, for example, was intended for the relatively affluent young woman whose plans included college and at least some years of independent living. The decline in the quality of the fiction that Friedan noted in the service magazines did not occur in *Mademoiselle*, whose annual short fiction contest for female college students launched the writing careers of such authors as Joan Williams and Sylvia Plath.

Plath's prizewinning story, published in the August 1952 issue, is interesting to read in the context of Friedan's commentary. Titled "Sunday at the Mintons'," the story is told primarily from the perspective of Elizabeth Minton, an unmarried former librarian who has returned to the family home to live with her retired brother, Henry. What seems outwardly the assumption of domestic responsibilities by a dutiful sister, however, quickly reveals that Elizabeth is utterly unsuited for and uninterested in domesticity. Although as a child Elizabeth had been "obedient and yielding," as an adult she resents Henry's fastidiousness, having to remind herself to dust the lamp shades in his study. On the Sunday of the story, she burns the dinner potatoes and daydreams while Henry lectures her on her inefficiency. Although in one sense Elizabeth seems stereotypically feminine in her penchant for daydreams and Henry seems equally masculine in his interest in the tools of precision—especially maps and compasses—the story actually depicts Elizabeth's defiance of Henry's expectations for her domestic behavior. Instead of the world of the efficient homemaker, "hers was a twilight world, where the moon floated up over the trees at night like a tremulous balloon of silver light and the bluish rays wavered through the leaves outside the window." Her secret fantasy is to "lift up the tops of people's heads like teapot lids and peer inside to find out what they were thinking." At the end of the story, Elizabeth's imagination temporarily takes command of the narrative. As she and Henry walk by the ocean, Elizabeth fantasizes that in attempting to retrieve a brooch she has dropped (significantly, a brooch that had belonged to her mother), Henry has drowned; rather than seeking assistance, Elizabeth feels herself being borne upward by the wind, free of Henry and all earthly constraints: "And that was the last anyone saw of Elizabeth Minton, who was enjoying herself thoroughly, blowing upward, now to this side now to that, her lavender dress blending with the purple of the distant clouds." Although the fantasy fades at the end of the story, Elizabeth's defiance has been made clear to the reader. At no point in the story does Elizabeth Minton lament her unmarried, childless state; on the contrary, the story emphasizes her yearning to escape the weight of domestic concerns, which both expresses Plath's own ambivalence about the future that seemed culturally mapped for her and reflects the widespread preoccupation with such concerns in the postwar world.

While *Mademoiselle* encouraged the talents of college-age women such as Plath, the mass-circulation service magazines also published fiction by writers who either had established or would establish notable careers as authors. In 1948, for example, *Good Housekeeping* published short stories by Pearl S. Buck, J. D. Salinger, Max Shulman, A. A. Milne, and Jerome Weidman, a novelist and playwright whose play *Fiorello!* won the 1960 Pulitzer Prize. In 1956, its last year of publication, *Woman's Home Companion* published fiction by Françoise Sagan, Shirley Jackson, and Laura Z. Hobson, among others. While the service magazines also published highly formulaic fiction by such authors as Faith Baldwin, whose happily-ever-after stories and novels were popular for decades, there is ample evidence to suggest that some readers of the magazines found such fiction unsatisfying. In the "Pats and Pans" section of the July 1960 issue of *McCall's* (a section that Friedan calls, in an interesting slip, "Pots and Pans"), two letters to the editor criticize the magazine's fiction. The first reader objects to what she terms "puppy-love" stories about very young couples, calling them "trite": "let's have some character stories, some stories with a little meat in them. Or just some plain stories about mature people." The second reader was even more blunt: "Why don't you cut out the stories? They're insipid."

Indeed, a close look at this issue of *McCall's*, which Friedan holds up as a particularly bad example of the feminine mystique, suggests that the magazine was not sending a monolithic message to women and that women did not read *McCall's* uncritically. Friedan mentions casually that the issue includes "columns by Clare Luce and Eleanor Roosevelt" (36); in fact, Clare Boothe Luce's "Without Portfolio" feature is a lengthy and cogent analysis of the effect of television on presidential campaigns, written, Luce says, because a number of *McCall's* readers had written her to ask about this phenomenon. Published in the same month that the Republican and Democratic Party conventions for the 1960 elections were to take place, Luce's column assumes a curious and politically aware reader. Noting that by 1956 three-fourths of American homes had television sets, Luce applauds television's power to serve democracy by bringing candidates and issues to the attention of so many voters, but she also warns that the cost of broadcast time drives up the cost of campaigns and that the medium forces the candidates to stress the entertainment value rather than the subtleties of their positions. A letter to the editor in the same issue congratulates *McCall's* on "pull[ing] off a novel editorial coup" by presenting both Luce and Roosevelt in each issue and expresses admiration for both women: "Mrs. Roosevelt for her unceasing efforts to humanize international relations [and] Mrs. Luce for her keen insight into a wide variety of matters."

During the summer of 1960, *McCall's* readers also wrote to criticize some of the very aspects of the magazine that Friedan deplored. In June, a letter-writer lamented the time wasted reading excerpts from a biography of Marilyn Monroe and expressed a preference for an article about Robert Frost, "who [does] so much to enrich our lives." In the June and August issues, readers expressed dissatisfaction with the emphasis on youth and slenderness in the magazine's fashion pages: "The feminine age average is rising, you know, and is mature," wrote one woman, and another echoed, "Do your fashion editors think that only young women read McCall's?" A third reader, representing the "forgotten ones," asked whether models could be "less slender and long-legged and more 'pleasingly plump.'" But most telling of all are two lengthy letters in the July issue that in different ways assert the readers' ability to think independently and thus tacitly refute Friedan's assumption that the overt messages of the women's magazines were those received, unmediated, by their readers. One writer, who essentially approved of *McCall's* and was tired of reading letters to the editor protesting the publication of various articles, used humor to declare her ability for independent thought: "1. Never once has any of *McCall's* staff forced me to agree with, buy, or indorse [*sic*] any article or product presented in any issue. 2. They have permitted me to consume the contents of each issue as I saw fit, to my individual taste, i.e., I have never been forced to copy any fashion or fad I didn't like. . . . 3. Never was I compelled to read any article by anyone I dislike or to agree with it if I did. 4. Never once has any of *McCall's* personnel pressured me into choosing sides on any Pro or Con material they have printed." The letter concluded, "I do not agree with everything you print. Please keep up the stimulation." The second writer, in contrast, wanted *McCall's* to be an entirely different magazine but struck a similar note of independence when she asserted, "we, the middle-aged, thickened, wise-by-experience women of this country are the ones with the money to buy your goods. We are not interested in making fools of ourselves." The long list of changes this Florida woman suggested would have made *McCall's* far more socially conscious and less youth oriented, and, like Friedan, this writer called for the magazine to pay attention to racism, as did another correspondent in this issue who complained that there was no reference to the civil rights movement: "Do you think that your typical woman reader, middle-income, white (like me) isn't interested in the burning social problems of a minority group, that we are so shallow we have no interest beyond the dress we wear and the dinner we cook?"

Despite the fact that the content of the women's magazines and their relationship to their readers was far more complex than Friedan posited in *The Feminine Mystique,* her characterization of the magazines as coercive and, by implication, of their readers as easily coerced went unchallenged for a long time.[2] This characterization also contributed to the popular impression not only that the postwar period was one of quiescent domestic conformity and segregation for American women but also that the situation resulted from an informal conspiracy among magazine editors, designers of suburban tract houses, and television programming. Serious challenges to this overly simplistic view of history emerged in the late 1980s and early 1990s, among them Joanne Meyerowitz's essay collection *Not June Cleaver,* in which studies of groups of women other than white, middle-class homemakers, in Meyerowitz's words, "displace the domestic stereotype, the June Cleavers and Donna Reeds, from the center of historical study" (5). Essays on immigrant women, professional women, and women as members of labor unions and political activists during the period from 1945 to 1960 present a more complex picture of women's lives, values, and attitudes than is available in either Friedan's *Feminine Mystique* or the leading women's magazines, which focused on middle- to upper-middle-class white women. Meyerowitz's essay in the volume, "Beyond the Feminine Mystique," expands on Friedan's research in popular culture by considering a wider range of periodicals published between 1946 and 1958, including "highbrow" magazines such as *Harper's* and *Atlantic Monthly,* African American magazines such as *Ebony* and *Negro Digest,* and middle-class magazines such as *Coronet* and *Reader's Digest.* Far from presenting a monolithic message, Meyerowitz finds that in this larger sample of periodicals, "domestic ideals coexisted in ongoing tension with an ethos of individual achievement that celebrated nondomestic activity, individual striving, public service, and public success" (231).

In addition to examining a wide spectrum of popular culture images of and commentary on women, Meyerowitz reflects recent approaches to popular culture that recognize that "mass culture is neither wholly monolithic nor unrelentingly repressive. In this view, mass culture is rife with contradictions, ambivalence, and competing voices. We no longer assume that any text has a single, fixed meaning for all readers, and we sometimes find within the mass media subversive, as well as repressive, potential" (231).[3] Not only, in other words, might a woman have read both *Good Housekeeping* and *Harper's,* but within each of these periodicals she would have found complex and even contradictory messages about her role and behavior. Further, as the letters to editors cited previously attest, readers were often selective in their responses to the texts they read, free to reject what seemed to them foolish, degrading, or irrelevant. Even those magazines expressly designed to appeal to the homemaker, Meyerowitz finds, did not uniformly glorify domesticity but often portrayed it as "exhausting and isolating" (242) and thus acknowledged the pitfalls termed the "feminine mystique." Meyerowitz concludes that Friedan's "forceful protest against a restrictive domestic ideal neglected the extent to which that ideal was already undermined" (250).

While I agree generally with Meyerowitz's critique, I wish to frame it differently. Rather than an opposition between a "restrictive domestic ideal" and material that "undermined" it, the magazines reflected an ongoing debate about how domesticity could and should be defined. Readers who found housework isolating and repetitive and visual images of women too young and slender—as well as writers for the magazines who critiqued the perfectionism the magazines tended to display (especially, although they would not have dared say so openly, in advertising)—were not attempting to deny the primacy of home and family in the postwar cultural ideology. To the contrary, the fact that the domestic was a contested site in the pages of the magazines that sold millions of copies testifies to the centrality of the issue in the public imagination. In addition, by the time that Friedan was writing *The Feminine Mystique* in the early 1960s, the concept of domesticity had become interwoven with the concept of upward social mobility, as I will discuss in chapter 4, so that complaints about homemaking standards can also be read as anxieties about social-class identification. Such complexity is at least implied in Daniel Horowitz's more recent studies of Friedan.

While Meyerowitz argues that Friedan read the women's magazines selectively, drawing attention to those portions that supported her thesis and glossing over those that would have challenged it, Daniel Horowitz, in his 1996 article "Rethinking Betty Friedan and *The Feminine Mystique*," questions both Friedan's identification with the unhappy housewives she writes about in the book and her claim to have awakened only shortly before to women's need for greater opportunity and fulfillment by pointing to her work as a labor journalist during the 1940s and 1950s. In 1941, Friedan (then Bettye Goldstein) participated in a workshop at the Highlander Folk School in Tennessee, which was helping to support union activity in the South, and wrote editorials attacking censorship and supporting labor unions in the Smith College newspaper. For a decade following her graduation from Smith, she wrote for the prounion Federated Press and then for the *UE News*, the publication of the United Electrical, Radio and Machine Workers of America, in both cases championing the cause of labor equity for women and African Americans. Horowitz's central point is that the civil rights and women's movements of the 1950s and 1960s had deep roots in earlier decades and that a close look at Friedan's personal history "offers vivid proof of the intertwined processes of containment and resistance of women in the

1940s and 1950s" (30). In his 1998 book *Betty Friedan and the Making of The Feminine Mystique*, Horowitz elaborates on a point that his article makes briefly: even though Friedan complained about the constraints imposed by the magazines for which she was a freelance writer in the 1950s, she actually wrote and published articles that described and celebrated the kind of female self-fulfillment that her book would declare that the magazines attempted to deny. "A central theme of Friedan's magazine articles from the 1950s," Horowitz writes, "was the ambition of independent women who achieved excellence in a career and raised a family" (*Betty Friedan* 184). Publishing in such disparate periodicals as *Parents', Cosmopolitan, Charm, Family Circle*, and *Redbook*, Friedan wrote admiringly of women's success in business, politics, and the arts—and in their domestic roles: "This was her dream, a kind of gestalt that integrated everything into a whole life" (Horowitz, *Betty Friedan* 184–85). The larger point is that this "whole life" gestalt, far from being unique to Friedan, was the promise of American culture in the 1940s and 1950s, and some version of domestic life was at its core.

The relationship between Friedan and midcentury women's magazines has by now been well documented and much debated, and by no means do I seek here primarily to challenge—except, perhaps, implicitly—her contention that these publications were complicit in creating what she called the "problem that has no name." *The Feminine Mystique* has served as a springboard for my discussion of the magazines because of its importance as a twentieth-century cultural document that inspired, among other things, numerous investigations of cultural messages and realities in two decades that were pivotal for American life in the remainder of the century. The germ of this book lies instead in a collection of articles from the midcentury magazines that I edited a few years ago (Walker, *Women's Magazines*). Reading back and forth between cultural histories of the period and the pages of the magazines themselves, with their ads for deodorant and linoleum, their pictures of women in aprons and high heels, their recipes for tuna casserole, their articles about film stars and marital harmony, I became convinced that the magazines were in no sense a separate reality but rather a part of an American culture attempting to re-create itself during and after a depression, during and after a world war. Rather than reading the magazines for their messages of either containment or subversion, then, I am concerned with them as a cultural phenomenon that interacted in complex ways with important aspects of American culture, including war, rapid economic fluctuations, an increased consciousness of racial and ethnic diversity, the proliferation of life-changing consumer goods, and heated debates about women's roles as workers, wives, and mothers. While the women's magazines—especially the four oldest with the largest circulations—were committed, as they had been for decades, to providing advice, entertainment, and information for the homemaker and family, at midcentury the concept of the domestic was complicated by the entry of many women into the paid labor force, by changes in household technology, by shifts from rural and urban to suburban living, and by a political ideology that equated the home with capitalism if not with democracy itself. Amid all of these changes, the editors of magazines and the advertisers that largely sustained them sought to appeal to an increasingly elusive but vitally important middle-class homemaker, in the process creating an often contradictory image of the domestic ideal. The home was a haven from war and strife, but marriage and motherhood were far from easy responsibilities. Women were smart and capable but needed instruction in accomplishing even the simplest tasks. The family was a self-sufficient unit but at the same time needed expert advice on everything from healing marital strife to purchasing washing machines.

In *The Way We Never Were*, Stephanie Coontz argues forcefully that the ideal "traditional" family of 1950s situation comedies has never been a reality for most Americans and that subsequent nostalgia for this golden age of the nuclear family is a yearning for a mythical past (8–22). I believe that such nostalgia did not develop in the 1970s and 1980s but instead was created in the middle decades of the century as popular-culture desires intersected with socioeconomic realities. As a case in point, in 1937, when President Franklin Delano Roosevelt proclaimed in his second inaugural address that he saw "one-third of a nation ill-housed, ill-clad, ill-nourished," the editors of *Ladies' Home Journal* had already decided that the fashion and house design pages of the magazine should present readers with images of clothing and homes about which most readers could dream but that they could not afford. In doing so, Bruce and Beatrice Gould were neither blithely ignorant of Roosevelt's assessment nor unaware of their readers' economic capacities. On the one hand, the editors wanted to offer hope to Depression-weary readers, but theirs was also a business decision, designed to alter the perception that the *Journal* had become frumpy and dull. Magazines, like film companies, television networks, and other aspects of popular culture, could survive only by appealing to those who supported them financially, and in the process these media endorsed ideologies, created fantasies, and engaged in dialogue with a host of other forces in the culture. Given the magazines' diverse contents, this dialogue brought magazine editors and writers in contact—at different times and to varying degrees—with political and military leaders, home economists, manufacturers of consumer goods (largely through the medium of their advertising agencies), educators, psychologists and members of the medical profession, fiction writers, and the readers themselves. Each issue of a magazine, then, was the product of negotiating a variety of often competing interests, and the result was a vexed but earnest, sometimes contradictory image of domestic America.

Women's Magazines at Midcentury

The interplay of these varied forces and women's magazines as a part of twentieth-century popular culture makes the 1940s and 1950s an appropriate period for study. As I will show in the chapters that follow, much of what can be observed in the magazines during these two decades originated in earlier periods of American history. Debates about domesticity and about the role of home and family in personal and national life can be traced at least to the early nineteenth century. The identification of the woman as household consumer was well under way by the late nineteenth century, and the modern advertising industry developed during the first decades of the twentieth century. Industrial production of household goods formerly made within the home, such as soap, cloth, and some foods, had begun to affect the life of the homemaker by the late nineteenth century, and in 1912 Thomas Edison predicted that electricity would soon alleviate all household drudgery. Magazines for women had been dispensing advice on fashions, home decor, and genteel behavior since *Godey's Lady's Book* in the mid–nineteenth century, and by the end of the century, *Ladies' Home Journal, Good Housekeeping,* and *Woman's Home Companion* offered assistance with cooking, cleaning, child rearing, and much more. To some extent, then, the midcentury magazines represented a culmination of trends that began much earlier.

But America's entry into World War II in 1941—anticipated by many for at least a year—brought profound changes in the lives of men and women alike. As Susan M. Hartmann puts it in *The Home Front and Beyond,* the war abruptly altered gender roles, changing dramatically the pace of what normally takes place "very gradually": "The 1940s contained developments which sharply set off that decade from the preceding one and which established patterns that would shape women's lives for some years to come. Most obviously, the second world war transformed the economy, made unprecedented claims on women and men, and disrupted social arrangements on a broad scale" (ix). The most dramatic and highly publicized alteration was the entry of large numbers of women into the paid labor force in war- or war-related work, a movement crystallized in the image of Rosie the Riveter. What made this change so significant was its reversal of the Depression-era ideology that effectively prevented most married women from working outside the home: the few available jobs were to be reserved for men, the "natural" family wage earners. If the late-1930s magazine fiction to which Friedan refers in *The Feminine Mystique* featured heroines with career aspirations, such stories either represented women's fantasies of public achievement or constituted a rejection of marriage: in 1940, only 15 percent of married women were wage earners (Hartmann, *Home Front* 16), and a disproportionate number of these women were racial and ethnic minorities. Even though the majority of American women did not become wage earners during the war, those who did were the focus of much public attention. The September 1943 issue of *Harper's,* for example, included an article titled "From Housewife to Shipfitter," the first-person account of a woman working in a shipyard. The exhilaration and sense of transformation in Virginia Snow Wilkinson's description of her first few weeks on the job are palpable. Even though she and the other women workers experienced some male workers' resentment, she noted with pride that "the responsibility placed upon these girls had made them almost in one day into serious workmen" (145). Personal pride in her own work was important to Wilkinson—her final comment is, "at last I had a job" (148)—but even more important was the sense of community as the women workers performed their duties as a team: "We became integrated persons working together on a project which focused all our interests" (144).

As I will discuss in chapter 3, the women's magazines immediately reflected America's engagement in the war and women's different responsibilities. By the beginning of 1942, issues bristled with images of women in military and nursing uniforms, and women who remained at home were addressed not as mere housewives but as contributors to the war effort through their frugality, cooperation with restrictions, and volunteer work. As Hartmann notes, "especially in the early years of the decade, media images of women were expansive, widening the range of acceptable female behavior, providing positive examples of unconventional women, and blurring traditional gender distinctions" (*Home Front* 189). It seems no accident, for example, that the "Wonder Woman" comic strip debuted in 1941; the opening text of the first strip reads in part, "At last, in a world torn by the hatreds and wars of men, appears a *woman* to whom the problems and feats of men are mere child's play—a woman whose identity is known to *none*, but whose sensational feats are outstanding in a fast-moving world!" Although the women's magazines tended to stress the feminine attributes even of women who worked in defense plants and to look forward to a postwar period when women would resume their "normal" role as homemakers, the war-intensified debates about women's public and private roles represented a new era for the magazines. With many of their readers functioning effectively as single parents and workers, no longer could the magazines assume that the nuclear family with a stay-at-home mom was the only viable domestic arrangement, even though the publications attempted to posit it as the ideal. Even when postwar American culture exerted many kinds of influence to return women to their proper duties as homemakers, there was no turning back the clock to 1940; increasing numbers of women attended college, and women's paid employment never dropped to prewar levels—facts that the magazines were forced to acknowledge and accommodate as the 1940s turned into the 1950s.

Also serving to set the middle decades of the century apart from earlier periods was the development of a national culture on a scale unprecedented in American history. The electronic media—chief among them, by the mid-1950s, television—played perhaps the largest role in this development, as millions of people saw the same films and listened to the same radio programs. But other factors came into play as well. In "Visions of Classlessness, Quests for Dominion," Roland Marchand points to the decline of foreign-language periodicals and entertainments, an increased homogeneity in clothing, and the fact that Sears, Roebuck ceased publishing regional catalogs, perceiving that taste in such items as furniture did not vary widely from one part of the country to another (164–66). In the mid-1930s, George Gallup had developed a reliable method of public-opinion polling that allowed advertisers, manufacturers, and politicians to take the pulse (Gallup's word) of the nation and thus plan strategies for marketing and policy. Gallup had worked at a major advertising agency in the early 1930s, and the advertising industry's increased power in the 1940s constituted yet another influence on American culture. As Jackson Lears states in *Fables of Abundance*, advertisers "played a crucial hegemonic role in creating the consumer culture that dominated post–World War II American society": "They rehabilitated and politicized the fiction of consumer sovereignty by broadening the practice of market research to include opinion polling; they democratized the imagery of the masses in promoting the ideological mobilization for World War II; they redefined the essence of the American Way of Life from a vague populism to an equally murky notion of free enterprise" (235). As widely circulated media themselves, women's magazines were deeply implicated in these changes, particularly in the way in which advertising scripted middle-class America during the war and postwar years. During the war the magazines' advertising pages encouraged patience and patriotism while holding out the promise of postwar material comforts; after the conflict ended, the "fiction of consumer sovereignty" (*Fables of Abundance* 235) held out the illusion of choice while at the same time fostering loyalty to certain brand names and aspiration to the standards of domestic life.

In *Where the Girls Are*, media expert Susan J. Douglas writes both as a scholar of American media and as someone who, growing up after the war, was conscious of their effect on her. Like Lears, Douglas perceives the postwar period as qualitatively different from preceding eras in the influence the media could exert on women's lives. Acknowledging that contradictory cultural expectations for women were not a new phenomenon, Douglas argues that the pervasiveness of such messages was unprecedented: "My point is that this situation intensified with the particular array of media technology and outlets that interlocked in people's homes after World War II. It wasn't simply the sheer size and ubiquity of the media, although these, of course, were important. It was also the fact that the media themselves were going through a major transformation in how they regarded and marketed to their audiences that heightened, dramatically, the contradictions in the images and messages they produced. Radio, TV, magazines, popular music, film— these were the *mass* media, predicated on the notion of a national unified market, and their raison d'être was to reach as many people as possible" (14–15). Douglas locates some of the most blatantly contradictory media messages in the women's magazines, in which editorial content and adver- tisements were often strikingly at odds. Citing a mid-1940s issue of *Ladies' Home Journal*, Douglas notes that "in between ads for Pond's cleansing cream ('She's Engaged! She's Lovely! She Uses Pond's!') and Ivory Flakes ('How to Bring Out the Wolf in a Man') were earnest articles about why women ought to get involved in national and international politics," and Eleanor Roosevelt's regular "If You Ask Me" column in the *Journal* conveyed such messages as "I think girls should have exactly the same opportunities as boys" (51).

In addition to pointing out such overt contradictions, however, Douglas makes an even more significant point when she suggests that in singling out teenage girls as a distinct market segment, especially by the early 1950s, the media gave young women a sense of identity as a group different from older women and thus a kind of power. Advertisers could profit from instilling in young women "a sense of entitlement, and a sense of generational power." Thus, ironically, "At the same time that the makers of Pixie Bands, Maybel- line eyeliner, Breck shampoo, and *Beach Blanket Bingo* reinforced our roles as cute, airheaded girls, the mass media produced a teen girl popular culture of songs, movies, TV shows, and magazines that cultivated in us a highly self-conscious sense of importance, difference, and even rebellion. Because young women became critically important economically, as a market, the suspicion began to percolate among them, over time, that they might be important culturally, and then politically, as a generation" (14). The success of such magazines as *Seventeen* and *Mademoiselle* bears out Douglas's con- tention that the media, in effect, created a generational group with its own products but, more importantly, with the sense that it could define its own goals and priorities. Thus, even more significant than the media's specific characterization of a group—which may involve negative or at least restric- tive stereotypes—may be its elevation of the group to a position of cultural importance. To a certain extent, magazines for homemakers set this process in motion during World War II: by celebrating women as patriots—whether working in defense plants, volunteering with the Red Cross, or growing and canning their own vegetables—magazine editors and advertisers promulgated the idea that American housewives and hence the home itself had agency and influence. Despite the fact that wartime images of patriotic women largely emphasized the domestic and the feminine—even a factory worker should be well groomed, and the war was being fought to protect the home—the women's magazines tacitly evoked the sense that women were deeply involved in the nation's political life. It is not difficult to imagine, then, that many readers saw as a betrayal the abrupt retreat from acknowledgment of women's public roles—however fabricated they might have been—that characterized the magazines by 1946.

Douglas points to the fact that alongside the mass media's presentations of "middle-class, sexually repressed, white-bread norms and values" there emerged a subculture, partly but not wholly led by young people, that included "rock 'n' roll, FM radio, 'beat' poetry and literature, and foreign films" (15). In *Deliberate Speed*, W. T. Lhamon Jr. investigates this culture, arguing that the 1950s not only were far from "a hole in cultural history" but in fact "were alive with vital art, new codes of behavior, and strong patterns of shape and energy that still survive without conventional acclaim" (2, 5). The concept that the '50s were a bland, conformist period with little cultural vitality, Lhamon believes, originated during the decade itself: "If there was no serious culture, if balm was everywhere in the land, if everyman might happily oscillate between job and hearth, then Americans had successfully turned the corner from the discipline, privations, and social commitment of the war" (3). Lhamon proposes that the popular culture and its mass media that could broadcast this sense of peaceful recovery via situation comedies and ads for electric mixers also fed the decade's vital culture, both by helping to solidify the youth culture that Douglas describes and by making available for public consumption the voices of those such as Flannery O'Connor and Chuck Berry, who "wrote about disenfranchised, displaced, and thus disordered people struggling to fix or simply understand their own place in a hostile or indifferent context" (6). In Lhamon's persuasive formulation, films such as *Rebel without a Cause,* the music of Elvis Presley, and Jack Kerouac's *On the Road* were not mere blips on an otherwise quiescent screen but instead constituted evidence—along with fast foods, interstate highways, and motels—of a shift from "folk or oral culture" to "popular or mediated culture," a transition similar to what Kammen identifies as the change from "popular" to "proto-mass" culture: "Lore, which previous generations had absorbed at Grandpa's or Uncle Remus's knee or on the store porch, was now absorbed basking in the blue glow of the TV, from the car radio, from comics and theme parks. Instead of producing and participating in their own lore, fifties people began buying it ready-made, became its recipients" (Lhamon 9). The fact that 1950s popular culture came to people ready-made in the form of recordings, television programs, and McDonald's hamburgers did not mean that the culture was inauthentic but merely indicated that the technological means for its rapid dissemination coincided with its development.

Of all the commentators on American culture during the period, Lhamon identifies Russian-born writer Vladimir Nabokov as the most perceptive about the shift taking place. The title character of his novel *Lolita* (published in Paris in 1955 and in America in 1958) is an adolescent girl who has known only postwar American culture and who has fully adopted its cultural style. "Lolita's life," Lhamon notes, "coincides with the fulcrum years of the country's tip from pre- into full-consumption economy, late forties to mid-fifties, about which Nabokov is carefully precise" (17), and the novel's narrator, Lolita's would-be lover, the fortysomething Humbert Humbert, understands both the culture and Lolita's immersion in it: "She it was to whom ads were dedicated: the ideal consumer, the subject and object of every foul poster" (Nabokov 148).[4] As Humbert and Lolita travel around the country in Part Two of the novel, Nabokov provides detailed glimpses of the mobile consumer culture that had begun to characterize America by the early 1950s: "The Lord knows how many nickels I fed to the gorgeous music boxes that came with every meal we had. I still hear the nasal voices of those invisibles serenading [Lolita], people with names like Sammy and Jo and Eddy and Tony and Peggy and Guy and Patty and Rex, and sentimental song hits, all of them as similar to my ear as her various candies were to my palate. She believed, with a kind of celestial trust, any advertisement or advice that appeared in *Movie Love* or *Screen Land*—Starasil Starves Pimples, or 'You better watch out if you're wearing your shirttails outside your jeans, gals, because Jill says you shouldn't.' . . . If some café proclaimed Icecold Drinks, she was automatically stirred, although all drinks everywhere were ice-cold" (148). In short, the messages that the adolescent Lolita appears to derive from movie magazines, signs, and popular songs differ in degree but not in kind from the messages that adult women were assumed to absorb from *McCall's* and *Good Housekeeping:* what to eat and wear, how to behave and be loved. Yet near the end of *Lolita,* Humbert confesses that despite his all-consuming love of Lolita, she remains something of a mystery to him: "it struck me . . . that I simply did not know a thing about my darling's mind and that quite possibly, behind the awful juvenile clichés, there was in her a garden and a twilight and a palace gate—dim and adorable regions which happened to be lucidly and absolutely forbidden to me" (284). Lhamon interprets Humbert's realization as meaning that the American Lolita finally cannot be dependent on and colonized by the European Humbert (18), but Humbert's epiphany also suggests the instability of the relationship between popular culture and the individual's response to it.

Nabokov's controversial novel may seem an odd text to draw into a discussion of women's magazines and the creation of a domestic world, but in addition to having an extraordinary perception of American popular culture and its power to conjure up habitable spaces, Nabokov saw—as perhaps only an outsider could have seen—the enormous significance of the domestic in postwar American life and understood its fragility and attendant anxieties. When Humbert marries Lolita's mother solely to gain physical proximity to her preadolescent daughter, his behavior is a travesty of the creation of the nuclear family, and ironic references to the domestic ideal permeate the novel. At dinner in Charlotte Haze's home, Humbert notes that the salad recipe was "lifted from a woman's magazine" (63), and shortly after their marriage, Charlotte begins redecorating and rearranging the house with the aid of "illustrated catalogues and homemaking guides" (78). After Charlotte's death, Humbert and Lolita travel across an America littered with temporary, even ersatz, renditions of home in the form of motels run by "the reformed criminal, the retired teacher and the business flop, among the males; and the motherly, pseudo-ladylike and madamic variants among the females," one of which offers "'raid-the-icebox' midnight snacks" (146–47). When finally the pair settles into an actual house, Humbert enrolls Lolita in the Beardsley School, where he is informed that the curriculum has "done away with the mass of irrelevant topics that have traditionally been presented to young girls, leaving no place, in former days, for the knowledges and the skills, and the attitudes they will need in managing their lives and—as the cynic might add—the lives of their husbands. . . . [T]he position of a star is important, but the most practical spot for an icebox in the kitchen may be even more important to the budding housewife" (177–78).

Nabokov's running parody of domestic culture was mirrored in the same period by satiric treatments of the women's magazines in other large-circulation periodicals. The fact that, as I will discuss in chapter 2, writers for *Esquire* and *Playboy* found the women's magazines worthy of satiric attention is just one indication of the fact that they occupied a position somewhere between what Lhamon calls the traditional "host" culture and the newly pervasive popular culture. Whereas Lhamon proposes that the host culture either ignored or suppressed the new cultural manifestations (3), the women's magazines by their very nature had feet in both worlds. At the same time that they remained committed to idealizing home and family and the woman's centrality within them, these publications also had a duty to inform readers about new cultural and technological developments that had a bearing on this sphere—everything from cake mixes to the Kinsey reports on American sexual behavior, from face creams to alarming statistics about divorce, juvenile delinquency, and the effects on young minds of reading comic books. The magazines often expressed dismay about these cultural forces but did not ignore them, instead seeking ways to integrate them into the domestic arena that had long been their concern. Indeed, this dual focus often led the magazines to deliver sometimes contradictory messages. In June 1954, for example, *Ladies' Home Journal* columnist Dorothy Thompson wrote enthusiastically about her visit to one of America's first shopping malls, a phenomenon that, as we now recognize, represented both consumerism and the displacement of human activity from the town center to the highway and the suburb; in the same issue of the magazine, an article on a troubled marriage located the central problem in the wife's tendency to overspend.

It is impossible to know precisely what led a thirty-eight-year reader of *Ladies' Home Journal* to write angrily to that magazine in April 1942 to complain about "almost obscene stories . . . sensuality—lust—ridiculous extremes." It is true, however, that sexuality was a staple element of women's magazines, and not simply as a means of having babies or keeping a husband. While *Lolita* would not have been serialized or condensed in their pages, the magazines often published fiction that dealt with sexual matters, including adulterous yearnings and relationships and premarital sex. Two stories in the

March 1957 issue of *McCall's* provide examples. In "Dream of Love," a medical intern considers becoming intimately involved with a married former patient but instead decides that he loves a nurse with whom he works; in "Another Man's Wife," a man comes close to having an affair with a married woman with whom he had been in love six years earlier. The August 1959 issue of *Good Housekeeping* includes the story "The Affair," in which a woman narrowly escapes having to tell her daughter that she and the girl's father had sexual relations before they were married. Magazines such as *Mademoiselle* and *Harper's Bazaar*, which assumed a more sophisticated readership, could afford to be somewhat more daring. In a May 1961 *Mademoiselle* story, after a couple has taken separate vacations, the wife tries to deal with her jealousy about a young woman of whom her husband speaks constantly after his return; at the end of the story, she decides that she needs "a life of her own that would not collapse" in the face of her husband's need for freedom. And while the magazines very rarely acknowledged any sexual orientation other than heterosexuality, the November 1955 *Harper's Bazaar* included a memoir by Mary McCarthy in which she recalled her grandmother and great-aunt reading Radclyffe Hall's *The Well of Loneliness* and coming to her to find out "what the women in the book 'did.' 'Think of it,' nodded my great-aunt, reviewing the march of progress, 'nowadays a fifteen-year-old girl knows a thing like that.' "

I do not claim that women's magazines were in the forefront of a sexual revolution; fictional characters tempted by adultery generally came to their senses in the end, and articles by doctors on sexual frigidity routinely concluded that an unaroused woman had only herself to blame. Yet in an era in which Elvis Presley and Marilyn Monroe became icons of sexual suggestiveness, the magazines published articles on the Kinsey reports and recognized sexuality as an inevitable part of human experience. In other ways as well, the magazines acknowledged a culture that existed outside the traditionally domestic but affected it. A story in the October 1949 issue of *Harper's Bazaar* features a lonely young woman who is comforted each night by the voice of a disk jockey taking song requests from people who, like she, derive a sense of connectedness from this late-night media presence. And while the Cold War and the McCarthy investigations of alleged communists encouraged the kind of conformity for which the postwar period became known, the magazines did not adopt a monolithic stance on either subject. In February 1952, *Redbook* reported admiringly on a woman who for seven years had posed as an official of the Communist Party while serving as an FBI informant. The author of "Secret Agent in Apron Strings" calls her a "heroine" and describes her testimony before the House Un-American Activities Committee. But in 1947, in her "If You Ask Me" column in *Ladies' Home Journal,* Eleanor Roosevelt spoke against loyalty oaths and commented, "I hope that the FBI will not do more than it is now doing about communism in this country. In fact, I would prefer to see it do less." And Dave Garroway, in his July 1960 "My World at Large" column in *McCall's,* expressed outrage that an Air Force manual had stated without any evidence that as many as one-third of the members of a National Council of Churches of Christ committee had "Communist affiliations."

In creating a domestic world during the 1940s and 1950s, then, American women's magazines conveyed complicated and sometimes contradictory messages precisely because such was the nature of the culture the publications reflected. World War II made Americans acutely conscious of involvement with the rest of the world, while the Cold War that immediately followed fostered insularity, both politically and within the family. Attitudes toward proper gender roles changed dramatically in some parts of the population during the war, and that change continued to affect women's lives into the 1950s despite the attempts of advertising-driven media to ignore it. Increased postwar prosperity focused the attention of white Americans on social-class mobility, while the civil rights movement forced recognition of politically sanctioned inequality. New appliances and convenience foods flooded the market, ironically resulting in more work for the American homemaker. As business ventures bent on economic survival, the women's magazines attempted both to honor their traditional advice-giving function, relying increasingly on "experts" such as doctors, psychologists, interior decorators, and home economists, and to alert readers to new developments in education, entertainment, and household technology.

It is impossible to know precisely what effect mid–twentieth century women's magazines had on their readers, although readers' responses to surveys, submissions to question-and-answer columns, and letters to the editors provide a glimpse of that effect. Instead, I intend to focus on the magazines themselves to analyze their depictions of the domestic between 1940 and 1960. What—and who—was included in and excluded from this portrayal? To what extent did the magazines mirror and to what extent did they depart from social realities? How did they respond to the period's many political and social upheavals? What did they perceive to be women's primary roles and responsibilities? How did they deal with such issues as race, social class, education, and women in the workplace? What changes did they register in women's lives and aspirations over this twenty-year period?

Crucial to such analysis are words such as *respond, perceive,* and *register.* If some who wrote for the magazines assumed a prescriptive role, advising readers how to cook a pot roast or avert marital disaster, the status of these periodicals as business enterprises and manifestations of an increasingly mass culture required editors to be attuned to alterations in the tastes, habits, and values of those people identified as the primary readership. The rate of change in midcentury American economic and cultural realities made such attention all the more important in the competition for subscription and advertising revenues. If, as I discuss in the following chapter, many of these magazines had origins in a period in which social-class markers and gender roles had a certain stability, such stability eroded quickly after 1940. As the magazines entered into the debate about the constitution of the domestic world at midcentury, their power to both mold and reflect public opinion encouraged prominent Americans to write for these publications and prompted satiric treatments of their contents and messages.

The World of Women's Magazines

Historically, magazines intended for women readers and the domestic life overlapped with other genres of popular culture—notably, the etiquette or "conduct" book and treatises on homemaking by such prominent authors as Lydia Maria Child and Catharine Beecher. While the home and family had become linked by the middle of the nineteenth century to the welfare of the nation as a whole, as was again true in the middle of the twentieth century, the domestic space was conceived ideologically as the domain of the woman in ways that seem straightforward in comparison to the role controversies of the 1940s and 1950s. The social-class consciousness of such publications was inherent in their focus on approved behavior, attire, and decor, and this emphasis both increased and solidified around middle-class standards (with the exception of such magazines as *Vogue* and *Harper's Bazaar*) as the production of widely distributed household products coincided with the maturation of the advertising industry. Although the magazines thus played a role in the creation of the domestic world well before 1940, the political need for a new American self-definition and a rising standard of living made this role both more insistent and more vexed after that point. A survey of the magazines' contents from 1940 until the late 1950s shows both an expanding definition of the domestic—to include national holidays and psychological adjustment—and an increased emphasis on the possibility of improvement in all areas of life.

Well before women's magazines became the target of Betty Friedan's scorn, they had assumed sufficient cultural force to be the subject of satiric treatment by well-known writers. The fact that the magazines were regarded as appropriate topics for humor during the 1940s and 1950s has at least two significant implications. One is that their formulations of the domestic were widely familiar to Americans who were not part of their female target audience, so that readers of such periodicals as *Esquire* would be able to appreciate the parody. Another is that in satirizing the messages of the magazines, such writers as Jean Kerr and Joan Didion became participants in the debates about these formulations. Although there is more than a germ of truth in these contemporary critiques, they fail to acknowledge that women's magazines were—and are—above all business ventures, attempting to survive and prosper economically by attracting advertisers, pleasing readers, and being watchful of competitors. In this respect more than any other, the magazines were necessarily attuned to cultural dialogues that affected their contents. As technology changed homemaking techniques, the magazines had to report this shift; as anxieties about education, juvenile delinquency, and the Cold War became part of the expanding definition of the domestic and as class consciousness spread through the burgeoning suburbs, the magazines ignored these developments at their peril.

Journals for Ladies

The role of the women's magazines as adviser to and definer of domesticity and women as domestic beings has its roots deep in the nineteenth century. A *Ladies' Magazine* began publication in 1828, and one of its editors, Sarah Josepha Hale, made it clear that the magazine was not intended to disturb what was then an increasing separation between men's and women's major responsibilities: "Husbands may rest assured that nothing found in these pages shall cause [their wives] to be less assiduous in preparing for his reception or encourage her to 'usurp station' or encroach upon prerogatives of men" (qtd. in Steinem 153). Hale is best known as the editor of *Godey's Lady's Book* from 1837 to 1877. With a circulation of 150,000 by 1860, *Godey's* was the first important American magazine for women, and there is much to suggest that its primary readership was at least upper middle class. The magazine printed elaborate sketches of the latest fashions but seldom offered practical advice on everyday tasks, assuming that its readers—like the characters in much of the fiction it published—had servants to tend to cleaning and cooking. *Godey's* addressed an audience educated enough to appreciate the literary criticism of Edgar Allan Poe, which sometimes appeared in its pages.

Like her contemporary, Catharine Beecher, Hale was eager for women to be educated not so that they could "encroach upon prerogatives of men" but so that they could be better wives and homemakers. Both Hale and Beecher respected women's talents and work but viewed them as quite different from those of men; both women subscribed to the philosophy that since woman's "natural" province was the home, she should be well equipped to discharge her responsibilities there. Given *Godey's* rather elite audience, the advice it supplied to women did not take the form of direct recipes (although Gloria Steinem cites a 1,200-word article on "how to maintain a goose quill pen" [153]) but emphasized instead women's behavior and demeanor. Much of what could be considered advice, in fact, is conveyed in the short fiction that *Godey's* published. A number of stories serve as cautionary tales, showing how the young woman who learns the proper lessons thrives in her domestic role, while the woman who is careless, lazy, or self-centered comes to a bad end. A story in the July 1845 *Godey's* is typical in its contrast between two cousins—Julia, a rather frivolous partygoer, and the more sober Fanny, who prefers to spend her evenings reading and keeping her parents company. Defending her preference to Julia, Fanny argues that women should be well informed but makes it clear that the purpose of such education is to improve domestic life: "I do not admire female politicians, Julia, but I think every American female should feel an interest in the welfare of her country, and should have enough information respecting the constitution and principles of its government to be able to listen intelligently to the conversations of those who have knowledge and wisdom on these topics." Because Julia does not learn to appreciate her husband's intellectual interests, he seeks companionship elsewhere and ends in "dissipation, . . . wasted fortune, [and an] early grave."

Not only does Julia's failure to develop an interest in political matters spell disaster for her marriage, but that marriage is tied—just as it would be a hundred years later—to "the welfare of her country." In 1845 as in 1945, the family was rhetorically posited as equivalent to the nation, so that a woman's domestic duty was also her patriotic duty. The *Godey's* story, in fact, resonates with the "Can This Marriage Be Saved?" article that Joan Didion cites in her 1960 *National Review* article: the woman whom the marriage counselor convinces to join the League of Women Voters regains her husband's affection in part by persuading him to "register and go to the polls" (90). That is, she does her civic duty by convincing him to do his.

The differences between 1845 and 1945, however, are equally striking. In the *Godey's* story, Julia's role is clear: she is expected to create a home environment that fosters genteel morality. The purpose of becoming well informed is to provide her husband with companionship that will prevent his "dissipations." Her place in the domestic arena is decidedly secondary; her part in conversation is to "listen intelligently" while others talk. Julia cannot vote, and her place in the nation's civic life is limited to exerting whatever moral suasion she can within her home and family. In 1945, in contrast, readers of women's magazines had been told for four years that they were integral not merely to the political process but to America's victory in World War II. The same magazines that advised women on the proper reception of returning servicemen encouraged female participation in civic organizations and published articles about the moral implications of atomic weapons. If women were urged to return to the kitchen after their work of the war years, it was not the same kitchen they had left; not only would it be stocked with products made possible by wartime technology, but within it they were to be as concerned with the quality of the educational system as with the quality of their casseroles.

Practical advice about the performance of everyday household tasks was available throughout the nineteenth century in such books as Lydia Maria Child's *The American Frugal Housewife* (1825) and Catharine Beecher's *Treatise on Domestic Economy* (1846 and 1868), but it became a staple of the periodical press only late in the century, with the advent of such magazines as *Ladies' Home Journal.* The success of such household "journals" and "companions" by the turn of the twentieth century can be attributed to several phenomena of the late nineteenth century. One, to which I have already alluded, was the increasing "professionalization" of housework, which was led by Beecher and others and had evolved into the "domestic science" movement by the end of the century. The application of scientific principles to the duties of the homemaker paralleled the "efficiency" movement in the nation's industrial production, assuring women that they too could benefit in their jobs from developments in science and technology. By the early twenti-eth century, the rhetoric of advertising reflected this correspondence. An ad for commercial laundries in the December 1929 issue of *Better Homes and Gardens*, for example, included the following text: "In the world of Business, men have banished the dragon of Drudgery. But what of *your* world? Are you still hampered by heavy household tasks that take your time and sap your strength?" (Marchand, *Advertising* 174). A second phenomenon was, ironically, the increased availability of products that should have—but did not—eased the homemaker's burden (just as canned soups and electric mix-ers later merely increased the standards for women's domestic perform-ance).[1] As Helen Damon-Moore points out in *Magazines for the Millions*, "As stoves replaced open fireplaces and products like flour were commercially produced, diets became more varied and cooking more complicated; as fab-ric was produced outside the home and paper patterns were made available for home use, wardrobes became more elaborate" (22). Damon-Moore notes yet a third phenomenon that increased women's need for printed homemak-ing assistance by the late nineteenth century: a decline in mother-daughter tutoring in a stable set of household tasks: "These new tasks and others meant that there were larger gaps between the experiences of one genera-tion of women and the next, a problem that was exacerbated in many cases by the physical separation of the generations resulting from migration. In a culture where at least some women were undertaking new tasks, and where women were often separated from traditional sources of advice and informa-tion, helpful-hints literature was potentially more and more relevant to many women's everyday activities" (22). Damon-Moore notes that in April 1884 the *Journal* reported with consternation that a survey of forty-eight girls at a Philadelphia boarding school showed that while all of them knew how to embroider and almost all could dance, only one could make bread and only three knew how to broil steak (46).

It is unlikely that Cyrus H. K. Curtis and his wife, Louisa Knapp Curtis, were aware in any very overt way of these trends when, in 1883, they de-cided to turn the "Women and Home" section of their weekly Philadelphia newspaper, the *Tribune and Farmer*, into a separate publication. Nor could either have dreamed that four years later the *Ladies' Home Journal*, as the new publication was called, would have more than 300,000 national sub-scribers. The Curtises did know, however, that "Women and Home," edited by Louisa, attracted increased attention—and increased advertising revenue—so that it seemed a sound business decision to establish first a women's supplement to the *Tribune and Farmer* and then a completely separate periodical. Cyrus Curtis proved to be a clever promoter of the magazine, and Louisa Knapp (her married name did not appear on the magazine) was equally talented as its editor, offering readers a mixture of domestic advice, fiction, and articles on topics of concern to women of the 1880s: for example, education, temperance, and women's organizations. The fact that "Practical Housekeeper" was the subtitle rather than the main title of the magazine suggests that household advice was a secondary concern, but in terms of space in the magazine, such was not the case. As Damon-Moore points out, however, the *Journal* also was not "simply a technical, how-to publication that corresponded only to the perfunctory aspects of woman's role" (37). Knapp recognized and addressed late-century instabilities in women's roles and aspirations and often sounded a progressive note, as when she argued that young women should be sufficiently educated to support themselves financially and wrote admiringly of advocates of female suffrage.

But along with such a forward-looking philosophy, which obviously resonated with the *Journal*'s rapidly increasing readership, the magazine also responded to women's increased purchasing power. Advertisers were interested in the women's magazines because of their ability to reach a particular group of potential consumers, and even in these early years, advertising revenue was crucial to a magazine's survival. All four of the magazines with the largest circulations by 1940 originated in some sort of commercial impulse: advertisers' interest primarily served to inspire Curtis to change the women's section of his newspaper to a separate publication within a few months in 1883; *McCall's*, begun by James and Belle McCall in 1876 as *The Queen, Illustrated Magazine of Fashion*, started as a circular to sell paper dress patterns; *Woman's Home Companion* and *Good Housekeeping* were established in 1873 and 1885, respectively, as mail-order catalogs.[2] Although each of these magazines developed a complex and in many ways sophisticated identity as a service magazine for the American homemaker, their ties with the sale of products remained strong, and because they matured at the same time that the development of advertising for print and other media itself became a big business, much of what the magazines taught women was conveyed in ads. By the 1920s, the trade magazines for professional advertisers commonly referred to the housewife as the "family G[eneral]. P[urchasing]. A[gent]." (Marchand, *Advertising* 168).

Just as the mixture of elements that would characterize the women's magazines—articles, advice, fiction (and, to a lesser extent, poetry), and advertising—was established early on, so too was the social class the magazines addressed and helped to define. Whereas *Godey's Lady's Book* had assumed an affluent reader (in part because that group possessed both literacy and leisure), Cyrus and Louisa Curtis targeted "white lower-middle-class to middle-class women from all over the country, women increasingly likely to live in towns and cities with populations of over ten thousand" (Damon-Moore 38). Not only did these readers have the potential for what was later termed upward mobility, they were, in Cyrus Curtis's view, solid, respectable citizens. Damon-Moore reports that Curtis was one of the first magazine publishers to do market research, studying areas that had large numbers of *Journal* subscribers. By the 1890s, he was satisfied that the readers of the *Journal* were "people who lived in the suburbs of large cities, and who were respected church-attenders; he also believed that the *Journal's* small-town readers belonged to the professional ranks in their communities" (38). Curtis's assumptions about his readership were echoed many years later by Herbert Mayes, who described *Good Housekeeping's* readers in the 1940s as "middle Americans. Middlebrow. In every way middle" (75).

But if magazine editors assumed their readers to be middle class (whether defined by income, geography, occupation, community standing, or taste), the editors also assumed that these readers aspired to improve their class standing, largely by improving their material surroundings. Editors Bruce and Beatrice Gould's decision in the mid-1930s to feature houses and clothing somewhat beyond those that *Ladies' Home Journal* readers could readily afford was in part a means of upgrading the image of the "Old Ladies' Journal," but it also tapped into the desire of Depression-weary Americans to dream of the more affluent lives they hoped someday to live. Nor were such perceived yearnings for improved social and material status merely a product of the Depression. Some version of the "rags to riches" story had been part of America's public rhetoric for at least 150 years, as the opportunities of capitalism belied the notion of a classless society. Well before the Goulds took over the editorship of *Ladies' Home Journal,* the advertisements in periodicals as diverse as *True Story, Literary Digest,* and *The Saturday Evening*

Post, as well as the major women's magazines, encouraged readers to envision themselves occupying a higher rung of society's ladder than most of them in fact did.

In *Advertising the American Dream,* a study of magazine advertising between 1920 and 1940, Roland Marchand locates the time of both dramatic expansion of advertising markets and a change in the way advertisers addressed consumers in the 1920s. Not only did the number of new products to be advertised increase dramatically during the period, but advertisers also embraced the concept of modernity, valuing "the new against the old, the modern against the old-fashioned" (xxi). This bias in favor of that which was new created a concomitant emphasis in advertising copy on "those styles, classes, behaviors, and social circumstances that were new and changing" (xxi). One effect of this focus on the modern, Marchand concludes, was to shift the emphasis from the product and its positive qualities to the consumer who would use it. "In their efforts to win over consumers by inducing them to live through experiences in which the product (or its absence) played a part, advertisers offered detailed vignettes of social life" (xxi), a social life that represented the tastes and activities of the upper-middle and upper classes, those who could most readily embrace the newest car, cigarette, or canned food. The change in focus is obvious in both the illustrations and the texts of advertisements. In the February 1886 *Journal,* for example, the Columbus Buggy Company ad features a simple line drawing of a buggy and a brief text that uses such phrases as "stands the severest use" and "absolutely reliable." In contrast, an ad for a Ford convertible in the August 1930 issue of the *Journal* shows what Marchand would refer to as a "tableau": the car is placed in a setting—specifically, on a boat dock—and the scene includes well-dressed people and yachts. Instead of pointing to specific attributes of the car, the printed text describes the experience of driving it in dreamlike terms: "the top down, the blue sky overhead, and the fresh, cool air brushing a rose glow upon your cheeks!" The text's tenor puts a dream within reach: "Rare indeed the woman who has not hoped that some day such a car might be her very own. That dream, long cherished, may now come true."

A common type of advertisement in the women's magazines of the 1930s and 1940s combines an interesting mix of elements: a visual appeal to the upwardly mobile, a textual appeal to the middle-class housewife, and a subtext of marital advice. A 1935 ad for Lifebuoy soap, for example, using the then popular multiframe "story" format, is titled in the first frame "True Life Experience No. 322," and text in the same frame tells readers that the story about to unfold is that of one of the "real" people who have written to the manufacturers of Lifebuoy. The couple pictured in succeeding frames are decidedly affluent for the 1930s, however—stylishly dressed and living in a comfortable home. In addition to presenting the "real" as an ideal, the ad's actual message is about personal hygiene, a message that the woman pictured would scarcely have needed. Although the woman is scrupulous about her cleaning and cooking, her husband has become distant, and when she asks why, he replies that it is important to a man that his wife be "sweet and dainty," which she properly interprets to mean clean. Her purchase and use of Lifebuoy soap is rewarded with a kiss and a bouquet of flowers, and she has learned her "lesson." Advertising, then, increasingly sold much more than specific products; it sold social-class aspirations, modes of behavior, and models of proper femininity.

Creating the Domestic Ideal

In his introduction to the 1960 *Good Housekeeping Treasury,* Donald Elder posits that many adult readers of *Good Housekeeping* were first acquainted with the magazine as children, not only because the magazine often included features designed for the young reader but also because of the world of possibilities displayed in its pages: "a whole fascinating world of fiction, illustrations, cover paintings, advertisements with pictures of houses, appetizing food, intriguing gadgets, far-off places, healthy babies in great numbers— there is hardly any childhood world comparable to it except that of the mail-order catalogue or a well-stocked attic" (13). Elder's comments suggest that *Good Housekeeping* and similar magazines offered the child a vision of what adulthood could be like—a time when the gadgets and babies would be one's own. He also suggests an interesting fusion of past and future: the "well-stocked attic" representing what had been saved by previous generations, while the "mail-order catalogue" offered consumer goods for tomorrow. In a very real way, the women's magazines sought to appeal to both nostalgia for former times and the desire to be up to date, and this dual purpose is also reflected in Elder's articulation of *Good Housekeeping's* definition of "home": "not merely . . . a shelter, but also . . . the fountainhead of social, cultural, and spiritual life" (13). The concept of the home as the wellspring of all of the affective areas of life harks back to nineteenth-century notions of the domestic space as the moral and spiritual counter to the evils of the public sphere and of the woman as its natural guardian.

But such a concept was alive with even greater force in the years during and after World War II, when *home* came to represent all that war did not: stability, peace, nurturance, and—one of the era's buzzwords—*normalcy.* In fact, by the end of the 1950s, the image of the idealized suburban family had entered the realm of international politics. In 1959, when Elder might have been writing his introduction to the *Good Housekeeping Treasury,* then Vice President Richard Nixon visited Moscow for the opening of a trade fair and engaged in what became known as the Kitchen Debate with Soviet leader Nikita Khrushchev. Nixon argued that the strength of American capitalism was evidenced by the freedom to choose one's own home and labor-saving devices. *Home* was thus the ideological opposition to communism, as a hundred years before *home* had been proposed as the moral antidote to business and political corruption. And, as Sonya Michel has pointed out, a public discourse that equated the family with democracy had gained force during the two decades that preceded the Kitchen Debate. At the White House Conference on Children in a Democracy in January 1940, President Franklin Roosevelt and others posited that the family was "the threshold of democracy . . . a school for democratic life" (Michel 155).

Just as the nineteenth-century concept of the domestic arena as America's moral center resulted in large part from certain conceptions of how women should (and should not) exert influence in the culture rather than from an objective map of reality, so cultural historians examining the mid–twentieth century have pointed out that the image of home and family as the source of all primary satisfactions was a construct created during and after World War II to promote the "American way of life" against external threat. In *The Way We Never Were,* Stephanie Coontz notes that the idealized midcentury family was not the culmination of a long tradition; instead, "the emphasis on producing a whole world of satisfaction, amusement, and inventiveness within the nuclear family had no precedents" (27). And Elaine Tyler May concurs in *Homeward Bound:* "[the postwar family] was the first wholehearted effort to create a home that would fill virtually all its members' personal needs through an energized and expressive personal life" (11).

If the idealized midcentury home and family was indeed a construction rather than a natural outgrowth of long tradition, who created this ideal? The question has no simple answer. A variety of forces, some easier to identify than others, converged before, during, and after World War II: the discrepancy between the hardships of the Depression and the rhetoric of the American Dream; wartime propaganda that valorized the home front as a site worth fighting for; governmental policies such as the Federal Housing Administration mortgage program; the development of new consumer products; the growth of the suburbs; the threat of the Cold War—all these factors and others played a part. The women's magazines were affected by these forces and in turn exerted their influence in combination with them. The magazines, in other words, became a lens through which numerous political, economic, and cultural developments could be focused on the American home and family.

There is ample evidence that the magazines played a role in defining the domestic long before 1940, and two particularly notable examples will serve to illustrate this phenomenon. One is the role of the *Ladies' Home Journal* in popularizing the simply designed, single-family suburban home in the early decades of the century. Edward Bok (son-in-law of Cyrus and Louisa Curtis), who edited the *Journal* from 1889 to 1919, was a social conservative who reacted against the turn-of-the-century "New Woman" by espousing the joys of motherhood and homemaking. Beginning in 1895, one of Bok's methods was to offer *Journal* readers inexpensive sets of complete plans for moderately priced homes: according to Kenneth T. Jackson in *Crabgrass Frontier*, "entire colonies of 'Ladies' Home Journal houses' sprung up" (186). Although architects initially were enraged at such an infringement on their livelihood, by 1906 architect Stanford White declared that "Edward Bok [had] more completely influenced American domestic architecture for the better than any man in [his] generation" (K. Jackson 186).

A second example of magazines' role in defining the domestic is the development of the Good Housekeeping Institute, which brought the concepts of scientific testing and product reliability to the American household in the early 1900s. *Good Housekeeping's* first publisher, Clark W. Bryan, was concerned that homemakers had little defense against unscrupulous manufacturers and misleading ads, so when readers reported to him problems with products advertised in his magazine, he made them the subjects of editorials. The magazine established fledgling testing facilities in 1900, and by 1902, *Good Housekeeping* offered to refund to readers the price of any inferior product advertised in its pages. By 1908 a full-scale testing "institute" existed; it was later administered by Dr. Harvey W. Wiley, who had drafted the legislation that created the Food and Drug Administration.

The original subtitle of *Good Housekeeping* was "A Family Journal Conducted in the Interests of the Higher Life of the Household." While it is impossible to know with any certainty what Bryan intended by the phrase "higher life," it seems clear that he meant something akin to Elder's later characterization of "home" as "the fountainhead of social, cultural, and spiritual life." While the relationship between house designs and product reliability on the one hand and with the "spiritual life" on the other might seem tenuous at best, women's magazines located the domestic precisely at the intersection between the realm of concrete, practical, useful advice and a set of values and beliefs. That is, the sum of the daily tasks involved in running a household was assumed to be far greater than its parts, creating an ethos that, however mythological we might today recognize it to be, could nonetheless exert great force on attitudes and behavior. Elaine May cites a fairly typical response to a longitudinal study of white suburban Americans conducted from the mid-1930s to the mid-1950s: one respondent stated that family life had "increased my horizons, defined my goals and purposes in life, strengthened my convictions, raised my intellectual standards and stimulated my incentive to provide moral, spiritual, and material support" (30). The increased role that women's magazines could play in the uplifting nature of domestic life by the early 1940s is encapsulated in a brief essay published in the March 1942 issue of *Woman's Home Companion.* The essay was written in response to a magazine editor's requirement that any women's club to which he was to speak must conduct an essay contest on the topic of why women bought and read magazines: "It seems to me we all want but one thing from our magazines: inspiration, if you will, or call it a new idea. Something that helps us make our lives better and richer with the beauty of living; something which will inspire us to a fuller, more comfortable life; something that will help us bring out the best in our homes, our children and ourselves.

You may find your inspiration in stories, musical articles, fashions or perhaps a linoleum advertisement. Where you have found this idea or inspiration matters not. You have got something out of these printed pages. They have made you a better person to live with. Perhaps the ideas have made your dinners more appetizing; your home a better place to live in; your clothes better styled to a particular type; or even made you a better wife and mother." The rhetoric of this peaen to women's magazines blends the specific and concrete (more appetizing meals, more stylish clothes) with the abstract ("beauty of living," "better person") in a way that suggests a causal relationship between *doing* and *being*—between cooking and morality, linoleum and a "fuller life."

The author of this essay stands at one end of a continuum of response to the women's magazines. At the other end, in addition to critics such as Jean Kerr and Joan Didion, were historians Charles A. Beard and Mary Ritter Beard, who, in their 1939 book *America in Midpassage*, excoriated the editors of the magazines for offering readers "fashion plates, fashion articles, society gossip, tepid fiction, bloodless sentimentality, Cinderellas, Fairy Princes, directions for the use of cosmetics, advertisements of the 'allure' " (741). Most readers doubtless fell somewhere between these extremes in their responses to the magazines, and there is no reliable way to ascertain their responses. Letters to the editor, which some of the magazines published, offer some clues, as do the questions that readers submitted to advice columns on topics ranging from personal appearance to cooking, but these sources do not constitute a representative sample. In addition, the magazine editors selected the letters and queries to be printed and thus exercised control over the written record that exists today. Only rarely did large numbers of readers of a given magazine respond either negatively or positively to a specific aspect of its content. One instance, recounted by Bruce Gould in *American Story*, occurred when the *Ladies' Home Journal*, profiling the family of a black Philadelphia physician in its "How America Lives" series in 1940, referred to the doctor's wife as "Mrs." rather than by her given name, prompting thousands of letters of outrage and a temporary drop of 200,000 in circulation, mainly in the southern states (Gould and Gould 204–5).

"In This Issue . . ."

A survey of the tables of contents of selected magazines provides insight into what editors assumed their readers wanted or needed to know as well as how such ideas changed from the early 1940s to the late 1950s. The contents pages of all the magazines were (and still are) subdivided by genre or topic, so that readers interested in short fiction, fashion, or cooking could see at a glance what a monthly issue offered. The January 1940 *Ladies' Home Journal* included one complete short novel, the fourth of five parts of a serialized novel, four short stories, and seven poems, including one by Paul Engle, who was then beginning a distinguished career as a poet and who later headed the Writers' Workshop master of fine arts program at the University of Iowa. As "Special Features," the issue included Dorothy Thompson's regular column, the results of a reader survey about psychic phenomena, an article by Rebecca West (who was then working on her 1941 two-volume study of Yugoslavia, *Black Lamb and Grey Falcon*), and an article titled "Your Chances of Making a Success of Marriage." Articles in the "General Features" category were those that appeared in each monthly issue; in January 1940, they included a doctor's article on child development, "As the Twig is Bent"; "The Sub-Deb," an advice column for teenage girls; a retrospective article called "Fifty Years Ago in the Journal"; and Gladys Taber's "Diary of Domesticity," a running account of life in the country that the *Journal* published from 1937 to 1957. The "Fashions and Beauty" section emphasized dressing for holiday parties and suggestions for last-minute Christmas gifts (the issue would have been delivered to subscribers and newsstands by mid-December), and the three articles on food in the "Food and Homemaking" section also had a holiday theme. The smallest group of articles in the issue was devoted to "Interior Decoration and Garden."

The July 1940 contents page of *Good Housekeeping* reveals a somewhat more utilitarian approach to domestic life. Like the *Journal, Good Housekeeping* at this time devoted a good share of its pages to fiction: this issue included portions of three serialized novels and six short stories, and the "Between the Book Ends" section offered eight poems. But of the eleven pieces in the "Special Articles" listing, most offer practical advice on such topics as "That Pain in the Pit of Your Stomach" and "How to Keep from Drowning." The "Special Features" offered information about "Incubator Babies" and "How to Visit an Invalid," the "Beauty Clinic" featured an article on "How to Walk," and the section devoted to fashion consisted primarily of patterns for sewing, knitting, and crocheting. Two of the largest and most directly instructive categories of articles were "The Studio," which focused on home design and gardening, and "The Institute," which dealt with cooking and appliances. Titles of articles in these sections suggest firm gender-role distinctions and posit the reader as needing advice: "Ask Your Husband To Make These Gates and Trellises," "How to Arrange Your Garden Flowers," "Look After the Man," and "When It's Hot, What to Eat." The single article in the "Babies" section is "Get Your Child through the Summer without Illness."

Woman's Home Companion provided similarly straightforward advice and information. The October 1948 issue, for example, included the usual complement of fiction—five short stories and portions of two serialized novels—and one article each on education, Hollywood, and politics ("The Democratic Party," by Arthur M. Schlesinger Jr.), but by far the majority of the articles instructed the reader on specific tasks, and the titles were often formulated as commands: the fashion section included "Take a Ball of Woolen Yarn"; the "Good Looks" section featured "Give Your Face a Lift"; and the homemaking section offered "Fix That Chair" and "Dye Your Faded Nylons." Also common in articles was the phrase "how to": "How to Fit a Foundation [Garment]," "Here's How" (recipes), "How to Keep Him Happy," and "See How to Knit a Baby Blanket." In November of the same year, readers were asked questions ("What's Wrong with Today's Family?" "Who's Your Favorite Hero?" "What's for Dessert?" "What Kind of Adult Will Your Child Be?") and given commands ("Reglue Those Rickety Chairs," "Cook Now for Thanksgiving," and "Stop That Leak!").

By 1951, *Redbook* had accomplished its transition from literary periodical to women's magazine, and while the questions its article titles asked the reader were not confined to household matters, the range of the magazine's concerns closely resembled that of the other periodicals for women. The November issue included "Are You Risking Cancer Because of False Modesty?" "Are We Starving Our Clergy?" "Psychologist's Casebook: No. 17," and "Toys for the Happy Child" as well as sections on current movies, radio programs, and fashions.

By the 1950s, not only advertising but editorial content reflected the postwar emphasis on family unity and home improvement. Women's magazines had long paid attention to seasonal cycles: fashion articles were keyed to changes in weather, and food and gardening features reflected the seasonal availability of produce (blueberry recipes in July, apple recipes in the fall) and cycles of planting, bloom, and harvest. But by the early 1950s, the magazines had intensified this seasonal emphasis, particularly in highlighting holidays and observances that could serve as occasions for family gatherings. Articles on cooking predictably presented special menus for Thanksgiving, Christmas, spring bridal showers, and the Fourth of July, but the magazines also advised on decorating and dressing for such occasions. The November 1950 issue of *Good Housekeeping* injected the spirit of Thanksgiving into even its fashion section, which featured such articles as "We Thank the Under-$20 Dress" and "We Thank the Shoe and Stocking." The July 1954 issue offered "A Guide to Entertaining: Family Fun for the 4th." The October 1956 *Woman's Home Companion* provided ways to share the "harvest bounty" with the family, and the December issue promised help with a "storybook Christmas," including setting up a "family theater" and an article on "The Folklore of Christmas." The May 1954 issue of *Ladies' Home Journal* followed a marriage theme. The "How America Lives" feature was "The Big Wedding," the fashion section advised on the "$100 Trousseau," and in addition to the regular "Making Marriage Work" and "Diary of Domesticity" articles appeared "Young Home-Builders" and "Happy Beginnings."

Even magazines not specifically identified as women's magazines reflected many of the same emphases in their contents. *Parents' Magazine*, with its focus on child rearing, promoted family life throughout the period. The majority of the August 1941 issue's articles were grouped under one of the following headings: "Feeding the Family"; "Family Home," which included products to buy for the home; "Family Fun"; and "Family Fashions." By 1953 the improvement of the home by the addition of appliances had become central to the magazine; the October issue's featured articles showcased the "Parents' Magazine Home" with its up-to-date equipment, and the issue offered readers a list of utility companies that were displaying the conveniences of this model home. In January 1958, *Parents'* included an article previewing that year's models of the essential family car, the station wagon. *Look*, which called itself "America's Family Magazine," was a photojournalistic competitor to *Life* and as such devoted a portion of each issue to news stories about politics, sports, and celebrities. But the emphasis on the domestic was unmistakable. The July 20, 1948, issue included an article about Shirley Temple as the mother of an infant, and the magazine devoted several sections to matters of particular interest to women: "Fashions and Beauty," "Food and Homemaking," and "Science and Medicine." By the early 1950s, *Look* had added a regular article on men's fashions and an "Entertainment" section that focused primarily on films and television programs suitable for family viewing. The November 18, 1952, issue featured articles about canned foods and dry soup mixes—convenience foods.

As more and more household appliances became available, the magazines touted their usefulness. Holiday and consumer themes merged in the title of an article in the November 1959 *Good Housekeeping:* "In Kitchens Like These, It's Thanksgiving Every Day." In November 1950 *Good Housekeeping* endorsed the steam iron; in July 1954 it described "More Small Electric Appliances That Work For You." By the mid-1950s, *Good Housekeeping* devoted a section of its contents page to "Appliances and Home Care," and *Woman's Home Companion* titled a similar section "Home Equipment." *McCall's* included product advice in its "Better Living" category, thus suggesting a link between household appliances and quality of life. The February 1959 issue of *McCall's* reported that homemakers felt the need for better household wiring to accommodate their electrical appliances and preferred appliances with "recognized brand names." By June 1960, so ubiquitous had washing machines, waffle irons, electric blenders, and other products become in the middle-class home that readers could relate to Joyce Lubold's article about the various repairmen who visited her house: "I am . . . a faithful, devoted, and loving housewife. Nevertheless, I must transform myself into the most flirtatious of plantation belles every time some major appliance breaks down. . . . Just now, the objects of my affection are three: Charlie Gant, who is tall and thin and repairs my washing machine; Huck Peters, who is short and heavy-set and tends to our television set; and Gus Marston, whose shape has always been hidden by loose-fitting coveralls hung with an electrician's tools." In addition to Lubold, writers such as Jean Kerr and Shirley Jackson made the appliance repairman a presence in their domestic humor, suggesting both a widespread dependence on these household fixtures and the woman's responsibility for overseeing their continued functioning.

In the world presented in such magazines as *Harper's Bazaar* and *Made-*

moiselle, neither washing machines nor those who used or repaired them were in evidence. Although these magazines, along with *Vogue,* were read by people at a variety of socioeconomic levels, the image they conveyed compounded leisure and affluence (less so in *Mademoiselle,* whose ideal reader was the young college woman). Primarily devoted to fashion and appearance, these magazines also provided features on travel, entertaining, and the arts. In the July 1949 issue, *Harper's Bazaar* published three short stories, an article on Maxim's restaurant in Paris and one on living in Barbados, and pictorial profiles of several wealthy couples in addition to many pages of the latest fashions for adult women and, in the "Junior Bazaar" section, the teenager. In November of the same year, *Mademoiselle* devoted its fashion pages to dressing for holiday parties and included articles on shopping for Christmas gifts, planning parties, and campus life. *Mademoiselle* and *Harper's Bazaar* presented different conceptions of the relationship between women and work—in the former, the young woman studied for her college courses, and each issue included a "Jobs and Futures" section for her postgraduate life, whereas the *Bazaar* woman might plan a charity ball—but they differed sharply in this regard from the service magazines, in which women's lives were an endless round of familial nurturance. The upscale magazines required certain domestic skills but did so for special occasions rather than for daily life: setting the table for a dinner party, making a fall suit for college football games, learning to make new drinks for summer entertaining.[3]

And yet, as magazines such as *Harper's Bazaar* and *Mademoiselle* instructed women on how to dress, select silver patterns, and function as hostesses, these publications participated in the creation of a midcentury domestic world. Like *Good Housekeeping* and *Ladies' Home Journal,* these magazines assumed the centrality of the nuclear family to the American way of life and carried the implicit assumption that if a few could possess mansions and social prestige, then the capitalistic system that was the subject of so much political rhetoric in the postwar years was vindicated. The women's magazines did not present a unitary, cohesive image of either domesticity or woman's role in the 1940s and 1950s. They acknowledged differences in social class, taste, values, and aspirations and responded to changes in them over the course of two decades. All the magazines shared, however, an abiding faith in the possibility of improvement, whether such improvement occurred in one's skin tone, pie crust, sex life, living room decor, health, or standard of living.

"Can This Marriage Be Saved?"

As the cultural emphasis on domestic life gained force by the 1940s in everything from political rhetoric to product advertising, the women's magazines responded by expanding their role as domestic advisers on both the practical and the affective areas of life. "How-to" articles took on an urgency that was thinly masked by a breezy style that suggested an immediate solution to every problem. If, as David Abrahamson suggests, the fabric of social reality was being rewoven, the magazines suggested that the average reader could accomplish the task in a matter of minutes, given the proper skills and equipment. The scope and repetition of such advice invited the criticism of some contemporary observers, a criticism that in turn testifies to both the visibility of the magazines on the national scene and their perceived power to affect the lives of women and men. While critics noted the contradictions inherent in some of the advice the magazines dispensed, they tended not to see what hindsight allows us to understand: that contradictions about, for example, the proper relationship between mother and child were not flaws in the magazines' editorial philosophies but reflections of an ongoing debate about defining domestic ideality.

In the January 1960 issue of *Esquire* magazine, Kerr published an article titled "Can This Romance Be Saved?" The article is a double parody: its title and format evoke the series "Can This Marriage Be Saved?" which began in the *Ladies' Home Journal* in the early 1940s and is still running. In Kerr's story, the clients who tell their stories to the marriage counselor are Lolita and Humbert, the central characters of Vladimir Nabokov's controversial novel *Lolita*, which had been published in America two years earlier. Kerr's humorous piece thus brings together the midcentury world of the popular women's magazines, with their emphasis on proper domestic harmony, and the consciously daring and sophisticated world of *Esquire* ("The Magazine for Men") and a novel about sexual obsession. Kerr's parody follows the by-then time-honored format of "Can This Marriage Be Saved?": the marriage counselor allows each member of the troubled couple to tell his or her side of the story and concludes with advice for resolution of the conflict. What makes Kerr's parody particularly rich is that, as in Nabokov's novel, Humbert, having murdered a rival for the affections of the prepubescent Lolita, speaks from his jail cell, so that a normal domestic reconciliation is out of the question. Also true to the novel is the fact that Lolita by no means reciprocates Humbert's adoration of her, so that although she promises the marriage counselor that she will await Humbert's release from prison (in forty-five years, when he is eighty-five), the twelve-year-old comments, "with my luck, he'll *get* out of the clink" (71).[4]

Later in the same year, Didion published her own send-up of "Can This Marriage Be Saved?" in the *National Review*. In "Marriage a la Mode," Didion claimed to be "incurably addicted" to women's magazines, an addiction that has allowed her to absorb the lessons they teach, especially about solving marital problems. The heart of Didion's article is a review of a published collection of twenty case histories from the *Journal* series, all presided over by Paul Popenoe, the *Journal*'s contributing marriage counselor for many years. Didion focused on the simplistic and blithely optimistic nature of Popenoe's advice, which usually required the woman of the couple to do most of the adjusting. One wife whose husband was about to abandon her for another woman was encouraged to engage in what Didion describes as "a cool battle which involved her losing eight pounds, learning 'to choose smarter clothes in more becoming colors,' and, I swear to God, joining the League of Women Voters" (90). Another woman in the same situation staved off disaster by planning more family activities and spending more money on herself and the children to give her husband "the satisfaction of feeling like an extra-good provider." Popenoe concluded that this woman "is sure there is no danger of [her husband's] ever becoming interested in another woman" because "she and the children occupy too much of his time." Didion commented wryly, "And, although Dr. Popenoe leaves the point implicit, his money" (90). After analyzing Popenoe's inordinate faith in "Talking Things Out," Didion concluded, "*noli me tangere*, Dr. Popenoe" (91).

These satiric treatments of the *Ladies' Home Journal*'s longest-running feature came from the pens of two authors whose concerns as writers were otherwise very different. Kerr, a playwright who sometimes collaborated with her husband, drama critic Walter Kerr, has become better known for her semiautobiographical works depicting humorously the life of the mid-century homemaker: *Please Don't Eat the Daisies* (1957), *The Snake Has All the Lines* (1960), *Penny Candy* (1970), and *How I Got to Be Perfect* (1978). The subjects of these books—parenting, housekeeping, and gender roles—allied Kerr, at least on the surface, with the agendas of the women's magazines, and Betty Friedan, in *The Feminine Mystique,* blamed both the magazines and writers such as Kerr for refusing to recognize women's real dissatisfactions with the homemaker's role. Didion, in contrast, is a novelist and social critic who depicts social and moral disintegration in modern life in such works as *Play It as It Lays* (1970), *A Book of Common Prayer* (1977), and *The White Album* (1979). Didion's grim analyses of decay are in many ways quite different from Kerr's comic accounts of suburban life. Yet, as I have argued elsewhere,[5] Kerr is in her own way a social critic, encasing in her humor a subtle protest against the trivialization of women's domestic lives.

In 1960, when Kerr was in her thirties and Didion in her twenties, *Ladies' Home Journal* had been a force in the lives of American women for more than seventy years, and these authors' responses to the magazine testify to its potential to influence women's thinking and behavior. Indeed, in both "Can This Romance Be Saved?" and "Marriage a la Mode," Kerr and Didion also address aspects of the women's magazines other than their marriage-counseling features. Didion distills some of the "tenets of contemporary life" in which the magazines have "schooled" her, including the fact that the magazines recognize two different kinds of women, "Homemakers" (those who are happy with their domestic roles) and "Housewives" (those who are not). No matter which kind of woman one is, "women carry on the world's work," and "that work is *never done.*" Men, Didion has gleaned, "are almost as amusing as children, besides being a help around the house, at least when they aren't out Gambling, Letching at Office Parties, or Taking Themselves Seriously." Didion was also perceptive about the magazines' function as purveyors of consumer goods, as she notes in another "tenet": "Although money never brings happiness, electrical appliances often do" (90). More subtle is Kerr's nod to the controversy about motherhood that had raged in the women's magazines for nearly two decades: women who were attentive to their children risked spoiling and smothering them, while the inattentive mother was assumed to create emotionally deprived juvenile delinquents. On either side of a narrow margin, then, lay failure, which Kerr encapsulates in the marriage counselor's concluding remarks. Humbert has had the ultimate in inattentive mothers—she died when he was an infant—"and so, quite naturally, he hated her." Lolita's mother, conversely, "danced attendance on her day and night. Naturally, she hated her" (71).

Several years before Kerr and Didion articulated their discomfort with the messages the women's magazines conveyed, those magazines had been the target of a very different kind of attack in the periodical press. In "The Pious Pornographers," published in the October 1957 issue of *Playboy,* Ivor Williams chastised the women's magazines for presenting sexuality as a problem rather than a source of pleasure. "For years," Williams began, "I have been bumbling along in the naive belief that the women's magazines were devoted solely to such matters as how to chintz up the living room and get a cake to rise. But it seems I was wrong—the most worrisome problem facing milady's monthly gazettes is how to muss up the marriage bed and keep one's mate aroused" (25). Williams's central argument was that, using the guise of dispensing advice, the women's magazines were at least as frank about sexual matters as were magazines such as *Playboy:* "By approaching the subject with a medical license and a little black bag, there were clearly no limits on how far the ladies' books could go" (62). In addition to articles by doctors, Williams found sex under discussion in the magazines' fiction and in features on marriage—including "Can This Marriage Be Saved?" which was devoted to "matrimonial rescue work, with a special disaster squad headed by Paul Popenoe" (26). The magazines' tendency to address sexual problems most bothered Williams and caused him to refer to "the sick, sad sex kick of the ladies' magazines" (64).

Williams's motivation for critiquing the women's magazines of course differed greatly from that of Kerr and Didion, who wrote as part of the potential audience for the magazines, aware of the contradictions of some of the messages they conveyed. In contrast, Williams wrote in large part to defend *Playboy*—which had begun publication four years earlier—against charges that it exploited female sexuality. Yet these articles share the perception that midcentury women's magazines were forces to be reckoned with, that they were sufficiently pervasive to have cultural power: Didion declared herself "incurably addicted" to them; Williams described women avidly reading *Redbook* and *Cosmopolitan* in his dentist's waiting room. This anecdotal evidence is supported by statistics. As early as 1940, *Ladies' Home Journal* claimed the largest circulation of any magazine in the world, and during the postwar period the other leading women's magazines—*Good Housekeeping, Woman's Home Companion,* and *McCall's*—had subscriber lists of between 2 and 8 million people, which did not count newsstand sales or multiple readers of individual issues.

Indeed, the fact that the editors of *Esquire,* the *National Review,* and *Playboy* saw fit to print articles critical of the women's magazines testifies to their perception that the magazines had wide cultural familiarity in mid-twentieth-century America. The target audience of *Esquire* and *Playboy* was composed of youthful, affluent, sophisticated men—and men who aspired to these attributes—who were nonetheless assumed to be familiar with the contents of magazines designed for female readers. Williams was not incorrect in his assumption that the magazines emphasized home decor and cooking; although he posits his cleaning woman as their likely reader in his household, the magazines—specifically *Redbook* and *Ladies' Home Journal*—are in his own kitchen. Even though such magazines assumed a largely female readership, the fact that they also assumed that women lived in families meant that they could be—and were—read by everyone in the home.[6]

In a sense, however, other family members did not actually have to read such magazines as *Ladies' Home Journal, Good Housekeeping, McCall's,* and *Woman's Home Companion* to feel their effects. As most of the titles suggest, these magazines offered readers guidance that could materialize in the form of a new casserole for dinner, a color scheme for the living room, the treatment of a childhood disease, or the purchase of a certain brand of soap or washing machine. Indeed, these service magazines sought to address nearly every aspect of women's lives, from how they dressed to how they could save their marriages, in a way unmatched by any parallel development in magazines for men. As Marjorie Ferguson points out in *Forever Feminine,* men's magazines have typically been more specialized, directed at some particular aspect of male life such as business, sports, or hobbies, not for "the totality of his masculinity, nor the male role as such" (2). Ferguson argues that the implicit assumption of magazines attempting to address the "totality" of women's experience is that "a female sex which is at best unconfident, and at worst incompetent, 'needs' or 'wants' to be instructed, rehearsed or brought up to date on the arts and skills of femininity" (2). Further, the magazines' heavy reliance on advertisements, which escalated during the first half of the twentieth century, adds the element of the woman as consumer, so that the magazines provided, in Ferguson's words, "a particular female world view of the desirable, the possible, and the purchasable" (2). In a 1970 article in the *North American Review*, Nora L. Magid put the matter succinctly: "Women's magazines teach women to be women" (25).

While Ferguson and Magid are correct in their perception that magazines intended primarily for women readers differ qualitatively from publications marketed to men, especially in the comprehensive nature of the advice offered, Ferguson's and Magid's observations are ahistorical, collapsing all women's magazines into the moment at which these authors wrote. As I suggested in the previous chapter, there are significant differences in magazines' content before 1940 and at midcentury, and one of those differences is a dramatic increase in the number of pages devoted to providing direct, practical advice on ever-increasing areas of domestic life. In contrast to the instructive nature of the midcentury magazines, reflected in the tables of contents surveyed previously in this chapter, the earlier magazines included perhaps half a dozen articles that could be considered instructional. The March 1924 *McCall's*, for example, included one article each on home decor, cooking, child care, health, and gardening and featured nine short stories or parts of serialized novels. The December 1926 *Woman's Home Companion*, a periodical that described itself as "The Indispensable Magazine," offered directions for making seasonal wreaths, several sets of embroidery and crochet patterns, a fashion section, two articles on cooking, and one on nutrition. The April 1934 *Companion* shows increased emphasis on instruction, but much of it applies to special occasions rather than daily living—for example, shopping for wedding gifts, a recipe for a luncheon party, and Paris fashions for spring social events. The shift in the 1940s to practical guidance for everyday domestic life received its impetus from the new prominence given the domestic in American culture and, perhaps most insistently, from the exigencies of World War II itself, which presented a host of problems to be addressed, including the rationing of products and materials, child care for working women, and an increase in single-parent households.

"What Every Woman Knows by Now"

The fact that "Can This Marriage Be Saved?" has been featured in virtually every issue of *Ladies' Home Journal* for nearly sixty years testifies to the perception of the magazine's editors that its ideal readers were, wanted to be, had been, or in any event should be married. This ideological location of the middle-class woman in a (heterosexual) relationship reinforces her domestic—as opposed to her intellectual or paid professional—life. The concept of the domestic had undergone both practical and ideological changes since 1869, when Catharine Beecher and Harriet Beecher Stowe published *The American Woman's Home*, dedicated to "the women of America, in whose hands rest the real destinies of the republic." In her *Treatise on Domestic Economy*, first published in 1846 and revised in 1868, Beecher outlined a woman's duties as including not only the care of husband and children—including the moral instruction of the latter—but also the supervision of servants, maintaining a proper social life, and duties to the larger community: "the poor to relieve; benevolent societies to aid" (156–57). As *The American Woman's Home* makes clear, the nineteenth-century homemaker's household responsibilities included many that had dropped away by the middle of the twentieth century, including the preparation of medicines for the ill, the maintenance of wood fires, the care of cows and poultry, and the making of butter. By 1940 the domestic was commonly understood to mean work performed to sustain the daily needs of family members, which rarely included servants or livestock; professionals largely took care of the ill and the indigent, and while a housewife was expected occasionally to serve as hostess, the etiquette of calling cards was a thing of the past. One area of responsibility that Beecher lists in her *Treatise*, however, had taken on renewed and altered importance. Her 1868 homemaker was "required to regulate the finances of the domestic state, and constantly to adapt expenditures to the means and to the relative claims of each department" (156). While the woman Beecher addressed in 1868 and the one the women's magazines addressed in the mid–twentieth century were both disbursing money earned by their husbands, the magazines had become such important vehicles of product advertising as to define the domestic to include the homemaker's purchasing power, as I will discuss in more detail in chapter 4. As the nuclear family and the material possessions of middle-class life became two of the central hallmarks of domestic culture, the magazines—in both editorial content and advertising—reflected the fact that women were to be rewarded for preserving them.

Also by 1940, the visual layout of women's magazines had completed an evolutionary change that mingled editorial and advertising content in a manner that mirrored the interactions between the home and the culture at large. In a study of *Ladies' Home Journal* between 1919 and 1939, Sally Stein has shown how the textual content (articles and stories) and the advertising portions of the magazine became increasingly interwoven with one another in terms of page layout, so that, pursuing an article or story to its conclusion, a reader necessarily traveled through many pages of advertisements for consumer goods. Stein links the increased emphasis on advertising to developments in workplace "efficiency" led by such people as industrial engineer Frederick Winslow Taylor; as factory workers could be encouraged to meet certain standards of performance and production given certain incentives, so could the American homemaker. Before 1940, Stein asserts, magazines such as the *Journal* were "rationalized as marketing vehicles, providing an optimal context in which to sell new domestic commodities" (148). Such commodities served both as tools of instruction and as rewards; the magazines "constructed a paradoxical vision of housework: scientifically reducible to its component parts yet containing still an irreducible quality of romance" (148). The physical format of the magazines' pages underscored both standards and rewards:

> The format could be made to mirror the compartmentalization of domestic tasks, while supplying instruction in all phases of this minutely detailed work. The magazine neatly categorized performance standards in matters of dressing, decorating, cleaning, cooking, child-rearing . . . and the repairing of home and marriage if constant attention proved to be insufficient. And unlike conventional instruction manuals, it provided a constant stream of promises—false promises, or at least inflated ones—of personal benefits that would result from tending new machines and using new materials. What these promises lacked in substance, they made up for in vividness—the kind of tantalizing but tawdry incentive proposed by . . . Taylor in his discussion of the "scientific management" of young, low-paid, female factory workers: "encouragement either in the form of personal attention from those over them or an actual reward in sight as often as once an hour." (148)

Stein's emphasis on the visual format of the women's magazines is well placed, for in addition to page layouts that led readers through multiple advertisements, both the editorial content and the advertising were (and are) heavily dependent on photographs and drawings to convey their messages.[7]

These visual images participated in the instructive function of the magazines—a recipe, for example, might be accompanied by photographs of its various steps and/or a picture of what the finished product should look like; articles on fashion or sewing necessarily featured pictures of apparel. But the promises of "personal benefits" that were to accrue to the conscientious homemaker were also conveyed visually. While getting a cake or casserole to look (and presumably taste) like the one pictured in the magazine might be a sufficient reward for following instructions, the magazines made clear that a woman's true reward was the approval of others. In both articles and advertisements, women who have mastered a household task are pictured receiving the admiration of their neighbors, guests, husbands, or entire families. A midcentury ad for frozen (then usually called frosted) green beans serves as an extreme—though not unique—example of this tendency: the homemaker, having managed to bring the beans to serving temperature, is drawn holding a steaming platter of them aloft, surrounded by her beaming family—including the dog.

Such rewards for domestic accomplishment are most obviously and fancifully rendered in the magazines' advertising sections, as Stein further notes: "Of course, since they were underwritten by advertisers, magazines were well suited to construct a visual argument for the rewards of modern domesticity. . . . Given their periodic appearance, the magazines were an especially effective means of inculcating new habits and standards. Once a month, the drilling and instructions were repeated, in slightly different form, and each repetition was accompanied by a new repetition of the rewards" (148–49). The repetition of domestic instruction that the magazines offered did not escape the attention of some readers. In "What Every Woman Knows by Now," published in the *Atlantic Monthly* in 1950, Marghanita Laski marvels at the fact that women continue to read the magazines, when "any one year's reading must inevitably give enough information about the technique of being a woman to see one through a lifetime" (90). Laski's summary of the magazines' instructions is drawn at least as much from the editorial content as from the advertising, but it reinforces the fact that women's success in following such instructions was to be measured by the external approbation of others—specifically, men. After noting the three remedies the magazines recommended for improving one's body shape (check for glandular problems, exercise, be fitted with a good corset), Laski concludes, "Men like good figures" (90). Regarding women's intellectual improvement, Laski sums the magazines' advice as "Read good books sometimes," but she cautions, "Men don't like cultured women much" (91). Laski's pithy summaries also point to the fact that the magazines often provided conflicting advice: "If you can't afford good furs don't have any, but there are some awfully good cheap ones in the shops"; "Choose the hair style that suits you *and* don't get into a rut" (90).

The imperative style that Laski chooses in her parody of women's magazines' advice reflects the commandlike titles of articles that appeared especially in such fashion magazines as *Mademoiselle* and *Harper's Bazaar*: "Slip into Silk," "Make a Blouse," "Keep Your Hair On," "Take a Lesson." The more general-purpose magazines, such as *Good Housekeeping* and *Woman's Home Companion*, also used this approach, using such titles as "Don't Put All Your Eggs in the Same Old Recipes," "Keep up with Medicine," "Make Your Mantel Count!" "Help Your Child to Wonder," and "Sew With an Eye to Summer." More common in the general-purpose magazines, however, were titles including the phrase "How to" (press a suit, make sense out of politics, bake a prizewinning cake) or asking the reader a question: "Are You Too Educated to be a Mother?" "Do You Make These Beauty Blunders?" "Are You Afraid of Childbirth?" "What's Wrong With Today's Family?" and, of course, "Can This Marriage Be Saved?" Such titles suggest an intimacy with the reader that is poised somewhere between helpful friend and intrusive judge, and Margaret Halsey terms the latter characterization the "Invisible Critic" that, she imagines, "inhabited a corner of the room, up near the ceiling" of her suburban home (141). Magid discerns an uneasy teacher-student relationship in the "service" area of the magazines: "It resembles the old one-room schoolhouse, in which the instructor had simultaneously to manage many learners at many stages. Some housekeepers are beginners, some have been at it for years. For each, different instructions need to be devised; and for all, convenience foods and new designs must be pushed. You may have a toaster, or even—heaven forfend—make toast in the oven. . . . You certainly must buy a blender, an electric can opener, an outdoor carpet. . . . Promotion is . . . the primary business of the women's magazines" (24–25). In the eyes of such critical observers, then, the domestic ideal fostered by the midcentury magazines was the woman as consumer—of products, certainly, but also of advice, instruction, enlightenment, and reassurance.

"The Prime Objective . . . Is to Survive"

Magid's use of the term *business* is telling: like all magazines, the women's magazines were (and are) businesses, with their primary product themselves. Thus when Herbert R. Mayes wrote in his autobiography, *The Magazine Maze,* that "the prime objective of a magazine is to survive" (88), he was stating a simple truth with complex implications. Mayes served as editor of *Good Housekeeping* and then *McCall's* between 1939 and 1969, and in reflecting on those years he assessed the content of these mass-circulation magazines with an eye to the bottom line: advertisers, subscription figures, circulation, and competition from other periodicals. Recognizing that such magazines "appealed to readers of varying interests, intelligence, age, and income and geographical demographics," he acknowledged that "it was as crucial not to talk up as not to talk down" (88). Whereas David L. Cohn, in his 1943 book *Love in America,* accused the editors of women's magazines of having "a corrosive contempt for the intelligence of their readers" (183), Mayes posited that an editor's job was to respond to, not to form, the reader's tastes: "The appetite for 'think' pieces and polished prose was relatively small; for the personality feature, insatiable" (88). Yet Mayes perceived the women's magazines as performing certain services, which he was fully prepared to defend: "It never occurred to us that advice on how to look and dress and cook better, how to make a home lovelier to live in, was less important than a polemic on the Christian ethic. The multimillion-circulation magazine was under no obligation, and isn't, to try to sway the populace with proposals for reforming society. It does not print for eternity, but for today. It performs its duty and performs it well if it offers an amalgam of fact and fiction, some of it entertaining, some enlightening, some defiant, and some practical. It fails in its obligation if it doesn't carry promise of hope and escape from the too generally depressing state of the world. . . . To cheer a little, inform a little, challenge a little—such tasks represent no mean achievement" (91). While Mayes saw his role as businessman cum domestic cheerleader, several decades earlier Gertrude Lane viewed her relationship with the reader of *Woman's Home Companion* as at once more intimate and more respectful. Lane, who served as the *Companion*'s editor in chief from 1912 until 1941, regarded her reader as holding her to high standards: "She is not the woman who wants to do *more* housework, but the woman who wants to do *less* housework so that she will have more time for other things. She is intelligent and clearheaded. I must tell her the truth. She is busy; I must not waste her time. She is forever seeking new ideas; I must keep her in touch with the best" (qtd. in Tebbel and Zuckerman 99).

As many who have studied the American homemaker over the course of the twentieth century have pointed out, women increasingly did more rather than less housework, despite Lane's perception of their desires (see, for example, Berch esp. chap. 6; Hoy esp. chap. 6; Mathews esp. chap. 8; Schwartz; Strasser, *Never Done*). In May 1930, midway through Lane's editorship of the *Companion*, a writer in *Ladies' Home Journal* described this escalation in terms that seem to link it to the very advice and information the magazines provided: "Because we housewives of today have the tools to reach it, we dig every day after the dust that Grandmother left to a spring cataclysm. If few of us have nine children for a weekly bath, we have two or three for a daily immersion. If our consciences don't prick us over vacant pie shelves or empty cookie jars, they do over meals in which a vitamin may be omitted or a calorie lacking." As one of the major means of disseminating information about household technology and scientific advancement, the magazines were, unwittingly, in the odd position of increasing the domestic demands on the readers they sought to serve. The magazines, however, continually promoted themselves as lightening the homemaker's burden, in concert with science and technology. In a retrospective look at the first seventy-five years of *Woman's Home Companion*, for example, Sophie Kerr, a former managing editor of the magazine, wrote of the decades during which Lane came to work for the *Companion*, "This first decade of the twentieth century began the decisive emergence of women from household drudgery. This was and still is a progressive movement. By improved house construction, labor-saving machines and devices, the ready-made clothing industry, the commercial preservation and distribution of all varieties of food, women's work in the home has been incredibly simplified and lightened."

When Bruce and Beatrice Gould took over the editorship of the *Ladies' Home Journal* in 1935, they accepted a mandate from the Curtis Publishing Company (which also published *The Saturday Evening Post*) to make the

Journal survive as a business. According to a Gallup poll (itself then a new phenomenon in American life), the *Journal* ranked fourth in the favor of American women, behind *Good Housekeeping, Woman's Home Companion,* and *McCall's.* In certain quarters—most damaging, among advertising executives—the magazine was nicknamed the "Old Ladies' Journal"; it was regarded as old-fashioned and stodgy, despite—or perhaps because of—its venerable reputation as one of the oldest extant periodicals for women.[8] The Goulds recalled the challenge as necessarily twofold: to provide a more "fresh" and "inviting" layout to entice advertisers and to alter the content to win the readers' "trust and affection" (164). The latter was the Goulds' higher priority, and they were fortunate enough to have the support of *Post* editor George Horace Lorimer, who was the final authority on the *Journal* as well.[9] "Advertisers, [Lorimer] believed, as did Bok and [Cyrus] Curtis before him, profit most from a magazine enthusiastically loved and trusted by its readership. No 'commercials' should be slyly slipped in to weaken the readers' faith" (Gould and Gould 171). This philosophy prompted the Goulds, early in their tenure as *Journal* editors, to decline the advertising revenue offered by a pharmaceutical company for a series of ads encouraging women to douche daily with a strong disinfectant.[10] Suspicious of the health consequences of such a practice—and repelled by the scare tactics used in the advertising copy—the Goulds insisted on consulting with a number of respected gynecologists, all of whom agreed that such a douche should not be recommended. The Goulds' decision lost the *Journal* half a million dollars in advertising income at a time when the magazine's financial situation remained precarious.

Rejecting advertising on the grounds that it promotes a dangerous practice is, however, a different matter than refusing to allow a magazine's editorial content to be dictated by its advertising or than failing to attract advertising for, say, a brand of electric stove if kitchen designs feature only gas stoves. Bruce Gould reported that he was determined to be independent of the *Journal*'s advertisers: "We knew early that we didn't want our magazine to be that deadening thing, a catalogue for advertisers. Ham recipes published opposite a page advertising ham arouse some skepticism. Uncritical puffs for dishwashers without realistic discussion of their home performance may please manufacturers, but owners of failing appliances may begin to feel, 'You can't believe what you read in the papers.'" Gould acknowledged, though, that the pressure to bow to the wishes of advertisers was greater for a women's magazine such as the *Journal* than it was for the *Post*, which did not "show pictures of ideal laundries (with trade-marked automatic dryers), did not use recipes (cake mixes, canned soups, coffee are advertisers)" (Gould and Gould 170). Gould here hinted at a problem for women's magazines that has since been fully explored in Gloria Steinem's classic essay, "Sex, Lies, and Advertising": without what advertisers term a "supportive editorial atmosphere" or "complimentary copy," the makers of consumer goods are largely unwilling to place ads in the magazines (131). In other words, unless the articles in the magazine endorse the use of certain products—from face creams to electric mixers—their makers assume that readers are not being sufficiently "instructed" in the products' benefits. The result, Steinem concludes, is that magazines for women have a "nothing-to-read" feeling that stems from "all the supposedly editorial pages that are extensions of ads" (157). In such a climate, the Goulds' declaration of independence seems noble but naive.

For late-nineteenth- and early-twentieth-century magazine editors and publishers, the advent of large-scale advertising was a great boon. Not only did it bring the magazines a steady stream of revenue, but many saw it as a means of improving society. For Frank Munsey, editor of *Munsey's Magazine* (1889–1929), advertising brought the manufacturer directly into contact with the consumer, eliminating several layers of middlemen and thus reducing costs. Further, in Munsey's view, such direct communication created a more trusting atmosphere between producer and consumer: "I don't believe there is a man anywhere who is manufacturing for the people, merchandising for the people, who can afford not to talk to the people about what he has for them—to put himself in touch with them, to make them know him and have confidence in him" (477).

Even the testing of products that the magazines claimed—often with justification—was a service to readers was sometimes posited as a similar link between producer and consumer. In an article describing the *McCall's* test kitchen in the January 1925 issue, the editor of the Department of Food and Household Management declared that one purpose of the kitchen was to "help the manufacturer to serve [the housewife] more directly and with greater satisfaction": "There was a time when the manufacturer turned out his product with little first-hand knowledge of its adaptability to the housewife's needs, and when the housewife accepted the product without being able to voice her suggestions or criticisms. That time has passed. Such a laboratory as the McCall kitchen serves as the practical link between producer and consumer." Two decades later, in a sixtieth-anniversary *Woman's Home Companion* retrospective, the editors praised advertising for providing a service to women by making possible the mass-circulation magazine: "We may appropriately recall, as part of our own history, that the first food advertising in magazines had appeared in 1870 and the first advertising of prepared breakfast foods in 1872. It is a tribute to the shrewdness of the founders of the Companion that they saw so immediately the approach of the great wave of national advertising which was to inform women widely and swiftly of their growing freedom and was also to make possible a new type of magazine, generous in content and low in price." Few people saw until later the ways in which advertising was implicated in social-class aspirations or its effect on the editorial content of the magazines. And, by mid-century, before television became the most attractive medium for selling products, advertisers increasingly regarded mass-circulation magazines as an effective way to reach large numbers of consumers. The total amount spent on such advertising increased from $140 million in 1935 to $730 million in 1955.

In contrast to former *Journal* editor Bok, Bruce and Beatrice Gould, like Lane, respected and felt they understood readers' needs and desires. Bok had written of himself in *The Americanization of Edward Bok* (1923), "He did not dislike women, but it could not be said that he liked them. . . . Nor had he the slightest desire, even as an editor, to know them better, or to seek to understand them" (168).[11] The Goulds, in contrast, believed that understanding the women who read their magazine was the key to its survival, and Bruce Gould attributed much of the *Journal*'s eventual success to Beatrice's valuable perspective: "I had the advantage . . . of a woman's true point of view—a woman who dared talk back, who didn't think women were dolts, shrews, or angels sheltered from the facts of life" (Gould and Gould 167). One of these "facts of life" in 1936 was that the rate of women's death in childbirth in America was six per thousand live births, higher than in most industrialized countries (Gould and Gould 172). The Goulds, though self-described as "not exactly crusaders" (172), were moved to launch a series of articles titled "Why Should Mothers Die?" that recommended full investigation of every maternal or infant death and that enraged many in the medical community.[12]

Other changes the Goulds made to revitalize the "Old Ladies' Journal" in the late 1930s had less to do with social reform and more to do with the quality of women's daily lives. Distressed by the magazine's architectural plans for modest homes that featured kitchens that were "small, efficient, antiseptic as a laboratory" (Gould and Gould 165) and that included only two bedrooms, the editors called for designs that enlarged the kitchen and had at least three bedrooms. They were similarly dismayed by fashion articles that featured "average-priced average clothes, photographed on average women, fitting them averagely well" (165). When the fashion editor protested that the clothes were "suitable for the ordinary housewife," Beatrice insisted that each issue of the *Journal* include "one beautiful spread of dream clothes" (166). While such changes evoked the approval of readers and advertisers alike, the *Journal* also was increasingly presenting what the reader should want and aspire to—a larger house, more stylish clothing—and thus helping to define domestic concerns in terms of consumer culture. As the Depression years wore on, few Americans were in a position to realize such aspirations, but in the period of relative affluence after World War II the fulfillment of such desires not only was within the reach of more people but had also come to represent the reasons why the war had been fought: for the way of life of the American family.

In constructing a particular version of domesticity during the 1940s and 1950s, then, the women's magazines were not fulfilling a stated agenda but instead, as business ventures, were responding to a variety of economic, social, and political forces that helped to determine the climate within which they published and, hence, what they published. Individual editors could— and did—affect the tenor of the magazines, of course. Bruce and Beatrice Gould introduced greater attention to political issues to the staid *Journal,* most prominently through a regular column by Dorothy Thompson; in the early 1960s, Helen Gurley Brown transformed *Cosmopolitan,* which had begun in the nineteenth century as a periodical for intellectuals, into a magazine for young women. But such editors did not work in a vacuum. During the late 1930s there was widespread concern in America about political upheavals in Europe and the possibility of the United States becoming involved in a second world war, and the greater openness about sexuality in the early

1960s convinced Brown—correctly—that there was a market among young women for a periodical that recognized them as sexual beings. Nor did the magazines speak with one voice. Although the reader market was nowhere near as highly segmented as it was by the 1990s—with magazines specifically designed for women who work outside the home, feminists, young mothers, and all manner of age groups and interests—the magazines were nonetheless divided along class and age lines. *Mademoiselle* advised young women on their college wardrobes, and *Seventeen* prepared their younger sisters for young adulthood; *Vogue* and *Harper's Bazaar* assumed an affluent, cosmopolitan reader, whereas the "big four" in terms of circulation—*Ladies' Home Journal, Good Housekeeping, McCall's,* and *Woman's Home Companion* (until its demise in 1957)—served middle-class domestic life. Amid these differences, readers of the women's magazines were assumed to have two things in common: they were predominantly white,[13] and they looked to the magazines for advice on everything from makeup and hairstyles to keeping a marriage together to feeding a family on a budget. As America's entry into World War II became a reality rather than a threat, the magazines would have more to advise readers about, and the presence of the war in the pages of the magazines—even in the form of its effect on fashions or recipes—is emblematic of the link between the home and the nation that made domestic concerns central to postwar American culture.

CHAPTER 3

"Portrait of, a Patriot"

The Domestication of World War II

World War II and the years immediately preceding it were crucial to establishing the women's magazines' central role in creating a complex and enlarged understanding of domestic life at midcentury. Early in 1940, sensing a need for a feeling of national unity and common purpose, the editors of *Ladies' Home Journal* launched its "How America Lives" series, which I will discuss in more detail in the following chapter. Although the series lasted until well after the war, its early articles provide a transition from the Depression years to the war years. One of the central themes of the series was socioeconomic: the families profiled each month were carefully categorized by income level, and part of each article was devoted to how the family spent its money, usually pointing to the thrift and restraint to which most Americans had become accustomed during the 1930s. The rhetoric of the articles tied the family directly to the nation as the series strove to introduce disparate people to one another as "neighbors" who had much more in common than their differences in geography, social class, and, to some extent, ethnicity might suggest. Above all, the series insisted on a core of shared values that could be considered middle class; whatever the income level, families were lauded for being industrious, unpretentious, civic-minded, moderate in their political views, and devoted to home and family.

Another way in which the magazines became a site of debate about the domestic was in their reliance on product advertising for business revenue. As Mark H. Leff has shown, the advertising industry received a much-needed boost at the start of the war when the War Advertising Council, an organization composed primarily of executives of advertising agencies, turned the industry into the largest single purveyor of domestic propaganda for the war effort by fostering the inclusion in advertising space of exhortations to buy war bonds, conserve food, and donate blood. By doing so, the industry benefitted in two major ways: manufacturers bought ads because they kept the brand names of even rationed or unavailable goods before the public eye, and the resulting show of patriotism caused the Treasury Department to allow businesses to deduct advertising revenues from taxable income, which further increased advertising sales. Thus it fell to advertisers to define the domestic war effort. As Leff notes, "their depiction of American war aims in terms of an 'American Way of Life' that encompassed abundant consumption and an absence of labor conflict reinforced other factors that cemented the postwar reputation and influence of 'free enterprise' and the advertisers who celebrated it" (1313). Hence, the war and consumption entered the home together, both promoting a domesticity that was national in scope yet focused on individual and family desires—especially as product manufacturers began predicting the postwar end of shortages and promised new and better products. Women were presented as participating in a national cause yet firmly placed within the home: supporting federal rationing policies in what they fed their families, trimming the household budget to buy war bonds. Nor was the power of advertising to manipulate public opinion limited to the war years. As Leff asserts, "the privatizing of the wartime propaganda apparatus and war aims through the advertising industry . . . resonated in the postwar consumer culture long after the war's end" (1318).

The most contentious and most long-lasting debate reflected in the women's magazines during the war concerned women joining the labor force (and to a lesser extent the armed services) as part of the war effort. Even though the percentage of women who did either was not large, the act had enormous symbolic significance—as the iconography of "Rosie the Riveter" attests—especially following the legal and psychological strictures against women doing paid work and thus taking a "man's job," during the 1930s. The arguments about the relative merit and morality of domestic versus public employment thus helped to set in motion the struggle to redefine the domestic world that continued after the war. Because of their primary audience, women's magazines were a logical location for this debate, and while during the war years it was couched in the specific terms of employment that supported the war effort, once the war was over it broadened into an ongoing discussion of woman's cultural role and thus her relationship to the domestic world.

Advertising the Domestic War

On the same page as the March 1942 *Woman's Home Companion* essay on why women buy magazines, quoted in the previous chapter, appears an advertisement for face powder. A little more than a year after the United States formally entered World War II, the ad appeals at least as much to patriotism as it does to vanity. One of its visual elements is a reproduction of an early-nineteenth-century portrait of a woman with pale, flawless skin, and the large print heading the ad evokes national history by touting "Early American Old Spice Face Powder for American Character Beauty." The text of the ad subtly refers to the world war and to women's role in supporting the American cause by referring to "these stirring times" that bring "a deeper beauty, bred of courage and unselfish service." Unraveled, the logic of the ad is as follows: American (white) women have long been known for their beauty; the current war effort has added the qualities of patriotism that bring "a new lilt to the chin"; women's duty during wartime is therefore to enhance that beauty with face powder. More than two years later, in the June 1944 issue of *Good Housekeeping,* an advertisement for liquid pectin also used the concept of the portrait, this time surrounding with a frame a photograph of a smiling woman stocking her pantry with homemade jams and jellies and titling it "Portrait of a Patriot." The advertising copy calls women to active service in the war effort by preserving the summer's fruits; although it may be "strange for women to think of *food* as a munition of war," the ad assures them that it is and that a woman who preserves it is "a credit to Uncle Sam!"

While preserving food amid shortages and rationing is easier to justify as a contribution to the war effort than is the use of cosmetics, these advertisements—and hundreds like them—share a translation of national defense into domestic terms. Whether maintaining her "historic" beauty or stocking up

food for the winter, the middle-class American woman is portrayed as working for the national interest, even though she is performing traditionally
feminine tasks. In *The Age of Doubt,* William Graebner characterizes the
1940s as being divided into two distinct half decades, split in 1945 by the
death of President Franklin Delano Roosevelt and the end of the war. The
first half of the decade Graebner describes as public, nationalistic, and prag-
matic, while the second was private, familial, idealistic, and domestic. Despite this split, Graebner maintains, women's roles did not alter significantly:
"Women spent the decade meeting the needs of men and capital; filling the
factories as producers, then, after the war, soothing the fragile male ego,
doing housework, and heading the family's department of consumer affairs"
(1–2). While Graebner is correct about the actual lives of the many women
who undertook jobs outside the home during the war, in the world of the
women's magazines—and particularly in their advertising—women's lives
were largely private, familial, and domestic throughout the decade, even as
women were described as patriots. Even advertisements that seem at first
glance to be exceptions to this pattern endorse women's domestic role. An
advertisement for Kleenex facial tissues appearing in the February 1944
issue of *Woman's Home Companion* bears the provocative heading "What to
tell your husband if he objects to your getting a war-time job," and the
successive frames of the ad's comic-strip format show an argument between
husband and wife, with the text providing the woman's answers to her husband's various objections and ending with the slogan "The More Women at
Work—The Sooner We'll Win!" But embedded in the text are suggestions
that in going to work, this woman would not really be leaving the domestic
arena. The ad copy supports women taking "civilian" jobs rather than joining
the "girls in war plants": the jobs enumerated are in restaurants, stores, and
laundries—that is, the service occupations—and women who take such jobs
are still referred to as "housewives." Finally, the fact that the ad is instructing women in how to win an argument with their husbands casts the magazine in its familiar role of giving women advice they presumably needed. As
Harvey Levenstein notes in *Paradox of Plenty,* "propaganda urging women
to join Rosie the Riveter was a mere trickle compared to that emphasizing
women's crucial role in keeping their families well fed and working for the
war effort" (85).

Of course, the businesses that advertised products in the women's magazines had a stake in women maintaining their domestic responsibilities even in a time of national crisis. Such businesses assumed that a woman who retained strong ties to household responsibilities during the war would remain the major purchasers of goods for their households. Advertisements frequently acknowledged shortages of consumer goods: the 1944 Kleenex ad, for example, notes that "there's not enough Kleenex to go around" because "paper, too, has a war-time job." Such statements made the products seem precious because scarce and also kept the brand name alive in the reader's mind. An advertisement for Canada Dry ginger ale appearing in the June 1944 issue of *Woman's Home Companion* brings together the various themes of women's wartime work, their consequent value as patriots, and their continuing responsibilities as domestic consumers. The visual component of the ad is a photograph of a woman serving her son a glass of ginger ale, which reinforces her responsibilities as a mother. But the ad praises her for taking a job driving a taxi, a civilian job that Canada Dry, like Kleenex, contrasts with more "military" pursuits such as being a WAVE or a WAC.[1] For this mother, there are "No parades. No bands. But because of this woman . . . America keeps on running." The text closes with an appeal to the reader's domestic and national responsibilities: she is admonished to be patient with shortages and to return empty ginger ale bottles to the store.

The magazines' editorial content also reinforced the homemaker as domestic consumer. An article in the August 1942 issue of *Good Housekeeping* advised readers on "Shopping in Wartime for the Men of the House," recommending that women purchasing men's clothing seek sturdy, conservatively designed garments to avoid waste. Even more common were articles on coping with food shortages and rationing. Articles in 1944 issues of *Good Housekeeping*, for example, advised homemakers on substitutions for meat and butter, promoting the use of soybeans, bacon fat, and the newly available margarine. Articles on food preparation often simultaneously linked women rhetorically to both a quasi-military and a domestic role. An article titled "Victory Lunches for Sturdy Men" in the March 1942 issue of *American Cookery* begins, "Mother, captain of the kitchen, guards the health and strength of the family these difficult days." Such cheerleading efforts may well have originated in the fact that Americans did not respond well to federal government rationing of such products as sugar, canned fish, and beef. As Levenstein points out, successive rationing programs were met with distrust, panic buying, hoarding, and a thriving black market (80–85). Women's fashions, too, were affected by government restrictions on the use of fabrics, but the author of an article in the September 1942 *Good Housekeeping* was determined to put the best face on this fact, declaring, "We can be grateful to the government for providing us with a silhouette that is really new." Such cheeriness about wartime consumer goods did not sit well with all readers. A British subscriber to *Ladies' Home Journal* wrote to the magazine in November 1945 to complain that when her family was reduced to eating "dregs" (dried eggs), the arrival of a *Journal* with displays of appetizing food "just sabotaged the whole morale of this family." Nor, of course, were product ads a comfort: "But those advertisements for Cannon towels, Pequot sheets and undies—my, oh my! I've one sheet that isn't patched and about two towels I could hand out to a visitor. At times it's really hard to know which hole to climb into in the undies."

In *Eating for Victory: Food Rationing and the Politics of Domesticity*, Amy Bentley emphasizes the fact that because of women's traditional association with the preparation of family meals, the rationing of food was the cause of some of the most conflicting media messages concerning woman's wartime role: "As both the government and the media declared home production and consumption of food to be decidedly political and patriotic (or, in the case of hoarding and buying on the black market, unpatriotic) activities, wartime food rationing campaigns collapsed the boundaries between women's public and private lives. In these campaigns, the family dinner became a weapon of war, and the kitchen a woman's battlefront. The media image of the 'Wartime Homemaker' defined as crucial American women's contribution to the war effort" (5). As Bentley demonstrates, the women the magazines presented as making "victory lunches" and preserving fruits and vegetables sometimes became directly involved in public-policy issues, campaigning for more informative labeling of canned foods, forming consumer groups to keep down the prices of staples such as milk, and complaining to their elected representatives that the rationing of sugar hampered their efforts to bake for their families.

Further, the wartime focus on the availability and preparation of food blurred gender lines at the same time that it sharpened racial and class distinctions. While products as disparate as Wesson Oil, Windex, and Kotex encouraged the planting of victory gardens in their advertisements in women's magazines, a 1943 Magazine Marketing Service survey revealed that the men of the family did 70 percent of the gardening (Bentley 126), and the gardens themselves were referred to in both government publications and the popular media in distinctly militaristic terms: as a "weapon of war," with vegetables "standing forth . . . in military rows" (127). Thus the man who was not in the armed services was encouraged to do his part in the domestic arena. The image of the "wartime homemaker" in magazine articles and advertisements was nearly always white, which not only reflected the magazines' assumed readership but also served as silent testimony to the fact that many African American women left domestic service for defense jobs, so that white women who had relied on black cooks were forced to join what one journalist termed the "WIKs (Women in the Kitchen)" (Bentley 48). Part of the magazines' emphasis on their readers taking volunteer or service-sector jobs during the war can thus be understood as a perhaps unwitting strengthening of class barriers—between the white and black women who joined the working class in shipyards and munitions factories and the middle-class women who waged war in their kitchens. Some of the mixed messages the magazines conveyed thus arose from a need to present stability in the midst of changes in the social order.

From Isolationism to the War at Home

During the years leading up to the December 1941 Japanese attack on Pearl Harbor, the possibility of American involvement in the conflicts that occupied much of the rest of the world loomed large in the pages of the women's magazines, but the overwhelming consensus in these pages, as in much public rhetoric, was that the United States must not enter into another world war, and one of the magazines' themes was that women were uniquely positioned to prevent such involvement. In its February 1940 issue, *Ladies' Home Journal* reported on a poll of its readers on the issue of war. To the question "Do you think the United States should go to war to help England and France?" a whopping 94 percent answered no, and when the question was rephrased to posit the possible defeat of those countries, 74 percent of respondents still answered negatively. A majority felt that the United States should fight only if invaded, and the *Journal* editors noted that "mothers, naturally, felt most strongly about this," with 79 percent of those with children agreeing. So strong was isolationist feeling that several of the letters published in the January 1940 issue of *Redbook* even urged the magazine to keep the war in Europe out of its pages. A woman from a small town in Oklahoma pleaded, "please, please, leave all record of the war and stories of the men who are responsible to the radio and newspapers," and another reader stated that "the affairs within another nation are not our affairs." Eleanor Roosevelt, in her July 1941 "If You Ask Me" column in *Ladies' Home Journal*, sounded a cautiously isolationist note in responding to a question about whether the United States should provide food to people in occupied countries. While Roosevelt reacted with "horror" to "the starvation of human beings," she nonetheless felt that "when we engage in war in any part of the world we cease to be civilized"; on a more practical political level, she expressed reluctance to interfere with the British blockade of Europe.[2]

Novelist Pearl S. Buck was one of those who felt that women could exert the moral force necessary to prevent war.[3] In her article, "Women and War," in the May 1940 issue of *Ladies' Home Journal*, Buck characterized the war in Europe as a conflict between the English and the Germans, people "so different that oceans should divide them." In terms of America's "natural" alliance with one country or the other, Buck cannot make a clear case, for "Germans make as good Americans as Englishmen do." She was clear, however, about the influence of women working together: "If the thirty-seven million women of the United States should will not to go to war on a particular occasion, there would be no war. Each day of delay in deciding our share in the European War has, therefore, been of inestimable value to us as women, because it has given us time to think for ourselves—and if not to think, since not all of us are given to thought, at least to feel about this war, and to come to wonder if it is ever going to be a war worth our fighting." Buck feared that because women were the "homekeepers," they would want men to fight if those homes seemed threatened, and she encouraged readers to use the "enormous, secret power of the home" to make a rational decision to reject war. Dorothy Thompson, a former foreign correspondent who began writing a regular *Journal* column on politics and other matters in the late 1930s, took a different kind of isolationist tack in the July 1940 issue. Responding to a number of letters complaining that women's clubs failed to discuss matters weightier than flower arranging and eighteenth-century English literature, Thompson defended the women's club agendas on two different grounds. One, which some readers must have found condescending, was that there was little point in fretting over problems beyond one's ability to solve: "Most of the great problems perplexing the world are beyond the solution of the statesmen and economists, and are certainly beyond the solution of the Ladies' Sodality of Grovers' Corners." Thompson's second point was that the arts traditionally practiced by women made an important contribution to civilization: "It is a noble thing to save mankind, but it is also a contribution to humanity to be able to bake a good coconut cake or a first-rate apple pie. No civilization can stand more than one Joan of Arc at a time, but it can do with an almost unlimited number of good cooks." Sounding a note that would gain force during World War II and the Cold War, Thompson argued for the domestic as the ultimate antidote to war: "Anything that increases consideration for human life helps toward the eventual abolishing of war." Even before America entered the war, then, the domestic world and the women responsible for maintaining it were directly implicated in the nation's well-being.

Robert B. Westbrook has argued persuasively that the arguments put forth by both the federal government and private propagandists for supporting the American cause during World War II—including being willing to die for the country—overwhelmingly stressed domestic rather than political interests. Westbrook points out that in a liberal society it is difficult to propose that citizens have an obligation to defend the state when a major function of the state is perceived to be the protection of its citizens. Thus, although the government sometimes appealed to such abstract concepts as "freedom," far more frequently the obligation to serve the war effort was couched in terms of the private and personal: "they appealed to Americans both as individuals and as families to join the war effort in order to defend *private* interests and discharge *private* moral obligations. . . . In the discourse of obligation during World War II, no private interest outranked that of the family" ("Fighting" 198–99).[4] The visual images that for most Americans served to anchor Franklin Roosevelt's abstract "four freedoms"—of speech, of worship, from want, from fear—were the Norman Rockwell illustrations published in *The Saturday Evening Post* in 1943, two of them scenes of family life (Westbrook, "Fighting" 202–3). Magazines for women, already positioned to champion the home and family, were logical sites for the quick shift from the ideology of women as keepers of the peace to the image of the family as both the justification for and a weapon in war.

A central transition point can be located in one of *Ladies' Home Journal*'s most popular series, "How America Lives," launched early in 1940. Editors Bruce and Beatrice Gould implicitly linked home and family to nationalism and democracy as a bulwark against the threats unfolding in Europe and Asia. In their memoir, *American Story*, the Goulds did not allude to the possibility of U.S. involvement in war as motivation for the series. Instead, they wrote of human interest and of wishing to present "a tapestry of American life" (203). But the rhetoric of the introduction to "How America Lives," in February 1940, clearly tied the American home to the concept of democracy. "This is America," the introductory essay began. "The America that is perhaps, as you hear on all sides, to be the last stronghold of democracy." And the essay ended with an emotional address to the reader: "Young, old, rich, poor, far from or near to where you happen to live, these people are as real, warm and American as pumpkin pie right out of the oven. They are yourselves. And you are democracy." The reference to pumpkin pie, the traditional Thanksgiving dessert, evokes the national holiday and locates the typical American firmly in a domestic setting. In a single paragraph, the editors—much like Richard Nixon debating Nikita Khrushchev nearly twenty years later—identify the American way of life with consumerism as well as with a kind of hometown dailiness: "Not the bare facts that these neighbors of yours own more cars, read more magazines, hear more radios than the rest of the world put together, that their national community leads the world in numbers of unemployed, millionaires, and middle class. How they live is the point—what they eat, drink, wear, and talk about, what gives them a kick, where the shoe pinches most and least, what they dream of and what they believe in. You already know those answers about some of your neighbors, because you know them well enough not to need to ask. You know how they live—next door." The purpose of the "How America Lives" series, as announced here, is to make America seem one big neighborhood, to inculcate a certain solidarity of purpose by introducing people to one another: "More than thirty million families, says the U.S. Bureau of Census. Each of them is the family next door, when you think of America as a whole. Each, if you knew them, would have more to show you about what democracy is." "Democracy," then, is a matter of families rather than of government and laws, and although the *Journal* series promised— and to a large extent delivered—the nation's diversity ("from the $1000-a-year farmer to the $25,000-a-year city big shot"), the magazine also proposed that such differences were eclipsed by the commonality of domestic life: "Mr. and Mrs. America are talking things over between themselves—the sun is long gone down and the children are in bed."

In selecting the first family to be profiled in "How America Lives," the Goulds deliberately sought out the average. As Bruce Gould recalled, "we wanted a family in America's population center, Cedar Rapids, Iowa; of middle years (late thirties) and middle income (then around $1,900 a year); a middle-sized family (two or three children)" (Gould and Gould 204). The Griffin family may or may not have been typical in naming two of their household pets for people prominent in recent world news—a monkey named Duchess after the Duchess of Windsor,[5] and a cat named Hitler, "because of his smeary black mustache"—but the *Journal* editors thought the Griffins fairly representative and sensible in their attitude toward events in Europe: "[T]he Griffins' interest in world news is hardly feverish. When the war broke they kept their radio red hot, like everyone else. But by now only the late bulletins from WHO, in Des Moines, get much attention. Cedar Rapids as a whole, Mr. Griffin says, has about decided to let the war take care of itself and go back to Charlie McCarthy and market reports." With Adolf Hitler present in the Griffins' lives only in the benign form of the markings on the family cat, the *Journal* article concentrated on their civic pride, how they spent their money, and how they raised their children.

Until late 1941, the focus of each segment of "How America Lives" remained much the same. But immediately after the bombing of Pearl Harbor, that emphasis changed. Bruce Gould wrote that "after December, 1941, we adapted the series to war problems—the lonely wife, the parted sweethearts, the disabled veteran" (Gould and Gould 205). In fact, all of the women's magazines quickly and uniformly turned from their isolationist stance to a wholehearted support of the war effort. As thousands of men were rapidly mobilized for military service, the magazines advised women on what to send to their loved ones in training camps. Men and women in uniforms became regular visual features of the magazines. Articles debated what part women should play in the war effort, and short stories depicted hasty weddings before heroic departures. Advertisements noted unfortunate shortages while keeping product brand names in consumers' minds.

Of course, the women's magazines were by no means unique in their support of the American cause in World War II. Virtually all media, from newspapers to films, carried the war message, from news bulletins to exhortations to buy war bonds. In *To Hasten the Homecoming*, Jordan Braverman examines how the war was "fought" on radio, in popular songs, and even in cartoons. Braverman notes that the *Chicago Tribune*, which before Pearl Harbor advertised its isolationist stance with the slogan "Save Our Republic," replaced this motto on 8 December 1941 with the words of naval officer Stephen Decatur: "our country, right or wrong" (10). Such a quick shift in attitude had many causes, not the least of which was the fact that while the bombing of Pearl Harbor was itself a shocking event, the years of hoping that America would not have to enter the conflict had built up a reservoir of national patriotism that the declaration of war unleashed in a variety of media. Even popular cookbook author Irma S. Rombauer, who was preparing a revised edition of *The Joy of Cooking* as the war broke out, quickly made adjustments to her book. As she writes in the preface to the 1943 edition, "When the revision of this book was begun a year ago we had no intimation that international obligations would lead our land of plenty to ration cards. It now goes to print with a number of emergency chapters added, written to meet the difficulties that beset the present-day cook" (n.p.).[6] Rombauer concluded her preface with language that reinforced the link between home and nation and that proposed—as the women's magazines would do throughout the war years—that the homemaker was important to the nation's victory: "It has been a pleasure to compile this record of our American way of life. Tradition speaks to us in its pages, a tradition of plenty which should always be ours, and which will be, with the intelligent use of our mighty weapon, the cooking spoon" (n.p.). As Anne Mendelson reports in her biography of Rombauer, *Stand Facing the Stove*, the "cooking spoon" provided by *The Joy of Cooking* was not wielded only by women at home. Letters from servicemen attested to the usefulness of the book in the theater of war. The chairman of the "Wardroom Mess Committee" on the USS *Independence* wrote to thank Rombauer for the "priceless guidance" of her cookbook (176).

Expressions of support for the American war effort were by no means always entirely voluntary. As part of national defense, a variety of federal and private agencies monitored and censored some kinds of information and promoted the dissemination of others. Of particular relevance to the women's magazines were the Magazine Bureau of the Office of War Information, a federal agency, and the War Advertising Council, an association formed by the advertising industry. The Magazine Bureau issued guidelines that affected the content of fiction and nonfiction features and the copy and illustrations of advertisements in America's magazines. From July 1942 until April 1945, the Magazine Bureau sent a monthly *Magazine War Guide* to hundreds of magazine editors. The function of the domestic branch of the Office of War Information was both to provide whatever timely information on the progress of the war could safely be released and to "energize the public's will to win the war despite privations and sacrifice" (Braverman 55). The *Magazine War Guide* advised editors of women's magazines to publish articles influencing women to cope effectively with rationing and shortages and to do volunteer work. Even before the *Guide* began publication, most of the magazines had already voluntarily enlisted in this effort: an article titled "Women Wanted" in the April 1941 issue of *Woman's Home Companion*, for example, encouraged readers to find ways to be of service in their own neighborhoods—leading a Girl Scout troop to provide "citizenship training," supervising playgrounds after school, providing meals for the poor. While none of these activities might seem directly related to national defense, the article sounded the "home equals democracy" theme that was reiterated many times during the next four years. The piece quoted Harriet Elliott, the only woman on the National Defense Advisory Committee, as saying, "The better our homes are organized; the more service our schools, churches and local organizations can give our communities, the better prepared we will be to meet whatever demands the future may make of us."

Regulating the content of advertisements was a trickier matter than influencing magazines' editorial decisions. First, magazine editors had far less control over the texts of ads than over the articles and fiction they chose to publish. Further, direct censorship of advertising—whether by the magazines or by the government—could be seen as interference with the system of free enterprise, which was, after all, a large part of the American way of life that the war was being fought to preserve. As had been the case during World War I, the advertising industry formed its own advisory group, the

War Advertising Council, both to provide guidelines and to actively promote support for the war. Organized very soon after the bombing of Pearl Harbor, the council took as its purpose "to mobilize the power of advertising for victory" and adopted the slogan "A War Message in Every Ad" (Braverman 236). Having learned during World War I that advertisements could have enormous influence in selling war bonds and promoting cautious use of resources, the creators of ads for everything from soap to automobiles sought to re-create the phenomenon. Certain forms of censorship did exist, of course, for the advertising as well as the editorial content of the magazines. No information could be printed that suggested troop movements or the development of weapons, and advertisers were not permitted to suggest that any branch of the armed services endorsed a particular product. But beyond these restrictions, advertising agencies and corporate ad departments for the most part voluntarily complied with the War Advertising Council.

The most common method of putting a war message in advertising was to include somewhere in the copy a box containing a slogan such as "Buy War Bonds," but most advertisers went much further in making their products relevant to the war. An ad for Kotex sanitary napkins in the October 1944 *Harper's Bazaar* is, appropriately enough for that magazine's fashion emphasis, a quiz asking readers to identify the dates of women's clothing in six periods between 1918 and 1944: the two women in the 1944 panel are uniformed as a nurse and a member of the armed services, and the text states that both they and Kotex perform a "service." The readers of the April 1944 *Glamour* could tie themselves symbolically to military service through cosmetics, as the text of a lipstick advertisement asserted that "Elizabeth Arden's newest lipstick color—Montezuma Red [is] inspired by the brave, true red of the . . . scarf and chevrons of the women in the Marines. . . . A tribute to some of the bravest men and women in the world." In the July 1942 issue of *American Home*, Dutch Boy paint is "right in step for home defense" as the Dutch Boy logo marches, shouldering a paintbrush as though it were a gun, against the backdrop of Uncle Sam's striped trousers. In the June issue of the same magazine a sheet-metal manufacturer, its product deflected from domestic to military use, demonstrates the present and future uses of sheet metal with drawings of a bomb launched from a submarine at the top of the ad and at the bottom a washing machine being admired by mother and daughter. A common tactic of wartime advertisers was to praise the homemaker for her part in the war effort. Sometimes she was commended for doing volunteer work; more often, she was cited for her work at home. An ad for Pequot sheets in the August 1942 *American Home*, for example, "hails the Great American Housewife—who has made our way of life worth fighting for!" The "way of life" intended here is clearly domestic; the ad shows a small boy saying his prayers while his mother watches, and the text touts women's "progressiveness": "our children have grown stronger and healthier each year. Our homes are the most convenient in the world, our standard of living the highest."

"Her Seven Jobs All Help Win the War!"

A Swift's Premium beef advertisement in the January 1944 issue of *Better Homes and Gardens* proposes the seven different "jobs" with which the American woman was helping to win World War II: wife, mother, purchasing agent, cook, salvage expert, war worker, and war bond buyer. By listing the jobs in this order, the ad gives primacy to the woman as nurturer and consumer; as a "salvage expert" she makes use of all leftover food and saves used fats for defense purposes. Her "war work" consists of volunteer efforts such as rolling bandages and donating blood, and the fact that she does not work for pay is underscored in the panel depicting her purchase of war bonds, where the text tells readers that more than 10 percent of "her husband's pay . . . plus dollars she saves in her household budget" goes for war bonds. Giving the woman titles such as "salvage expert" and "war worker" lends her a professional status that is in turn undermined by the overwhelmingly domestic nature of her "seven jobs" and by the language of the ad's text, which emphasizes that she "keeps . . . home a peaceful, happy place . . . a loving and lovable person, doing a fine job of homemaking."

The plethora of messages suggesting that women's contributions to the war effort were best accomplished as volunteer activities rather than paid employment no doubt had some effect on what women chose to do. But such choices were also influenced by socioeconomic levels and race. In *Women at War with America*, D'Ann Campbell demonstrates that most volunteer work, such as rolling bandages, knitting warm clothing for servicemen, distributing ration coupons, and working for the Red Cross, was organized by and for relatively affluent white women, who had the necessary time, resources (such as automobiles for transportation), and social networks to become involved. Campbell further posits that most wartime volunteer work was of little real value to the war effort and "absorbed energies that would have been more effective in the production of war materials. Volunteerism was an obsolete policy in a professionalized, industrialized warfare state, as the British and Soviets fully realized" (71). The real value of volunteer work, Campbell argues, was more affective than practical: "The real contributions of volunteer work to the patriotic cause were to raise participants' morale, to demonstrate that the rich were doing their share, and to heighten the sense of awareness throughout the community that the nation was involved in a total war" (71). Volunteer work thus served a purpose parallel to the congratulatory articles and advertisements in the women's magazines: bringing the war truly home.

In reality, large numbers of women joined the paid labor force and the various branches of the armed services during the war years. From 1940 to 1945, the number of women working outside the home grew from 12 to 18 million, and of these, 5 million had industrial jobs; 17 percent of shipyard workers were female (Braverman 22). More than 350,000 women served in the military, with the largest number joining the Women's Army Auxiliary Corps (WAAC) (after 1 July 1943, supplanted by the Women's Army Corps [WAC]). More than 30 percent of America's professional nurses served in the military during the war, and the number of women employed in agriculture increased from 8 percent in 1940 to more than 22 percent by 1945 (Litoff and Smith 35–36, 167).

Despite these impressive statistics, it is important to note that the majority of women did not engage in paid employment during World War II. As William M. Tuttle Jr. points out in *"Daddy's Gone to War,"* "in 1941, about 30,000,000 women were homemakers, with no paid employment; in 1944, seven out of eight of these women were still engaged entirely in homemaking." Furthermore, women between ages twenty and thirty-four—that is, women in their peak childbearing years—were least affected by the increase in female paid employment (71). As John Modell notes, "whatever the pressures, whatever the opportunities for attractive or rewarding gainful employment during the war, marriage and particularly parenthood militated heavily against employment" (170). Public opinion about married women working outside the home—at least as measured by the Gallup Poll—had changed dramatically between the mid-1930s and the early 1940s. In 1936, 82 percent of respondents opposed the paid employment of married women (and more than half of the then forty-eight states had laws prohibiting such employment in at least some circumstances), whereas in 1942, only 13 percent expressed opposition. Despite this shift in opinion, however, both practical considerations (such as the lack of adequate day care for children) and ideological pressures (such as the messages of the women's magazines) combined to reinforce the domestic ideal, especially for married women with children.

An advertisement for Windex in the April 1944 issue of *Better Homes and Gardens* strongly urged women to take war jobs, admonishing, "it's your duty to take a war job NOW!" But the ad divided the women it addressed into several categories, making it clear that only women without children under fourteen should take full-time jobs. Those who had young children should seek part-time jobs only if they could leave their children "in competent hands" for part of the day; if such help was unavailable, these mothers should provide it for others so that they could go to work. Appearing on the same page as the Windex ad was the second half of one of the magazine's regular wartime features, the "Young Mothers' Exchange," a column in which mothers shared hints for caring for small children effectively, economically, and often as (temporarily) single parents. Advice in this installment included wrapping a child in a sheet before administering oral medication and a speedy method of hanging diapers out to dry to avoid missing a phone call from an absent husband.

While such articles offered practical advice for mothers dealing with wartime challenges, a number of prominent people used the pages of the women's magazines to warn mothers not to abandon their primary responsibilities. In the January 1944 issue of *Woman's Home Companion*, both J. Edgar Hoover and James Madison Wood warned of the dangers of increased juvenile delinquency if women abandoned their children to work outside the home. The editors' introduction to these two articles urged women to read the pieces "with the utmost attention" because juvenile delinquency was "probably the most important crisis on the home front today."[7] What the editors termed "two prominent authorities" spoke with impassioned rhetoric about this "crisis." In "Mothers . . . Our Only Hope," Hoover argued that juvenile delinquency was actually "adult delinquency," although it is clear that the adults he meant were mothers rather than fathers:

"If the drift of normal youth toward immorality and crime is to be stopped," Hoover announced, "mothers must do the stopping" by not working outside the home: "The mother of small children . . . already has her war job. . . . *There must be no absenteeism among mothers.*" But "small children," it turns out, were not Hoover's primary concern; as the article continues, he increasingly focuses on teenagers, who needed a "decent" rather than a "clandestine" place to meet their friends. Wood sounded the same note when he stated that "children between fourteen and eighteen are the very ones who need parental attention the most," and he, like Hoover, warned women not to "swap their aprons for overalls and trade their homes for auto-trailers." Echoing many other voices both before and during the war, Wood declared, "The American home . . . is the very foundation of our way of life." The answer to the question in Wood's title, "Should We Draft Mothers?" was yes—"assigned to duty in their own homes."[8]

Both Hoover and Wood acknowledged that some women needed paid employment for financial reasons, but these authors suggested that such women constituted only a tiny fraction of the whole. In so doing, Hoover and Wood reveal their—perhaps correct—assumption that their audience was white, middle class, and married. In fact, large numbers of women outside this segment of American society worked to support themselves and their families. In 1940, for example, two of every five African American women—or 1.5 million—participated in the paid labor force, most of them as domestic or agricultural workers, cooks, and waitresses. World War II afforded many of these women better-paying industrial jobs (Tobias and Anderson 359). For these and other women disadvantaged by racism and poverty, paid employment—when they could secure it—was not an option but a necessity, and the years of economic depression preceding the war had made their circumstances more desperate. Coupled with discrimination was the widespread Depression-era philosophy that available jobs should be reserved for men, the "natural" providers. As Sheila M. Rothman points out in *Woman's Proper Place*, during the 1930s the notion that even "single women who had traditionally been employed in schools, offices, stores, and factories might want to continue to work promoted widespread objections." When companies and government agencies were forced to lay off workers during the decade, women were often the first to go (221–22). When the war created a demand for women's participation in the paid labor force, concern about the fate of their children, such as that expressed by Hoover and Wood, was focused almost entirely on the white middle-class family. As Tuttle puts it, "With little fanfare, African-American mothers had long before faced the problems caused by leading dual lives. Although black mothers had worked throughout the nation's history, few lamented the fate of black latchkey children. And during the war, in the voluminous periodical literature published on the topic of latchkey children, white children were really the subject of concern. Black children's unique circumstances were seldom explored in the magazines; segregation's effects on child development, for example, were never seriously discussed" (78). By insisting that the middle-class white mother's wartime job was parenting, articles such as those by Hoover and Wood simultaneously drew on Depression-era thinking about women's paid employment and helped to create the mythology of the "traditional" nuclear family of the postwar period that Stephanie Coontz analyzes in *The Way We Never Were.*

There is no doubt that some children—particularly infants—were neglected during the war years, although it is equally clear that the cause cannot be reduced to women's eagerness to take jobs in factories. In an article titled "War Babies" in the April 1944 issue of *Woman's Home Companion,* as the "baby boom" had already begun, Alfred Toombs reported his observations of infants left alone in cribs while their mothers went to work. Toombs at first sounded accusatory, writing that with men going into the service and women going to work, "normal patterns of family life are being destroyed. . . . And the fact—which must be faced—is that America's babies often become victims of this chain of circumstances." But Toombs did not blame mothers for this state of affairs or assume that the problem was caused solely by women entering the labor force. Indeed, Toombs noted that "children born to the wives of men in the armed services have been among the worst sufferers," pointing out that the allotment given by the government to servicemen's dependents is "only a pittance." Toombs also identified, as have many people since his time, the lack of adequate day-care facilities, so that mothers who either were forced to work to augment the military dependent allowance or chose to take jobs to support the war effort had few options for child care. Toombs concluded by calling for action at both the local and federal levels to alleviate the problem, "lest in our haste to destroy our enemies we injure ourselves."

From the perspective of later decades, it seems that the failure of state and federal authorities to provide adequate child-care programs during the war years was not merely the result of shortsightedness about the need for such assistance but rather the consequence of prevailing attitudes toward mothers working outside the home. Rothman reports that not until 1943 did the federal government begin establishing day-care centers, and as of the spring of 1945, such centers met less than 10 percent of the need. Not only were these day-care centers often poorly run and regarded as temporary, but federal agencies recommended that they not be located close to defense plants, "for then they might become *too* convenient, outlive the emergency, and encourage women to stay at work" (Rothman 223). Citing comments by Hoover similar to those published in *Woman's Home Companion,* Tuttle puts the matter starkly when he writes that "at issue for Hoover and others was male power; many saw the entry of millions of women into the paid labor force as threatening to the patriarchal goal of relegating women to the life-time performance of unpaid, largely domestic, tasks" (70). Tuttle further notes that between 17 and 18 percent of American households lacked male wage earners, and women in these homes had to work (71). Thus, when the women's magazines published articles urging women to stay home with their children, the publications were effectively addressing only those readers who were sufficiently privileged to do so.

With the stresses and shortages of wartime, the advice-giving function of the women's magazines took on a particular sense of urgency. Both articles and advertisements offered information on product rationing, tips on keeping the family healthy, guidelines for thrifty shopping, counsel on parenting, warnings about the black market and the censorship of mail, and, of course, advice on how to look good through it all. The ideal middle-class homemaker that emerges cumulatively from the pages of the magazines is efficient, vigilant, self-reliant, and at the same time the emotional center of the home. Much of the information the magazines provided was straightforward and probably fulfilled actual needs. An article in the July 1942 issue of *Good Housekeeping,* for example, told readers how to use less bleach in doing laundry and how to care for rayon stockings, since chlorine, silk, and nylon were all in limited supply; the same article reminded readers that new rubber belts for vacuum cleaners could only be purchased if the worn belts were turned in to the dealer. In September of the same year, the Good

Housekeeping Institute urged the woman as "salvage expert" to save used cooking fats and empty cans for the war effort. The information for such articles came from various government bureaus and agencies, often conveyed in the *Magazine War Guide*. In a somewhat more intimidating manner, some articles invoked the federal authorities themselves rather than the friendly chat of a magazine staff member. Also in the September 1942 *Good Housekeeping*, for example, an article on nutrition bore the stern-looking photograph of Paul McNutt, director of the Office of Defense, Health, and Welfare, whose question provided the article's title: "In Which Half Are You When It Comes to VEGETABLES?"—the half of American homemakers who served their families fresh vegetables or the half that did not? In the December issue, *Good Housekeeping* admonished, "Plan your holiday meals this way and you'll meet UNCLE SAM'S RECOMMENDATIONS for nutritious meals"; the article included advice on shopping, menus, recipes, and the by-then standard reminder to recycle tin cans.

While magazine articles often invoked authorities and experts to lend weight to wartime pronouncements, advertisers commonly presented the homemaker as the expert, frequently in a quasi-military way. A 1942 ad for Lysol disinfectant offered a free "War-Time Manual for Housewives" with each purchase of the product. The cover of the manual featured an attractive woman saluting, and the rest of the ad showed that the smart woman knew how to use Lysol to disinfect cuts and sickrooms to prevent the "incendiary bomb" of infection. While women in the ads were most commonly pictured wearing aprons or nurses' caps, looking busy and useful, a few ads for household consumer goods reminded readers of women's sexual potential. A 1942 advertisement for Cannon sheets pictured a shapely young woman reclining seductively (although fully clothed, including high heels) beneath the question "What *else* could a good wife do?" The text at the top of the page explained why buying new sheets even in wartime was a smart consumer move, and the bottom block of text provided hints—presumably those of the woman pictured—for making sheets last longer. Advertisements in magazines aimed at upper-class readers featured more subtle messages but still suggested that women were on duty even while at home. A woolen manufacturer's ad in the February 1943 issue of *Harper's Bazaar* pictured two slender women wearing handsome wool suits in front of a sign saying "Buy War Bonds," and the text read in part, "Military and Civilian: A Uniform for civilian war activities . . . a favorite Suit or Coat for day-in, day-out service! A costume to live in, for the duration, if necessary—." In contrast to the busy women pictured in the pages of *Good Housekeeping* and *Woman's Home Companion*, these women's "service" consisted of wearing "costumes."

Indeed, class differences are strikingly apparent in the ways that editors and advertisers responded to the war years. While readers of all the magazines were encouraged to buy war bonds, *Harper's Bazaar* reported in January 1943 on a mass debutante party held at the Ritz-Carlton Hotel in New York; the party was sponsored by the Coty cosmetics company, and the parents of the debutantes bought war bonds for their daughters with the money they would otherwise have spent on hosting private parties. The following month, the *Bazaar* published an article featuring two women working in defense plants. While the editors praised the women for their contributions to the war effort, the real focus of the article—as signaled by its title, "Hands on the Job"—is on how nicely manicured their fingernails are. The text points out their "neatness, feminine charm, the grace with which they go about their highly skilled tasks," with fingernails as "beautifully manicured as if their owners had spent the morning at home and had nothing more on their minds than an afternoon of bridge or a cocktail party."

The middle-class magazines did not ignore women's appearances during wartime but tended to emphasize dressing well on a budget. A fashion sequence in the October 1942 issue of *Good Housekeeping*, for example, features six "war wives" as models for sensible clothing, all of which had been tested in the Good Housekeeping Textile Laboratories for "fiber content, color resistance to light, [and] shrinkage." Most of the wives were engaged in volunteer work, and one ran the family farm in Pennsylvania while her husband was in the Coast Guard. Even articles on dealing with food rationing and shortages reflected great differences in income levels and tastes. Whereas recipes in such magazines as *Good Housekeeping* and *Ladies' Home Journal* urged readers to make casseroles using hot dogs, soybeans, and macaroni as major ingredients, menus appearing in *Harper's Bazaar* both required more sophisticated cooking techniques and frequently used wines and liqueurs as ingredients. The April 1943 issue of *Harper's Bazaar* proposed solutions to five situations when dinner had to be prepared for unexpected guests with supplies on hand: one scenario involved hungry cyclists who have turned up at the family's "week-end farm," and in another the homemaker had to use "leftovers that your maid was to finish up over the week-end." A coping-with-shortages article in the January 1943 *Bazaar* included a recipe calling for saffron, possibly the world's most expensive spice, and part of the piece was flanked by an advertisement for leisure wear made by a firm associated with Sun Valley, Idaho.

Readers at all social levels were encouraged to avoid purchasing goods on the black market that emerged simultaneously with governmental restrictions on civilian use of such products as metals, fabrics, rubber, meat, and gasoline. Levenstein notes that whereas the British took pride in adhering to rationing guidelines, "Many Americans questioned the necessity and even the legitimacy of rationing, refusing to believe that certain foods were really in short supply" (81). Those in the "land of plenty" resisted what they viewed as governmental interference in their lives, creating an atmosphere in which shopping for black-market goods could be excused, perhaps especially by women, who were continually advised to provide the best for their families. Yet here, too, class differences are apparent in the magazines' approach to the subject. The tone of Patricia Lockridge's article "I Shopped the Black Market" in the February 1944 issue of *Woman's Home Companion* was one of shock at the extent of available black-market goods, and Lockridge saw her duty as informative: to "report to the nation on how that black market actually operates today." Thus she reported on her purchases of meat, sugar, and nylon stockings in various parts of the country and ended by stating, "My tour convinced me that each of us must stand fast and refuse the temptation to buy illegally." In contrast to Lockridge's article is the almost conspiratorial title of "How Black Is Your Marketing?" in the May 1943 *Harper's Bazaar*. The author, Mary Frost Mabon, assumed that her readers were likely to be consuming more meat and butter than the ration coupons would legally allow, using such excuses as "that gem of a butler who can always produce a steak," and "I don't *like* to do this, but the children must eat." The fact that the well-heeled shopper could readily work around rationing was borne out in Lockridge's account: she reported meeting a "bank president whose bottom desk drawer was full of nylons for sale at five dollars a pair to his best depositors." Both articles, however, instructed the family "purchasing agent" in how to help with the war by resisting the temptations of the black market.

"What Are You Doing about the War?"

Despite the many ways in which the women's magazines supported domestic ideals for their readers during World War II, the periodicals did not do so consistently and uniformly. Most of them had for decades prior to the war celebrated women's professional achievements: they profiled women who were prominent in business, entertainment, and politics; they engaged well-known women such as Roosevelt and Thompson to publish regularly in their pages, and they regularly published fiction by prominent women writers, including Carson McCullers, Jessamyn West, M. F. K. Fisher, Katherine Anne Porter, Jean Stafford, Pearl S. Buck, Shirley Jackson, Kay Boyle, and Katherine Mansfield. It is not surprising that editors continued these practices during the war years, and if the accumulated weight of the majority of the magazines' content still promoted women's accomplishments within the home, at least a portion of it showcased women's work in the public arena. Indeed, even articles admonishing women to stay home with their children served as a tacit acknowledgment that many of them were not doing so.

Even before the United States entered the war, many of the magazines published articles about how war was affecting the lives of women in England and Europe. While such articles contributed to the isolationist stance the magazines assumed before December 1941 by portraying various hardships, these pieces also frequently praised women for active participation in war-related endeavors. The February 1940 *Good Housekeeping* article titled "Housewives and War," for example, was intended to inform American women about the lives of women in England, France, and Germany, especially their war work, whether as uniformed members of one of Britain's many women's service organizations or driving trucks as part of France's civilian workforce. The author wrote admiringly of the French Women's Auxiliary Aeronautic Corps, which trained "thousands of women mechanics to replace ground crews in the men's aviation service," pointing out that the youngest pilot to do such training was only fourteen years old. He concluded the article with a prediction of women's continued role in national affairs: the war "is bound . . . to develop women's abilities as never before—and give them major roles in world reconstruction once the struggle ends." Also forecasting women's lives in a postwar world was a 1944 article in *Seventeen* magazine. "What Are You Doing About the War?" applauded young women for volunteer work but encouraged them to engage in work and training that could prepare them for careers after the war—not only in nursing and child care but also in aviation and agriculture. The author of the *Seventeen* article could not resist inserting a "boy-meets-girl" note at the beginning of the section on aviation by writing, "The air age is upon us and you'll want to speak the language of the returning flyers," but the next sentence cited airline executives as predicting "a tremendous future for women in all phases of post-war aviation"—not, in other words, just as flight attendants.

At times, the magazines offered their services in helping women to find war jobs. *Woman's Home Companion* for December 1941 (an issue that would have been prepared for printing well before the bombing of Pearl Harbor) included "Women Work for Their Country," describing a series of defense-related activities—from keeping fit to learning automotive mechanics—in which groups of women engaged. The article offered readers a booklet of suggestions from the magazine's Service Bureau. A year after America entered the war, *Good Housekeeping* spoke with a more urgent voice in "We Are Trying to Find One Hundred Thousand Women," an article addressed to graduates of nursing schools who were not employed in the profession and who were needed in war work. Qualified women were invited to fill out a form on the same page and return it to the magazine, which would in turn give it to the National Nursing Council for War Services, the headquarters of which, the editors noted, was "just around the corner from *Good Housekeeping's* main office in New York City." In August 1942, *Good Housekeeping* offered advice on "How a Woman Should Wear a Uniform," intended to overcome men's objections to women wearing uniforms.

Even while helping to recruit women for war work and extolling the virtues of those who engaged in both voluntary and paid service, however, the magazines conveyed the sense that such work was temporary and that women's "real" lives involved home and family. Just as the *Good Housekeeping* article on the proper way to wear a uniform emphasized women's feminine appearance—"use any make-up you require to get the fresh, pretty, mind-on-the-job appearance you should have"—so a February 1943 *Harper's Bazaar* profile of a woman pilot who was teaching flying to Army Air Cadets mentioned that "the men have taken kindly to their dazzling teacher." Furthermore, in noting that she had once made the U.S. Olympic ski team, the emphasis was again on her appearance: "she had all the other skiers beaten hands down for looks." A profile in the same issue of a woman serving as a courier in the Civil Air Patrol ended by placing her squarely back in her traditional role: "At home in Huntington, Long Island, she is domestically pleased with a handsome colonial house and inordinately proud of her designer-inventor husband." Less glamorous than these two women was Mary Godfrey Berckman, whose family was the subject of the October 1942 segment of *Ladies' Home Journal's* "How America Lives." Although she was employed full time in the Colt firearms factory in Hartford, Connecticut, the article's title signaled that instead of trading one job for another, Berckman had added work in a munitions plant to her career as a homemaker: "The Story of a Mother Working on Two Fronts." Captions accompanying two photographs on the first page of the article revealed the deep ambivalence the magazine editors—and the culture at large—felt about the wartime lives of the Mary Berckmans of America. The caption under a photograph of Berckman with her family reads, "Neglected family? Mary claims her war job makes her a more efficient homemaker," but beneath a photo of Berckman sitting in front of a factory machine, she was quoted as saying, "Makes a woman forget her worries at home." Within the text of the article, she expanded on this comment in terms that resonated with the thesis of Betty Friedan's *The Feminine Mystique:* "It's good for a woman to get out and do something away from her family. You get irritable sticking with housework, especially with a lot of children. I know women who've gone so stale raising a family and polishing furniture they won't give you a civil answer to a civil question. If you can't stay home brooding over what's wrong with the kids, it works out better. You go to your job, meet a different crowd, get your mind right off it. Then things are much easier when you do get home."

Contemporary sources other than the women's magazines also suggest that many women found great satisfaction in taking on traditionally male jobs during the war. For Berckman, an Irish immigrant, work was in part an expression of patriotism: "When you're in war work, you're in the Army now!" Earning their own money could provide a sense of power and agency. As Gulielma Fell Alsop and Mary F. McBride put it in *Arms and the Girl,* "She has money in her pocket, she has more money to spend than she has had in all her life that has covered the great depression period. . . . She is the womanpower of the war" (44–45).[9] For African American women, who were largely absent from the mass-circulation women's magazines, war work also contributed to self-esteem, a sense of being involved in an important enterprise. The author of a 1945 publication of the Women's Bureau of the U.S. Department of Labor quoted a black female shipyard worker as saying, "I have a job to do in this great scheme of production" and noted that a black woman made the highest score of the 6,000 women who took the 1942 civil service examination for jobs in navy yards (Blood, excerpted in Litoff and Smith 176–77).[10] Augusta H. Clauson, whom the government hired to investigate shipyard working conditions during the war, summed up the rewards of engagement in war work: "We are worth something. We're building ships" (Litoff and Smith 201). Shortly before World War II increased women's paid employment, Alsop and McBride published *She's Off to Work*, a guide for the young career woman in which they were enthusiastic about what they saw as a dramatic change in the way women would find self-fulfillment. In the past, they stated, women had to depend on their husbands' relative success to define their lives: "It was by the position of her home in society and by her place within the home that the woman received . . . basic human satisfaction. And now she does not." The authors proposed that enough women had entered the paid labor force to constitute a critical mass: "Before her a girl can hear the tread of the millions of marching women who have gone into modern business and the professions. These women have set up signposts along the way for her help and direction—sharp curves, hill, steep grade, detour. And by a girl's willingness to follow the signs and to accept the help and experience of others, she, too, will find her place in the exciting and adventurous work of the modern world."

Women who had no children or whose children were grown could enjoy such rewards without accusations that they were traitors to their real jobs: the major lightning rod for criticism of women's war work was motherhood. A note of concern creeps into the "How America Lives" article about Berckman, who is otherwise depicted as a patriotic heroine. After reporting that the four Berckman children (ages seven to twelve) seem bright and well adjusted, the *Ladies' Home Journal* author mused, "Many a worried mother would regard their spontaneous well-being as an utter mystery, considering that for the past five years their mother has been on a factory job at least five days a week." Indeed, the fact that Berckman seemed to manage well her dual set of responsibilities may have prompted the inclusion in the same issue of the *Journal* an article titled "Can Women in War Industry Be Good Mothers?" written by a psychiatrist at Johns Hopkins University. The answer to the title's question is yes, but only under very special circumstances. The author described with barely concealed disgust the circumstances of a Baltimore mother of two who had hired an "irresponsible" woman to care for her children while she worked in a factory. Compounding this sin was the fact that the woman spent most of her earnings on clothes and evenings out with her husband. In contrast to this "poor excuse for a mother," according to the psychiatrist, was Berckman, who worked an early shift so that she could be home when the children returned from school and whose husband came home from his job to prepare their lunch. For 1942, the author is surprisingly supportive of women having jobs outside the home, believing that "women are made more interesting to their girls and boys by an outside job," but only if two conditions are met: "it is absolutely necessary for husbands to help their wives with home duties and with the children's training," and "war or no war, outside work should never be undertaken by mothers until adequate care and training of their young children are assured."

Product advertisements echoed the dual nature of women's wartime work, serving the country and preserving the family. A General Electric ad in the October 1942 issue of *American Home* suggests this duality in its opening line—"This Fight is a Family Affair!"—presumably spoken by the smiling woman in uniform. The rest of the ad consists of vignettes of families contributing in various ways to the war effort. The only woman with a factory job has a son in the navy; women with younger children are pictured with them in the kitchen or around the dinner table. Another General Electric ad, this one in a 1943 issue of *Better Homes and Gardens*, links the woman pictured to both war and domestic responsibilities: she is pictured working at a factory machine, and the text is headed "This *was* her Washday"— suggesting that after the war is over, it will be again. A Swift's Premium meat ad in the June 1944 issue of *Better Homes and Gardens* tells the story of "Betty Wins a Bet," in which Betty proves that she can take a job as a bus driver and thus "release a man to fight" yet still provide a good dinner for her father every night.

Preparing for the Postwar World

The women's magazines tried in a number of ways to prepare readers for the changes that would take place when the conflict ended. Advertisements during World War II for products whose manufacture had been suspended—either because the necessary materials, such as metals, were diverted to military use or because factories were converted to produce munitions—kept the reader's eye constantly on the eventual end of the conflict and hence the renewed availability of consumer goods. Magazines featured plans for postwar houses, published articles on how to deal with returning servicemen, and in general predicted a rosy domestic future that would be unlike both the war years and the economic depression that had preceded it. Significantly, the rhetoric of wartime popular periodicals, in an attempt to include all Americans in such a future, forecast the transition to mass culture that took place following the war. The 29 August 1942, *Saturday Evening Post*, comparing the goals for which America and its enemies were fighting, announced, "Our [people] are fighting for a glorious future of *mass* employment, *mass* production and *mass* distribution and ownership" (emphasis added). In keeping with the magazines' tendency to look to the past and the future at the same time—for example, pudding like grandmother used to make using a convenient new mix—the postwar period was paradoxically forecast as a "return" to the "new." The concluding paragraph of the General Electric ad that begins "This *was* her washday" manages to convey this complex message in a single sentence: "So when peace is here again and things like washday and baking day and bridge day assume their old place in your life, General Electric, too, will be ready—ready to equip that wonderful new home your War Bonds will buy." The woman pictured sitting at a machine, in other words, would be back in her "normal" routine but would be in a setting that as yet could only be imagined. Thus, when Rothman comments that "the war was not so much a transformative experience as an interruption, after which women returned to pursue an inherited role" (224), she is only partly correct. Women had indeed inherited the role of homemaker, but in the postwar period they would play out that role in a culture that was busy reinventing itself. And just as they had in previous decades, the women's magazines advised women after the war.

The "How America Lives" feature in the November 1945 issue of *Ladies' Home Journal* invited readers to "Meet a Demobilized Housewife." The woman profiled in the article not only had combined marriage and motherhood with a job as a welder but had borne her two children during the war years. The headnote to the article reads, "In two years of marriage, Ruth

Tillson had two babies, helped build fifty-five submarines, earned twice the salary of her bos'n's-mate husband!" The author of the article, Elizabeth Janeway,[11] described Tillson's arduous days as a factory worker, rising before daylight to take her infant daughter to her daytime caretaker, working from 6:45 until 4:00, and fitting her household responsibilities into the day's scant remaining hours. Like many such women, Janeway noted, Tillson "worked too hard, slept too little, ate on the run." But far from denouncing Tillson as a bad mother and homemaker, Janeway wrote with admiration of Tillson's transformation from domestic worker to welder: once in her work uniform, "there was no trace left of Mrs. R. W. Tillson, housewife. For the next five hours, with one fifteen-minute rest period, she would make the sparks fly and the air hum. . . . She was a welder, a builder of submarines, good enough and experienced enough to work on the ways with the men." While the photo captions that accompany the article (and which in all likelihood were not written by Janeway) stress Tillson's relief at being able to quit her war job—for example, "Hurrah for a full-time wife"—the article itself instead emphasizes the importance to her family of Tillson's wartime income, especially since her husband's postwar navy salary would cease to be supplemented by a family allotment. At the end of the article, the Tillsons face "the unknown world of after-the-war," a phrase that suggests far more than economic uncertainty.

Approximately 2 million women left the paid labor force when World War II ended. While the overall percentage of women in paid employment increased as the 1940s went on, the nature of and the rewards for women's work had changed by the second half of the decade. A combination of government and business policies and public opinion favored men in industrial jobs, so that even when America's Ruth Tillsons wanted or needed to continue to earn income, they were deflected into lower-paying jobs in the clerical and service sectors. According to Elaine Tyler May, women's average weekly wages dropped 26 percent following the war. Further, public attitudes that could countenance women in military positions during the war could not do so in peacetime, so that most women left the armed services. "To make matters worse," May notes, "these female veterans were considered dependents rather than providers in their homes, and therefore were ineligible for many of the important veterans' benefits that were available to their male counterparts." Finally, the federal day-care centers that had opened during the war closed when it ended, so that women with small children found it increasingly difficult to work outside the home (76).

This was not the future that many had envisioned during the war, when *Seventeen* magazine counseled young women on postwar careers in aviation, and advertisements for window cleaner and facial tissue urged women into war work and hailed them as patriots. Yet memories of the conclusion of the World War I, when women had turned from war work to the domestic arena, prompted some to express fears—well founded, as it turned out—that the phenomenon would repeat itself. In her 1943 book *Out of the Kitchen—Into the War*, Susan B. Anthony II, niece of the nineteenth-century women's-rights advocate, both articulated these fears and issued a call for women's right to choose their postwar occupations. "The conditions of war," Anthony wrote, "are definitely pulling women out of the house and into the world. The peace must not push them back into the house, unless they wish to go there" (excerpted in Litoff and Smith 217). Anthony expressed concern that uncertainty about their postwar futures could prevent women from entering wholeheartedly into training for wartime jobs: "The woman riveter, the seaman, the farm laborer are wondering, 'Are we living only on borrowed time?' " (excerpted in Litoff and Smith 213). Anthony was sufficiently prescient to see that only with the continuation of such wartime emergency measures as day-care centers would women with children achieve economic security and the nation make full use of its potential labor force, and she called for an end to distinctions between "men's jobs" and "women's jobs": "Personal ability and choice, not sex, must determine the jobholder" (excerpted in Litoff and Smith 217–18). Anthony was not alone in seeing a time of transition for women at war's end. In 1944 and 1945, the Women's Bureau of the Department of Labor sponsored six conferences on postwar work, and in 1944 the bureau issued *A Preview as to Women Workers in Transition from War to Peace*, which argued that steps should be taken to ensure that women who needed paid employment would be able to benefit from all of the "four freedoms" to which President Roosevelt had declared Americans entitled, including "freedom from want."

Alsop and McBride attempted as early as 1943 to imagine what the war would do to women's aspirations after the war, and they were in remarkable agreement with Anthony. In the penultimate chapter of *Arms and the Girl*, "A Woman's Postwar World," the guests at a wartime party discuss what peacetime might be like, and a young woman who works in a munitions factory delivers an impassioned speech to a naval officer:

> It's not only opportunity I want, Commander Jackson. I want better pay. I want a fairer adjustment of wages for equal work between men and women. I'm doing David's job now, exactly the same job he had before he enlisted. My output is exactly the same that his was, and I am getting less money. I know all about discrimination and favoritism. I know how all the underdogs feel. I know how the slaves feel, how the Jews feel, how the women feel. The men have the power. And power is heady stuff and precious. And it takes war after war to make the powerful willing to give up their power.
>
> But suddenly women were wanted in this war. We were desirable from a labor point of view. We were valuable. (281)

The woman's sense that she is being used but not rewarded is clear, and at the end of the chapter, in the "Plans for Action" section that concludes each chapter of the book, the authors call for postwar changes in women's involvement in public life: "Make a state where opportunities for work for women are equal to the women wanting to work. Plan for equal pay for equal work. . . . Put women into politics. . . . No world will ever be built for peace unless women are participating in its planning" (295).

The women's magazines also expressed the sense in 1944 and 1945 that a time of transition was imminent, but in their role as advisers on domestic life they played a part in affecting that transition that was very different from what Anthony and the Women's Bureau might have wished. As the issue of women's paid employment became a topic of much debate in the latter years of the war, the magazines often reminded readers of their domestic responsibilities. The influx of women into the workplace in the early years of the war had revived interest in the Equal Rights Amendment to the Constitution, which had first been introduced in 1923. The July 1945 issue of *Ladies' Home Journal* included the article "Why I am *against* the Equal Rights Amendment," by Alice Hamilton, the president of the National Consumers League, an organization founded in 1899 to foster citizen participation in governmental and industrial decision making regarding such matters as fair labor standards and product safety. Hamilton argued, as would others several decades later, that the amendment would remove certain protections for women in the workplace and would force women to bear equal responsibility with men in the economic support of their families, thus causing women to abandon their children to earn money. Two articles in the January 1944 issue of the *Journal* took opposite sides in the debate about working wives. The author of "Working Wives Make the Best Wives" took the approach that women who feel an individual sense of accomplishment are happier and more interesting people, whereas the author of "You Can't Have a Career and be a Good Wife" argued that a woman who works outside the home is in many ways avoiding her primary responsibilities: "Why . . . do women have this suicidal hunger for success outside the home? Why do they crave so deeply to 'go out to business' instead of making a business of their homes?"

Even more overtly related to women's postwar domestic lives are such articles as "When Your Soldier Comes Home," which appeared in the October 1945 *Journal*. The author, who described himself as an infantryman wounded in the Battle of the Bulge, advised women to be patient during the ex-soldier's readjustment period and to forgive any sexual indiscretions he might have committed during the war, which, "in the soldier's unwritten code of morals" are "perfectly excusable."[12] The fact that men in the armed services might be anxious about what women were doing during the war years is expressed in a short story in the November 1942 *Good Housekeeping,* "The Girls We're Going to Marry When the War Is Done." The story consists of a conversation among several servicemen about the reversals of male-female roles that have occurred as a result of the war. At first the soldiers tease each other about the "feminine" skills, such as cooking and making beds, that they have developed as soldiers, anticipating that they will criticize their future wives' efforts in those areas. But the talk turns a bit more serious when one of the men ventures the opinion that after the war women will in fact not be doing such domestic chores at all. "I've been reading up on what happened with women after the last war," says Sergeant Sher, "They got suffrage out of that one. That ain't nothing to what they're going to get out of this one. Here's the way I figure it. Everybody but the 4-F's and the old fellows are in the Army or on the way in. Already we got women driving streetcars and running filling stations and working in the steel mills. . . . They got girls doing everything. So you get out of the Army, and you look for a job, and they tell you they already got a good woman doing it. You know what else they'll tell you? They'll tell you that a man's place is in the home!" For female readers already receiving messages about what to send and write to servicemen and how to maintain a feminine appearance while working in factories, such a story could well have served as a cautionary tale about not straying too far from accustomed roles.

If the magazines envisioned one of woman's postwar jobs to be that of nurturer, restoring or creating family life after years of disruption, her other job was as a consumer, purchasing not only those products that had been unavailable during the war but also the many new or improved goods marketed after the war, some of them developed with the help of military technology. Advertisements were, understandably, a major means of conveying such messages; manufacturers were eager to keep their brand names alive in the public eye and to benefit from the sales of previously scarce commodities that were sure to take place after the war. As early as December 1943, the manufacturer of Hotpoint appliances tantalized readers of *Better Homes and Gardens* with a "Victory Kitchen" and offered to send them a "House Planning File" to store ideas for their postwar dream homes. The makers of the Easy Spindrier washing machine encouraged 1944 readers to envision the day when they could say "good riddance to all the pesky problems of wartime washing." And in June 1944 General Electric promised "Everything Electrical for After-Victory Homes," especially for the woman who has become accustomed to the mechanized factory setting; the woman in the ad looks forward to a future in which she will not be doing "the same old kind of housekeeping." In a similar spirit of a brand-new world to follow the war, Delco Appliances promised in 1943 that when the "great day" of peace arrived, the company would "utilize all its experience to build new and finer appliances for your home and farm."

Articles as well as advertisements played into the sense of a brave new world of consumer goods to follow the war. The pent-up desire for everything from automobiles to musical instruments is reflected in "When Can We Buy It?" in the September 1945 issue of *Redbook*. Using information provided by the War Production Board, the article offered a chart predicting the availability of twenty categories of products, including radios, sewing machines, and children's toys. Although the article was generally cautious in tone, warning of continuing shortages of automobile tires and vacuum cleaners, it nonetheless predicted a rosier Christmas than in the preceding years, noting that "Christmas shopping for children should be easier this year," and commenting about electric stoves, "Maybe you can get one for Christmas this year." Both during and after the war, the magazines touted products for civilian use that had been made possible by military technology. "Things to Come," in the March 1944 issue of *Better Homes and Gardens*, pointed to chocolate bars that did not melt, clothing made from fabrics developed for parachutes, and a confection made from dehydrated sweet potatoes. As was commonly the case during the war, the article promised that investors' returns on war bonds would make purchasing these and other products easy: "Things you can't have today you can have tomorrow. And money put into War Savings Bonds today will buy them tomorrow, better things and more of them." In January 1946, *Redbook* predicted that military innovations in processing and preserving foods would lead the homemaker to "Better Meals with Less Work." The woman whose husband brought home unexpected dinner guests would be able to order complete frozen dinners from her local market; bacon would be canned, requiring no refrigeration; and a forerunner of the microwave oven had been developed, although at $12,000 per unit, it was not envisioned for home use.

As abruptly, then, as the women's magazines had turned in 1941 from promoting nonintervention to supporting America's war effort, they recovered their emphasis on the primacy of domestic life at war's end. While the Cold War would make its presence felt in the decades to come—especially in expressions of concern about the adequacy of the American educational system—the magazines primarily went about the task of helping to create the postwar home and family, featuring articles on housing shortages and suburban developments and bringing in increasing numbers of "experts" to counsel readers on marriage, child rearing, shopping, home decor, and nutrition. As the birthrate increased from 18.4 to 25.3 per 1,000 women from the Depression to 1957 and the financial status of millions of Americans improved so that by the mid-1950s almost 60 percent of families could be considered part of the middle class, the magazines celebrated the white nuclear family as an antidote to more than fifteen years of economic deprivation and social disruption.

CHAPTER 4

"Do You Have a Radio in Your Kitchen?"

Class and Consumerism at Midcentury

If, as Robert Westbrook argues, the appeal to American citizens to support the country's involvement in World War II was couched in terms of private interests rather than the welfare of the state, implicit in such an appeal was a connection between domestic life and the material goods that anchored it. Jean-Christophe Agnew cites the comment of one serviceman that "I am in this damn mess as much to help keep the custom of drinking Cokes as I am to preserve the million other benefits our country blesses its citizens with" (14). Such a comment, Agnew suggests, has important implications for the formation of political thought. Like other historians, Agnew sees the midcentury period as pivotal in America's cultural reformulation, positing that the citizen's relationship to the nation became articulated through consumer goods: "Depressions and wars are by definition moments of crisis, moments when a society is potentially open to radical definitions of its political, social, and economic foundations. And what the history of twentieth-century consumption is telling us is that a far-reaching ideological redefinition of polity and society did begin to take hold during the 1930s and 1940s: the promotion of the social contract of cold-war liberalism, which is to say a state sponsored guarantee of private consumption. But, more importantly, we are also being told that this redefinition of rights and obligations articulated itself in the seemingly innocuous language of soft drinks, arms, and household appliances, and that it therefore occurred . . . privately, imaginatively, and incon-spicuously—in short, without discussion" (14). An understanding of the nation in terms of private consumer goods was discussed in public, however, not only in Franklin Roosevelt's identification of one of the "four freedoms" as freedom from want and later in Richard Nixon's conflation of democracy and domestic consumer goods in his 1959 debate with Nikita Khrushchev, but, I would argue, also most consistently in the pages of the women's maga-zines, where the domestic world was portrayed as insistently material. Read-ers were told to both buy and budget, to strive for improved class standing yet maintain certain core values, to respect America's ethnic diversity but emulate the white middle class.

The very contradictions inherent in such a discussion suggest that the magazines assumed a more diverse readership than would be implied in their visual presentation of this middle-class ideal. The essays in Joanne Meyerowitz's collection *Not June Cleaver* argue that the previous tendency to define the postwar period in terms of the white suburban homemaker obscured the lives of women who were immigrants, labor organizers, rebels against convention, and marginalized by race and ethnicity. But even within the apparent homogeneity of the women's magazines are clear acknowledg-ments of differences in social class, ethnicity, and race. Indeed, the presenta-tion of an ideal domestic life and many kinds of advice on how to obtain it suggest the presence of readers for whom such was not a reality, just as the many articles urging women to remain homemakers during World War II suggests that many were not content to do so. Much of the iconography of middle-class suburban life also was contributed not by the magazines' edito-rial content but rather by the advertisers, who were understandably invested in presenting images of the domestic lives their products promised to achieve. Thus the magazines' status as business ventures depended on ad-vertising revenue that has helped to obscure whatever inclusiveness they embodied.

Selling Mrs. Consumer

Midcentury women's magazines were often overt—and certainly unapolo-getic—about helping their readers acquire the values, behaviors, and above all the consumer goods that represented middle-class life. Particularly after

World War II, both editors and advertisers were committed to offering keys to a way of life that had been deferred for many people for fifteen years of economic depression and war. A 1954 advertisement for the National Broadcasting Company is emblematic of this philosophy. Designed to encourage the purchase of radios, the ad inquires of the homemaker, "Do you have a radio in your kitchen?" Like the titles of magazine articles that often asked questions of readers, the advertisement's query suggests that there is only one correct answer. In addition to urging consumption, the ad reveals what the housewife could listen to if her kitchen radio were tuned to NBC: in the morning, quiz shows named "Break the Bank" and "Strike It Rich" and in the afternoon, soap operas that included "Life Can Be Beautiful" and "Right to Happiness"—the American Dream with its dual components of material prosperity and emotional fulfillment.

The particular focus on the relationship between class and consumption in the postwar magazines must be understood as the result of several developments during prior decades, among them the increasing sophistication and professionalization of the advertising industry, the dashed expectations of the stock market crash in 1929, and advancements in household technology that provided widespread improvement in the quality of domestic life. All of these events participated, in turn, in the steady march toward the "proto-mass culture" that Michael Kammen describes, which was firmly in place in the postwar years. Kammen notes that "the commercialization of culture accelerated rapidly after World War II" and that the 1950s "marked the true beginning of mass consumption as we know it, and henceforth mass markets swiftly became a 'real fixture' in national life" (60). Although Kammen wisely cautions against equating "mass culture" with "standardization" (185), it is nonetheless true that advertising and marketing on a truly national scale—very much the position of the midcentury magazines—required imagining, even creating, a large median population with predictable tastes, values, and economic means.

The assumption that readers of women's magazines wished to improve or solidify their social-class status was not new in the 1940s and 1950s. *Ladies' Home Journal* founder Cyrus Curtis had noted with some satisfaction in the 1890s that *Journal* subscribers tended to be solidly middle-class citizens, and when Bruce and Beatrice Gould began editing the *Journal* in the midst of the Depression, among the first changes they made in the magazine were fashion pages and home designs that represented what most readers could only aspire to rather than what they already possessed. In between, in the early twentieth century, *Journal* editor Edward Bok revealed just as clearly that his audience embraced a certain class status. Editing the magazine through the Progressive Era, Bok was in many ways a reformer who assumed that his readers could exert influence in such matters as temperance, educational reform, and public health. But he also took for granted the existence of class differences; while he urged readers to be considerate of those on lower rungs of the social ladder and even crusaded for better treatment of domestic servants, he spoke about rather than to the laboring class. As Salme Harja Steinberg notes in *Reformer in the Marketplace,* "During his thirty years as editor [1889–1919] Bok tried to adapt middle-class values to the exigencies of a changing society. . . . The *Journal*'s emphasis on women's fashions, home decoration, good taste over bad taste, and etiquette fostered the image of a woman whose behavior was superior to those who either could not or did not conform to the prescribed life-style. In this way Bok's *Journal* aided in the uniformity of middle-class life" (144–45). Bok's class stance was in part a matter of his personal conviction about the proper ideals of American life and in part a response to the needs of advertisers, who, increasingly during his editorship, influenced the content of American periodicals. And it is no surprise that those who had products to sell wished to address an audience that not only could afford to buy them but also found positive social value in doing so.

A great deal of the groundwork for the consumerism and class consciousness that were manifest after World War II was laid in the 1920s. The decade was one of relative prosperity, advertising had become a significant part of American culture, and, as Ruth Schwartz Cowan has pointed out, the role of women as homemakers/consumers that Betty Friedan would later characterize as the "feminine mystique" became well established. Prior to the 1920s, housekeeping and child care were acknowledged to be chores that families of sufficient means readily hired servants to perform. Even though the majority of Americans could not employ others to accomplish all the tasks of homemaking, having hired help for cooking, cleaning, or child care was presented as a norm in magazine fiction and advertising. But by the end of the 1920s, Cowan notes, "the days when a housewife of moderate means fully expected that she would have at least a maid of all work, and probably a laundress and nursemaid, were clearly over" (149). As factory work and immigration restrictions diminished the supply of household servants, most women assumed responsibility for all aspects of homemaking.[1] No longer, however, could housework be presented as drudgery; if women were willingly to take full charge of household tasks, such work must take on added dimensions. As Cowan states, "housework was no longer regarded as a chore, but as an expression of the housewife's personality and her affection for her family. . . . Laundering had once been just laundering; now it was an expression of love. . . . Diapering was not just diapering, but a time to build the baby's sense of security" (150–51).

At the same time that housework was touted for its creative and emotional rewards, the homemaker was nearing the end of a long transition from producing goods (food, clothing, cleansers) to consuming them. By 1928 *Ladies' Home Journal* reflected this change in an article on the purchase of linens: "A woman's virtue and excellence as a housewife do not in these days depend upon her skill in spinning and weaving. An entirely different task presents itself, more difficult and more complex, requiring an infinitely wider range of ability, and for these very reasons more interesting and inspiring." Just as they had previously offered women advice on the production of household goods, the magazines now stood ready to instruct them as consumers. As Cowan remarks, "In earlier days the young housewife had to be taught to make things well; in the 20's she had to be taught to buy things well" (152). And during the post–World War I years, there were many more things to buy. Although Thomas A. Edison was mistaken when he predicted in 1912 that electricity would entirely free women from household drudgery, he was correct in assuming that the force he had put to practical use would bring enormous changes to the home. Whereas in 1907 only 8 percent of American homes had electricity, by 1925 more than half did, making possible the use (and hence the purchase) of electrical appliances such as irons, sewing machines, toasters, and vacuum cleaners. The availability of such technology coincided with the maturation of the advertising industry, which brought the manufacturer's brand name to consumer consciousness. In 1929 former *Journal* editor Bok hailed homemaking as "the most outstanding phase of modern civilization" and credited for this development the manufacturers who had "carefully studied" the "beauty and convenience and efficiency of home equipment" in order to "meet the demands of the modern housewife" ("American Home" 287). If the modern housewife were "demanding" such products, it was in large part because advertising—largely, in that pre-television era, in the women's magazines—told her that she should do so.

The gendered nature of domestic consumerism had itself been established decades earlier—specifically in the 1880s and 1890s, during the period when the major middle-class women's magazines were beginning publication. In *The Adman in the Parlor*, Ellen Gruber Garvey describes the process by which product advertising became a part of female domestic experience between 1880 and 1910. Even before the magazines became major repositories of product advertisements, the manufacturers of such products as soap, thread, coffee, and patent medicines produced "trade cards" to promote their brands; resembling calling cards in size and appearance, these colorful bits of advertising were intended to appeal to the collecting mania of Victorian Americans and were often pasted into scrapbooks by girls and young women alongside the calling cards they imitated. Young women were thus encouraged to develop brand loyalties, which in turn became expressions of taste. As Garvey explains, being educated to shop was one way to express social-class identification: "For middle-class families, consumption became a way to actively articulate their class position; they consolidated class definitions by establishing taste markers, and then by choosing appropriately among them. Learning to shop as a middle-class woman, then, expressed both gender and class position" (18; see also Merish).

At one point during his editorship of *Ladies' Home Journal*, Bok hired Christine Frederick as director of the Applecroft Housekeeping Experiment Station, which tested consumer products for the magazine. By 1929 Mrs. Frederick (she preferred the indication of her marital status) had served as a housekeeping consultant and editor for several magazines (including *Ladies' Home Journal*), had lectured widely on home economics, and had published such books as *The New Housekeeping* (1913) and *Household Engineering: Scientific Management in the Home* (1915), advocating the application of "scientific management" to the home. Using the observations she had accumulated in these various roles, in 1929 she published *Selling Mrs. Consumer*, a four-hundred-page volume intended to advise the advertising industry on how to appeal to the American woman. Combining statistics, the fledgling field of psychology, and her own experiences, Mrs. Frederick produced a detailed analysis of the values, habits, and tastes of the American woman that is valuable today as a sociological document both describing domestic life in the late 1920s and identifying class and consumer trends that were intensified twenty years later. Early on in *Selling Mrs. Consumer*, Mrs. Frederick asserted that women at all socioeconomic levels wielded the family's economic power, spending a minimum of 80 percent of all family income (12). "Every article of family use," Mrs. Frederick asserted, "even those beginning with exclusively male interest, like automobiles and radio, have slowly come into woman's purchasing field, and their design, distribution, sales and advertising vitally affected by the fact of woman's purchasing standards" (12). The "purchasing standards" that Mrs. Frederick describes were a curious mixture of intuition and practicality; women often made purchases for emotional reasons but at the same time were apt to exert rational control over the family budget. Mrs. Frederick made it clear that these two attributes were put to the service of upward social mobility when she asserted that "a civilization like ours . . . *centers its genius upon improving the condition of life*" and that such improvements involve the purchase of consumer goods when she speaks of bringing "more news and entertainment to the family fireside" and reducing "the labor and hardship of living" (15; emphasis in original).

To give advertisers a clear picture of the American consumer, Mrs. Frederick paid a great deal of attention to variations in socioeconomic levels as a means of pointing out where purchasing power resided. She divided the nation's 28 million families into ten income levels, ranging from the "Croesus Level"—an annual income of more than $50,000, representing .125 percent of households—to the poverty level, the nearly 7 percent of families and individuals earning less than $500 per year. More than half of Americans occupied what she termed "subsistence" and "minimum comfort" levels, with incomes between $1,000 and $2,000. While most of the money earned by these two groups was devoted to the purchase of "necessities," members of each group nonetheless had small amounts for what she termed "advancement" and thus were worth advertisers' attention, not least because people at these levels were particularly eager to improve their status (66–71). Coupled with such desires for "improving the condition of life" are the changes that Mrs. Frederick discerned in American women themselves, which she described as the "six new criterions [sic] of American women." One of them was "a new kind of adulthood," in which women "consider themselves individuals, citizens and responsible persons." Closely related are better education and increased sophistication and a desire to have a part in eradicating such evils as child labor, malnutrition, and disease. The final three characteristics were related more directly to women's role as consumers, one of them the desire to be free from "the crushing, age-old burdens of the home," which necessitates more labor-saving devices. The second was a heightened aesthetic sense, so that women want "more beautiful goods of every variety, even more colorful and decorative kitchen utensils." And finally, women were "resolved to enjoy more of the good things of life," including travel, art, and music (29–31).

Christine Frederick assumed—correctly—that the advertising industry to which she spoke in *Selling Mrs. Consumer* had an important role in patterns of consumption and hence the quality of American family life. Far from accepting uncritically the practices of manufacturers and advertisers practices, she sought to protect female consumers as much as she did to advise industry on how to appeal to them. She was particularly critical of the manufacturers of canned food for not providing more content information on labels. Noting that in 1928 the per capita consumption of such food was thirty-one cans, she chided producers for failing to describe accurately what was inside: "A tin can is literally a dark, sealed mystery until it is opened" (157). Mrs. Frederick believed women's magazines performed one of their great services in helping to remedy such failures. She praised the "combined wisdom of the periodicals" for establishing "high standards of advertising acceptance": "I still remember the sense of relief and gratification I felt when the first large magazine—I think it was *Good Housekeeping* or *Ladies' Home Journal* [the latter]—announced it would guarantee all its advertising to its readers. This stand broke down consumer resistance to a minimum and began a new era of domestic progress, since women could now give a far larger amount of credence to what advertising told them" (334). Even more important than their role in protecting women from misleading advertising, however, was the magazines' function as educators in domestic matters. Mrs. Frederick singled out in particular the Good Housekeeping Institute, which had made the magazine "the equivalent of college text-books and curricula in all the special interests of house, home, and family" (284). A note of national pride entered *Selling Mrs. Consumer* at this point, as Mrs. Frederick identified the domestic education in such magazines as a particularly American phenomenon; in the absence of such periodicals, England had yet to learn about "intelligent feeding, pure milk, and the desirability of warm houses," and France would not "emerge from its mediaeval indifference to hygiene" (284).

In 1929, the same year that *Selling Mrs. Consumer* was published, *Ladies' Home Journal* announced a new educational service for readers. In "The Household Buyer," in the November issue, household editor Lita Bane outlined twin obstacles for the homemaker as purchaser: the lack of sufficient standards of quality in some industries and the lack of awareness of such standards when they did exist. "For the household buyer [buying on the present market] is manifestly an extremely complicated task because of the great variety of things she must judge and select, ranging from a baby's dress to a cookstove, the limited nature of the budget in most cases, and the few standards of quality at her disposal." Bane advanced three solutions to this dilemma. The first was the increasing role of federal bureaus in establishing standards—"the Federal Government . . . keeps in its vaults in Washington a yardstick and a pint measure by which others throughout the country can be checked to test their accuracy." The second solution is advertising; Bane quoted a University of Chicago home economist who had great faith in the advertising industry: "an ever-growing volume of advertising . . . gives this essential information. The accuracy of the information is probably becoming greater and greater."[2] And finally, the *Journal* itself would cooperate with "various agencies in collecting, sorting and presenting for the use of its readers the standards and specifications that may better enable the household budget to yield the satisfaction and enjoyments sought by the family."

Near the beginning of *Selling Mrs. Consumer,* Mrs. Frederick brought together themes of nationalism, the importance of home and family, consumerism, and anxiety about gender roles in a manner that presaged the way these topics would be even more intensely interwoven following World War II. Having asserted that post–World War I concerns were overwhelmingly domestic, she quoted an unnamed writer who expressed fears that postwar American culture had become "lush soil for the feminine, but barren soil for the masculine characteristics of history and legend. . . . The Anglo-Saxon male tradition is slipping!" Responding as "Mrs. Consumer," Frederick defended peacetime values in a way that would be echoed less than twenty years later:

> [B]oth men and women seem to be agreed upon what constitutes real civilization, especially since the World War so apparently finally warped and destroyed the last vestige of the male's romantic notion about war. Man has decided to glorify the fireside rather than the God Mars, and to graft upon himself some of the more humanitarian principles with which women have always been concerned. He will fight nature, not himself; make war upon disease, discomfort, ugliness, hunger, ignorance, poverty and misery rather than upon other men. He will live gorgeously and imperiously, not upon goods taken from others in conquest, but upon goods which he himself manufactures and distributes. If this be feminine, then make the most of it! is woman's reply to the iconoclast. If it seems to some to lack the lift and glory of traditional war and conquest,—then we should admit that a new concept of glory which is neither male nor female but *human* is being substituted by the American man, in which the prize is the lifting of living standards in this country. (16)

Mrs. Frederick's exhortation bears traces of the Progressive Era in its emphasis on eradicating social evils and thus illustrates the prewar ethos that Lary May terms an "ideology of republican citizenship" rather than the "ideology of consensus" that characterized postwar culture (2–5). The corollary message, however, is that the goal of a newly enlightened American "civilization" was to live more comfortably with the aid of consumer products—the "American way of life" that by the late 1940s was viewed as a bulwark against communism and as the nation's defense in the Cold War.

"How America Lives"

As most recent cultural historians agree, American culture in the postwar period was far more diverse—in tastes, values, political philosophies, and economic levels—than the popular media of the time projected. The anxieties expressed especially during the 1950s about conformity to an emerging "mass culture," which Kammen explores in chapter 7 of *American Culture, American Tastes,* served to obscure such differences and suggested a homogeneity that persisted in characterizing the period for several decades. By the late 1930s, social class and race had become particularly implicated in women's lives through debates about whether the "right" elements of society were reproducing themselves by bearing children; not only did such discussions continue into the postwar period, but the influence of these concerns can be seen in the fact that the postwar focus on the middle class was equally a focus on the middle-class family. The *Ladies' Home Journal's* long-running series "How America Lives," which began in 1940, is central to the creation of the domestic world at midcentury in its embodiment of a paradox: while it promised to reflect the diversity of American life, the editors tended to define diversity within fairly proscribed limits; more importantly, the *Journal* insisted on a community of shared values that crossed economic lines: hard work, morality, the centrality of family life, and aspirations for a better future.

Although Christine Frederick does not claim in *Selling Mrs. Consumer* that the various socioeconomic levels she identifies are fixed, allowing no movement up or down on the income/consumption scale, she could scarcely have foreseen in 1929 the dramatic fluctuations in economic and hence social standing that would affect American families during the next two decades. Published shortly before the stock market crash, *Selling Mrs. Consumer* shares in the general post–World War I sense that widespread social catastrophe was a thing of the past. The Depression threw into reverse the pattern of "the lifting of living standards" that Mrs. Frederick so rosily predicted, and the radical restructuring of the American economy during and after World War II created enormous changes in what status in society Americans could expect as well as how that status would be defined. Seldom before had Americans—particularly those not members of identifiable racial or ethnic groups—been so conscious of their relative socioeconomic standing. Morris Dickstein, in "Depression Culture: The Dream of Mobility," describes two kinds of movement observable in American culture during the 1930s: the wandering of those who "took to the road" in an era of widespread unemployment, and the images presented by escapist films of the decade, epitomized in the dances of Fred Astaire and Ginger Rogers. The freedom embodied in the latter, Dickstein writes, "suggests that the real dream of the expressive culture of the 1930s was not money and success, not even elegance and sophistication, but mobility, with its thrust toward the future" (239). The future, in the form of World War II, brought near-full employment by 1943, and, Dickstein suggests, "perhaps the most far-reaching legacy of the depression was the consumer culture, the automated culture, the suburbanized one-family house culture that followed the war" (240).

But far from blurring socioeconomic lines in the interests of patriotic nationalism, the war introduced new fluctuations in the fortunes of Americans. Not only did large numbers of women join the paid labor force, either in response to wartime need or to supplement the military allowances of male family members, but many immigrant workers benefited from the improved salaries and benefits of war industries, allowing them to feel they had a chance at social mobility. As Gary Gerstle notes, "by itself this economic experience would not have been enough to bring about inclusion of workers who had keenly felt their marginality, but in conjunction with the wartime celebration of the nation's multicultural character it allowed European ethnics to believe that the American dream was finally within their grasp" (116). As Gerstle also points out, however, some of this promise was illusory; for a variety of reasons, labor unions failed to secure for workers the gains that might have resulted from the country's desperate need for industrial laborers, and although 1.5 million immigrants became citizens during the war years (115), there was substantial labor unrest both during and after the war. Further, although these workers, like middle- and upper-class Americans, supported the war effort by buying war bonds, the appeals to such workers to do so reflected a class bias on the part of the advertising agencies the government engaged to market the bonds. Gerstle cites as examples two 1944 ads for war bonds appearing in different publications in the textile-manufacturing city of Woonsocket, Rhode Island. The advertisement in the *Woonsocket Call*, a middle-class newspaper, stressed the bonds as an investment for a better way of life in the future: "When they mature, they mean new machinery and equipment, new conveniences for the house, money for the children's schooling, funds for retirement." In contrast, the ad in the *ITU News*, the city's labor paper, appealed not to visions of an improved lifestyle but rather to concerns for "religious tolerance, racial equality, and cultural pluralism." War bonds, the working-class citizens of Woonsocket were told, would enable America to "show [Hitler] that ethnic and racial diversity was a source of strength, not weakness, and to preserve America's historic role as a land of freedom and opportunity for all" (111–12). The appeal to consumer gratification in the *Woonsocket Call* is the same one that appeared in the women's magazine advertisements for shiny postwar kitchens, in which the whiteness of the appliances matched the skins of their proud owners. Periodicals other than city newspapers and women's magazines reinforced the concept during and after World War II that the white middleclass family represented the American norm. Wendy Kozol's study of the midcentury *Life* magazine argues persuasively that editorial decisions about the photographic representation of American "life" amounted to an ideology: "*Life*'s determination of what constituted the ordinary, and how the ordinary was presented, shaped the ideological perspective of the magazine. . . . Ideology is . . . constructed and reinforced through the camera's presumably objective gaze by mapping out a selective cultural space that privileges one way of life as representative of the nation" (9–10). Kozol points out that although *Life* began publication in the 1930s, the magazine achieved wide readership during World War II, in large part because of its ability to bring the war visually to its audience. When depicting the home front, "the editors increasingly relied on images of the white, middle-class family to signify national ideals" (56). In addition, this family's role as purchasers of goods would ensure the survival of democracy. *Life* publisher Henry Luce, in his 1941 editorial titled "American Century," equated democracy with capitalism. As Kozol notes, "Advertisements and photo-essays in *Life* aligned democratic rhetoric with capitalistic objectives, frequently through families who were exhorted to consume as a patriotic duty" (67).

With women already identified as the household's "general purchasing agents," advertisers logically saw the women's magazines as the most direct conduit for messages about consumption and their implications for class status. Women were assumed to be particularly implicated in issues of social class, most obviously because, as purchasers of clothing and household goods, they were uniquely positioned to express the family's tastes and aspirations. Typical of such assumptions is an advertisement for Wamsutta towels in the February 1958 issue of *House Beautiful* magazine encouraging the reader to "put fashion in your bath" with towels called "chinchilla" and "ermine": the utilitarian bath towel is visually linked to the world of elegant fashion with a drawing of a woman wearing a fur stole. Before World War II, those who advertised in women's magazines often acknowledged differences in socioeconomic levels among product users. An ad for Royal Baking Powder in the December 1933 *Delineator*, for example, highlights the fact that the product is used in "123 out of 150 homes in lovely Sewickley, exclusive suburb of Pittsburgh," and quotes "Mrs. C. E. I., prominent in Sewickley society," as saying that she "always take[s] the trouble to make sure that Royal Baking Powder is used," which suggests that servants do the actual baking. But the ad also includes an endorsement from "Mrs. E. M. V., whose home is a modest 5-room cottage, and who does her own housework and cooking." After the war such frank admissions of class distinctions gave way to a single middle- to upper-middle-class model. Roland Marchand points to a shift in the way advertisers portrayed social class between the prewar and postwar periods: "Advertisers [by the 1950s] cast affluent suburban families not only as models of appropriate consumer styles but also as realistic portrayals of average Americans. In the 1920s and 1930s, Americans had known that they were seeing explicit models of high society 'smartness' in many ads. Now they were encouraged to see the advertising models as mirrors of themselves" ("Visions" 169).

Women were also connected to class and consumerism in their role as mothers, not only in their aspirations for their children and as purchasers of products for children but more fundamentally in debates about what kind of women should bear children. Even as Adolf Hitler was implementing his plans for a pure "master race" in Germany, discussions of U.S. birthrates were tinged with the language of eugenics and social engineering, and the views of the determinants of human intelligence that prevailed into the 1940s and 1950s were derived from research that betrayed a large component of class (not to mention racial) bias. As Hamilton Cravens has shown, such influential works as Alice M. Leahy's 1935 *Nature-Nurture and Intelligence* were premised on studies that relied on existing social-class structures: John E. Anderson and Florence L. Goodenough of the Minnesota Institute of Child Welfare "created an occupational scale, drawn from the 1920 federal census. They devised a hierarchy of eight groups, the most prestigious white collar occupations at the top, with those at the bottom requiring the least skill and education. To assess the home environment they used a sociologist's rating scale that assigned different weights to various types of material possessions in the home. Thus the higher the occupational and educational level of the parents, and the more highly ranked material possessions they owned, the higher the social status and, therefore, argued Goodenough and Anderson, the innate intelligence of the parents and their relatives—certainly their children, but all to whom each parent was biologically related." Such theories, Cravens notes, were "comforting" to those "firmly committed to the social class and caste order of contemporary America" (154–55).

By the late 1930s, anxiety about whether the "right" women were reproducing themselves had become a theme in the women's magazines.[3] In her inaugural May 1937 monthly column in *Ladies' Home Journal,* Dorothy Thompson warned middle-class women against refusing to have children in order to afford more of life's luxuries. Thompson noted with alarm that birth rates in countries such as Sweden and England were falling and cited a professor of anthropology who believed that "humane measures to keep alive the unfit and prolong old age—while the birth rate declines—were increasing the numbers of the inferior, giving us an old population and diminishing the level of general intelligence." In her preference for the middle-class values of *Journal* readers, Thompson did not agree with Anderson and Goodenough that the top of the social scale produced the best citizens; instead, she asserted that the people "whose achievements adorn our society" do not come from either "wealthy homes" or "deeply impoverished ones" but instead come from middle-class homes with "cheerful, robustly sensible parents." A dozen years later, Thompson was still concerned that the proper people were failing to have enough children, but she was less worried about the cultural pursuit of luxuries and—reflecting the changes caused by World War II—more preoccupied with what she terms the "so-called 'emancipation' of women." Thompson's starkly titled "Race Suicide of the Intelligent," published in the May 1949 *Journal,* chided educated, childless women for "violating their own biological natures." Whereas "the intelligent of the nineteenth century used their relative prosperity to feed, house and educate substantial families," Thompson was distressed that in the middle of the twentieth century, "every year thousands of women leave our colleges and universities determined to make careers for themselves. They marry, but find many reasons to postpone having children." While Thompson devoted much of her article to outlining the negative effect that having few or no children would have on the women themselves—"psychoneurosis," unhealthy (because late-born) children, loss of the mother-child bond, disappointed husbands, and the loneliness of the only child—it is clear that her real concern was the diminishment of a ruling elite who can "leaven and lift the level of the masses, who never can lift themselves alone."

Thompson was by no means a lone voice. The editorial in the June 1946 *Ladies' Home Journal* asked readers "Are You Too Educated to be a Mother?" Citing a Census Bureau study showing that a college-educated woman was likely to have, on average, one child and a high-school graduate two, while a woman who made it only to the fourth grade produced four, the *Journal* editors warned that "educated women, potentially mothers of children with greater native ability, are guilty of squandering their genetic inheritance." The editors' stance is a variation on the decades-old argument that women should be barred from higher education because it would "unfit" them for motherhood. In 1916 Leta S. Hollingworth, writing about the forms of social control used to convince women to bear children, noted that "those in control of society yielded up the old prescribed education of women only after a stubborn struggle, realizing that with the passing of the old training an important means of social control was slipping out of their hands," and she was optimistic that once women realized the methods used to control their behavior, such methods would cease to have any force (25). Yet Helen H. Franzwa, studying motherhood in the fiction appearing in *Ladies' Home Journal, McCall's,* and *Good Housekeeping* between 1940 and 1970, found that even as the actual birth rate fell steadily after the mid-1950s, the fictional birth rate increased, and "most childless women were portrayed as dependents who had no outlets for self-expression save the unfulfilled one of motherhood" (73). Pondering the discrepancy between real and fictional motherhood, Ellen Peck speculates in *The Baby Trap* that magazine editors, on behalf of their advertisers, wanted to present women as mothers/consumers:

> So, inasmuch as we're selling domesticity, I guess we're selling motherhood. The situation is kind of a paradox since no matter how merchandisers try to show that being a mom and a homemaker is fascinating, it's essentially not. Breeding is not chic, it is not fun, it is not glamorous. . . .
> But the simplest way out of the problem is through spending. I mean, the old saw about the wife feeling depressed, buying a new hat, and feeling better. Well, it's true. Spending money is therapeutic. If we can keep her spending, she'll be more satisfied with her role. Now, doesn't that make sense? (50)

By midcentury, then, concepts of family, social class, and consumerism had become as inextricably interwoven as the various elements of the magazines themselves.

The "How America Lives" series that began in *Ladies' Home Journal* in 1940 provides an interesting case in point. The term *how* in the series title points in multiple directions, as the series explored Americans' values, activities, economic conditions, and what we would now term lifestyle by focusing on a different family each month. Family income and spending were central to the series; many of the articles included a yearly budget for the featured family, and many were accompanied by editorial commentary indicating what proportion of Americans occupied the same socioeconomic level or providing other statistical information. In October 1941, for example, such commentary focused on the ownership of electrical appliances, noting that in homes with electricity, 59 percent had washing machines, 95 percent had irons, and 48 percent had vacuum cleaners. Echoing Christine Frederick's emphasis on women's purchasing power in *Selling Mrs. Consumer*, the *Journal* noted that "U.S. Housekeeping is today Big Business, indeed—all in the hands of 28,581,680 housewives who, to keep their homes in apple-pie running order, spend a total of $5,285,000,000 yearly." During the early 1940s, when economic depression still gripped the United States, the *Journal* reported that nearly 96 percent of American families had incomes of less than $4,000 per year, with 17.6 percent earning between $1,250 and $1,750, 12.85 percent between $2,000 and $3,000, and 15.3 percent receiving some sort of government welfare. At the other end of the economic scale, 1.1 percent of families lived on incomes higher than $10,000, including .001 percent of Americans who were millionaires. By noting such statistics and reading the household budgets of the profiled families, readers of "How America Lives" could readily compare their own circumstances to those of their contemporaries.

"How America Lives" was, from its inception, devoted to displaying the nation's socioeconomic diversity. During the first year of the series, articles focused on the very wealthy and the poverty-stricken as well as more typical families earning $2,500 a year. The December 1940 segment featured the family of a Chicago meat-packing company executive whose $80,000 Depression-era salary (down from $250,000 in the 1920s) maintained homes in both the city and the country and six full-time servants. The decline in income had not curtailed the Wilsons' lavish way of life, which included entertaining and vacation trips. In August of the same year, the series visited four families at the other end of the economic scale: an out-of-work painter in

Brooklyn whose family of seven depended on welfare, a Pennsylvania man whose Works Progress Administration job barely sustained a family of ten, a West Virginia coal miner, and a black sharecropping family in Mississippi.

Yet despite these extremes, the *Journal* authors were intent on pointing out what made these people similar rather than different. The editorial headnote that preceded the story about the millionaire Wilsons, for example, began with the rhetoric of social leveling: "America is proud to have no aristocracy; she has a sense of humor. Steel tycoons and waiters scream themselves hoarse at the same football games, get wet feet and colds, read the same three-cent newspaper, the same best seller, worry about the state of the world, the kids' chicken pox, and what to give the wife for Christmas." In describing the Wilsons' lives, the author repeatedly stressed the family's lack of ostentation. "Pots of money" have allowed the Wilsons to live "comfortably, . . . sensibly, and with a cheering lack of swank," the article reported, and the author was careful to include the fact that when Tom Wilson proposed to his wife, when he was earning $6,500 a year, she told him that "any time it was indicated, she could feed him and keep him well and comfortably on $100 a month." The Wilsons' country house, with its twenty-one beds, was described as comfortable rather than elegant, and the *Journal* author noted that the towels in the bathrooms did not match and had "obviously been laundered again and again." While the Wilsons made do with unmatched towels, the four families whose poverty is described in the August 1940 issue were presented as earnest, hardworking people temporarily down on their luck but possessing values that differed little from those of the wealthy Wilsons: "courage for the future and loyalty to the wife and kids . . . survive—with astounding vitality."

Again and again in "How America Lives," the family unit was portrayed as the key to social mobility and security. In a sidebar article that accompanied the April 1941 profile of two young immigrant couples, a psychiatrist answered the title question, "Are America's Foreign-Born a Problem?" with a paean to the American Dream: "Those who are badly and permanently warped by living on the wrong side of the railroad tracks are far outnumbered by those prodded into taking advantage of the abundant opportunities in America to jump across to the less-cindery side." To enable this "jump," the psychiatrist identified the "central unifying forces" of success as "family life" and "universal education." At the center of family life, the *Journal* agreed with its sister magazines, was the woman, who exerted her force as moral influence as well as consumer. In the rhetoric of patriotism so common to the war years, the preface to the June 1942 article about a Rochester, New York, couple with eight children mixed living standard and moral suasion with national defense: "The American housewife is not only the best dressed, best fed, best cared for in the world; she also wields incalculably greater powers than women of any other nation. Slums are cleared, schools and hospitals built, the Red Cross pours its vans of mercy across a blood-streaked world, because she wants it that way. Now she realizes that in this war she stands to lose more than men and country, more than all the brave women of China, England and Russia put together, if Hitler conquers. 'Our' way of life means all she lives by. Above all others, she has the right to defend the priceless privileges of democracy." The "priceless privileges" of "our" way of life were not identified specifically, but the evidence of the "How America Lives" series, combined with other magazine content in the years during which it ran, suggests a combination of material goods and values and behaviors that would be associated with "middle America" whether one lived as a millionaire or a sharecropper. The mother of eight in Rochester summed up this idea when she was quoted as saying about her children, "We just want them to be healthy and clean-thinking and that's just what they are. They'll find their niche in life." Despite maintaining ten people in a four-room house on just over $3,000 a year—a feat for which the *Journal* author displayed considerable admiration—this woman expressed calm optimism that God and her husband's employer would take care of the family.

To at least the same degree that the *Journal* series described how America lived during the war and postwar years, it worked to teach Americans how to live. While few readers could aspire to the way of life of the Chicago Wilsons, and none would have wished to live like black Mississippi sharecroppers, the *Journal* editors clearly saw their mission as educational, not only in helping Americans to know their neighbors but also in promoting certain domestic values. Striking evidence of this philosophy is provided in the February 1941 editorial in which the Goulds announced that the *Journal* would continue the "How America Lives" series into a second year. "We go through life," the column began, "trying to learn how to live":

> At sixteen, it's what shade of lipstick is right for you, and what can you say to the boy next door when he tries to kiss you goodnight. At twenty-five, it may

be what kind of refrigerator shall you buy, and how can you stop Junior's temper tantrums. At thirty-five, perhaps it's how can you lose fifteen pounds, and must you tell Janie the facts of life now. . . .

It is to answer these questions that women's magazines exist. They must help women to make roast beef and a happy marriage. Tell them how to give Junior a warm sweater and sound teeth; Janie, a curl over her forehead and a straight and honest approach to marriage.

There is considerable evidence to suggest that many readers of women's magazines welcomed such instruction in how to live. Fairly typical is a June 1942 letter to the *Journal* in which a reader testified to the magazine's value in her family's life. The letter, like the prose of the magazines themselves, blended material acquisition with behavior and values; growing up in Iowa, the reader reported, she was taught by the *Journal* about "hardwood floors and bathrooms and a lot of the now necessities of life," and her Aunt Maggie "raised her family by the *Ladies' Home Journal*," even to the point of accepting her children's fondness for playing bridge when she found that the *Journal* sanctioned such activities.

One woman who seems to have taken the women's magazines' homemaking instruction very much to heart is Marjorie Reeves, of Peoria, Illinois, whose family was featured in the September 1946 "How America Lives." This "perfectionist housewife," as the title of the article called her, embodies our stereotypical notion of the postwar housewife utterly devoted to her role—cleaning, cooking, sewing, painting, decorating, and raising two children with an almost fanatical zeal. The article describes a sparkling house utterly without clutter or disorder, and the author noted that the Reeveses appeared to belong to a higher economic level than they actually did: "At first glance it might seem that the Reeveses have an income of between four and five thousand dollars a year. This effect is achieved and maintained on a net income . . . of $2830." In a tone approaching awe, the author described the family's standard of living: "Practically every gadget for keeping house is there. The children have excellent toys. They all have good clothes." If Marjorie Reeves was often tired, the author explained that "she is driven by the unrelenting compulsion of a true craftsman." Yet the *Journal* editors did not wholly endorse Reeves's perfectionism. A second article in the same issue (written by a different staff writer), titled "The Price of Perfection," suggested, albeit gently, that Reeves and her family might be better served with a bit more spontaneity and humor and a bit less order and perfection. "Doing a woman's work," the author commented, "is like blowing up a balloon: you've got to know when to quit." That this second article is meant to provide a "corrected" Reeves is clear from accompanying photographs showing her reading to her children and playing chess with her husband, as photographs in the first article had shown her sewing, scrubbing, and dusting. The middle-class ideal required a proper balance between industriousness and emotional fulfillment.

The second article about Reeves resembles the magazines' popular "makeover" articles, in which selected readers had their appearances transformed by new hairstyles, makeup, and clothing. In fact, most of those whose lives were featured in "How America Lives" were subject to routine makeovers before the *Journal* told their stories. Despite the editors' February 1941 statement that the series presented "a picture of life as it is really lived in America," an article in the May 1949 issue revealed just how carefully constructed was the America the *Journal* presented to its readers. In "How the *Journal* Lives," the magazine turned the lens of its series on the *Journal*'s new offices and testing facilities in Rockefeller Center in New York, offering a visual and verbal tour of both its facilities and its editorial processes. The article pointed out that the assistant editor who served as the "talent scout" for "How America Lives" interviewed between three and six families for each segment, "and of course no family is chosen which does not enter into the idea with wholehearted enthusiasm." Introducing the work of the interior decorating editor, the article revealed that the homes of "How America Lives" families as seen in the magazine were not precisely the ones in which they had previously lived: "Miss Murdock visits them for several days to discover how they would like their living or dining or bedroom to look. Sometimes all the redecorating is done on the spot." But if the redecorated room would be difficult to photograph for the feature, a model would be constructed in the New York offices, "and later the room is completed in the family's own home, an exact replica of the photograph." The women, like their houses, were made over for the articles. About the *Journal*'s beauty editor, the article stated, "One of the greatest pleasures of her job . . . is 'beautifying' How America Lives housewives. She has never seen an HAL housewife yet who made the best of her good points, nor one who, after a strict regimen of dieting, exercise and advice on hair and makeup, didn't gain an immeasurable lift of spirit." The beauty editor's telling summation was, "They seem like different people." Evidence that the *Journal* editors recognized the somewhat fictive nature of the series is afforded by the editorial response to a letter published in the September 1951 issue. The reader expressed her happiness that an article had described a mother "who does more yelling and spanking than I do," to which the editors commented, "Most popular How America Lives stories are, invariably, those about wives up to their eyes in trouble. Is this because women love soap opera? Or do women love soap opera because it's so much like life?"

Given the women's magazines' long history of providing instruction in "better living," it is doubtful that many readers were disillusioned to learn that the homes and housewives of "How America Lives" were to some extent a creation of the *Ladies' Home Journal,* and the families who were "redecorated" as part of the series surely were grateful for these improvements. Nonetheless, by turning them into "different people," the *Journal* tacitly acknowledged that their "real" selves were not quite worthy of being publicly displayed and furthered an ideology of self-improvement that had distinct social-class implications, as is underscored by the fact that the poverty-level families featured in August 1940 did not receive household and personal makeovers. Because—apart from their exhibitions of family loyalty and courage—these ways of life were not to be aspired to, no effort was made to beautify the O'Briens' ground-floor Brooklyn apartment, with its "dangling electric bulb in a cold, windowless room"; the wife of the Pennsylvania WPA worker was described as "in need of teeth"; and the article about the Mississippi Braceys was illustrated with photographs of an outhouse without a door and of a dog peering into an empty kitchen cupboard. While readers were expected to be saddened by and sympathetic to the plight of these families, they were at the same time not part of the pattern of upward mobility that characterized the rest of "How America Lives."

Another aspect of the selection process for families in the *Journal* series is evident in the fact that with very few exceptions, the families had children—usually three or more. Childlessness, whether by choice or necessity, was not part of the picture of America that the series wished to present, except in such cases as the unmarried draftee profiled in the March 1942 issue or the June 1947 story of New Orleans newlyweds—and this young couple was "eager to save [money] against the arrival of children." The couple featured in March 1940 were expecting their first child, which they hoped would eventually be one of three—"just the number," the *Journal* author wrote, "experts recommend if this country is to maintain a healthy population level." The articles sometimes noted that women who had fewer than three children had been advised against further pregnancies for health reasons. Large families were consistently presented as desirable no matter what the family's income level; the article about the Rochester, New York, family of ten made this attitude part of the first paragraph: "John and Geraldine Seefried, experts in living, have a small gray house a few miles south of Rochester, New York. Their first real worries developed only seven or eight years ago, after more than a dozen years of married life. They were afraid that, although still in the lower thirties, they were not going to have any more children. Up to then, they had had only five—three girls and two boys." During the war, such families could remind readers of what was to be protected from Hitler and the "Japs"; after the conflict ended, such families served as the consumers of both the goods advertised in the magazines—the production of which, in turn, provided jobs for returning veterans—and the advice on child rearing, family harmony, and education that the magazines dispensed in copious quantities. For parents who had lived through World War II and the Depression, peace and relative prosperity would allow their children fully to embrace the American Dream. In this sense, a childless couple or a single person offered no future.

In the first years after World War II, "How America Lives" introduced readers to returning veterans and war brides and welcomed women back to the home from their factory jobs. The economic emphasis of the series continued, though its focus became the pent-up desire for consumer goods still in short supply and the postwar economic inflation. In August 1946 the series featured an Englishwoman who had married an American paratrooper in London in 1944 and had settled with their infant son on a chinchilla farm in California. Much of the article points to the ease with which Norma Domina had entered American culture, hardly seeming "English" to her American neighbors; when Max Domina teasingly called Norma a "Cockney" for referring to a roast as a "joint," the author hastened to state that "there's no hint of cockney in her warm voice or her well-pronounced syllables." A second article about Norma Domina in the same issue showed the *Journal* helping her to become an American consumer by seeking items necessary to outfit her American kitchen. While the article stressed that many basic goods remained in short supply—"such backbones of the nation as rotary egg beaters and potato mashers we never could track down"—the photographs that accompanied the article showed Norma looking delightedly at an automatic dishwasher and a below-counter refrigerator displayed at a model house in Los Angeles. While manufacturers tantalized consumers with such products, postwar inflation took its toll on the average family's income; the *Journal* noted in November 1946 that since 1938, food costs had increased by 49.7 percent and clothing costs by 55.7 percent.

By the early 1950s, with the specter of the previous economic adversity held at bay by increasing national prosperity, "How America Lives" lessened its emphasis on how Americans managed their financial lives, and articles in the series sometimes featured ways of life that would have seemed to most readers unusual or exotic. In August 1952, for example, "Child of Nature" profiled a six-year-old girl whose mail-carrier father and journalist mother were raising her on a farm in California without running water but in the company of fifty-six animals. The following month, the series featured a pair of aspiring young actors living on a shoestring in New York City. By 1953 the series was retitled "How Young America Lives" and usually focused on young married couples, such as the Navy electronics technician who, with his wife and two small children, lived in a thirty-three-foot trailer so that the family would not be separated as he was transferred from one base to another. Although such ways of life were far from typical, the series' emphasis remained on family solidarity, hard work, and gentility.[4]

Race, Consumerism, and Status

Despite clearly regarding the white middle-class family with several children and a stay-at-home wife as the American cultural norm, "How America Lives" nonetheless presented a more diverse nation than was commonly seen in women's magazines of the period.[5] In addition to featuring members of vastly different socioeconomic groups, the series profiled recent immigrants (primarily from Western European countries) and African Americans as well as people of European origin whose families had been U.S. citizens for many generations. One important reason for this openness was the spirit of nationalism that characterized the country on the eve of World War II and that constituted a major impetus for the series itself. In the interest of unity, it was important that all Americans recognized each other as neighbors; the editorial preface to each article in the series during the first half of the 1940s typically concluded, "They are yourself. And you are democracy." Nor did such refrains cease when the war was over. In the March 1946 issue of the *Journal*, Struthers Burt, who wrote regularly for the magazine, reminded readers that each of them belonged to a religious, racial, political, or economic group that had at some point been persecuted and warned that "prejudice is a prairie fire; a spark can make a conflagration."

As late as 1955, when many Americans—and certainly most of the *Journal's* readers—were benefiting from postwar prosperity, "How America Lives" continued to present an economically diverse America. In March, in "My Sons Live On Misery Street," the series profiled a family of five living in a Manhattan slum. The story of an unemployed father, periodic welfare dependence, and three boys living largely on the streets to escape a crowded three-room apartment was told primarily in the words of the mother, who provided whatever support—both moral and financial—the family had. Yet even in presenting this picture of dire poverty, the *Journal* series exercised a certain selectivity. Although article's introduction mentioned that most of the residents of this portion of East 101st Street were Puerto Rican, the Schaefer family was of Irish and German descent. Mrs. Schaefer, described as having "a strong spirit . . . apparent in her eyes," worked hard to teach her sons to be honest and avoid drugs and to hope for a better future: "I think the most important thing to teach a child is to do the right thing, and if you don't have what you want, maybe you will have it tomorrow." Although neither parent had lived in much better circumstances than the family's currently ones, both express faith in a brighter tomorrow. Mrs. Schaefer told her boys that "if you're poor maybe later you can go to work and have the things you don't have now." and Mr. Schaefer, a German immigrant with little education, lectured his sons about doing well in school: "Learning to read and write is the most important thing in the world, unless you want to be a truck loader like me." In short, middle-class aspirations existed even on "Misery Street."

During the war, "How America Lives" even pointed out economic diversity among African Americans, profiling both the family of sharecroppers in Mississippi and that of De Haven Hinkson, a major in the Army Medical

Corps and the first "colored" doctor to head a U.S. Army hospital. The article about the Hinkson family was candid about the fact that racial prejudice affected the life of this successful West Philadelphia doctor and his wife, who had one daughter at Cornell University and a second about to enter the University of Wisconsin. When he was appointed to run the military hospital near Tuskegee, Alabama, Major Hinkson wrote to both the Philadelphia Red Cross and Red Cross headquarters in Washington to inquire about volunteer work for his wife and was stung but not surprised when neither letter was answered.

While the vast majority of the fiction published in the magazines told stories in which young white heroines found domestic happiness and improved their social and economic status, there were exceptions, and here, too, the *Ladies' Home Journal* demonstrated greater willingness to deal with racial themes than did the other magazines. In August 1953 the *Journal* published the story "D.P." by Kurt Vonnegut Jr. Set in Germany during World War II, the story concerns a young black boy in a Catholic orphanage who becomes convinced that a black American serviceman is his father because the boy has never seen anyone else who looked like him. And in June 1951, the *Journal* published "See How They Run," by a previously unpublished young black woman, Mary Elizabeth Vroman, based on her experiences as a young black elementary school teacher in the segregated southern educational system. Alongside the first page of the story, the *Journal* editors printed the letter that had accompanied the story, in which Vroman asserted that she wished the story to call attention to the conditions under which Negro students and teachers attempted to create an environment of learning; the letter also testified to some degree of black readership of the magazine, as Vroman wrote, "Need I say that I think the *Ladies' Home Journal* is wonderful, when I'm entrusting you with my first precious brain-child?" While there is no record of the overall reader response to Vroman's story, the August 1951 issue carried two letters to the editor from readers who praised the story. In *American Story,* Bruce and Beatrice Gould describe the *Journal* fiction editor taking a chance on this unpublished writer, noting with pride that Vroman's story was subsequently made into a film starring Dorothy Dandridge (261–62).

Such sensitivity to racial inequality was, however, relatively rare in the women's magazines of the 1940s and 1950s. Occasional articles drew attention to what was called the "Negro problem" or encouraged tolerance of others in a general sense. In July 1941, a brief *Journal* article described the founding of Meharry Medical College in Nashville, Tennessee, in 1875 for the education of black doctors, noting that the school owed its continued existence to "white man's largesse," most recently a grant from the Rockefeller Foundation. In December 1947, a *Journal* article reported on the Fellowship Commission in Philadelphia, which had significantly reduced what would today be called hate crimes in that city. *Coronet* magazine devoted a December 1953 article to a black Alabama widow who with her ten children had developed a thousand-acre plantation that grossed more than $130,000 a year. But for the most part, appearances or mentions of African Americans in the magazines served to emphasize racial and class distinctions. Typical is a comment in a June 1942 letter to the editor of *Ladies' Home Journal*. The author, who served as chairman of industry of the Texas Federation of Women's Clubs, wrote to lament the fact that a national defense program designed to teach young women homemaking skills for domestic employment was having difficulty attracting white students, whereas fifty black women had signed up: "the young white women's objection to it is that the word 'housemaid' or 'cook' carries a social stigma." As though the futures of the enrolled black women were of no significance, the writer worried that "our [white] girls" will have "neither the skill nor the desire to create homes."

Product advertising, more than any other magazine feature, reinforced the white, middle-class ideal. Perhaps the apotheosis of this tendency was reached in a Maytag washing machine ad in the May 1960 issue of *McCall's*. Posed with a gleaming white washer and dryer are a woman and two children, all dressed in white, including the woman's gloves and the shoes worn by all three. The ad also reinforces stereotypical gender roles: the woman and the little girl have their hands on the washing machine, suggesting their involvement in doing laundry, while the little boy sits on the floor playing with a toy truck. When blacks appeared in advertisements, they were typically cast in the role of servants or presented as iconic representations of servants, such as the familiar "Aunt Jemima" and "Uncle Ben." Ads featuring blacks as consumers of products were extremely rare. In *Aunt Jemima, Uncle Ben, and Rastus*, Marilyn Kern-Foxworth cites studies showing that between 1946 and 1956 the number of such ads in national magazines ranged between .57 and .88 percent (140). More commonly, blacks in magazine advertising were cast in the role of helping white Americans lead happier lives even when such blacks were not portrayed as servants. The beaming face of a black man wearing a chef's hat announced the "new 5-minute Cream of Wheat" cereal for a quick and nutritious breakfast for a white family in the October 1959 issue of *Good Housekeeping*.[6] In the November issue, an equally cheerful Aunt Jemima rescued a woman with unexpected dinner guests, saying, "Don't you fret, honey! Jus' feastify dem wif my pancakes!"[7] A black railroad porter was similarly helpful in a Sanka coffee advertisement in the December 1941 issue of *Woman's Home Companion*, introducing a traveling actress to decaffeinated coffee. (The color line was drawn even more sharply when the white actress ordered a "white-meat sandwich.") The use of blacks in such advertising was more complex than mere stereotyping. As Jackson Lears posits in *Fables of Abundance*, "It is easy to dismiss these figures as emblems of white disdain, but their meanings were multivalent. Without question, they epitomized a whole constellation of nurturant values associated with preindustrial household and community life. They provided sustenance; they took care of (white) people" (384). By 1949 such overt servility was less common, but the face of Uncle Ben dominates the box of rice pictured in an ad in *Ladies' Home Journal*. Thus, at the point in the twentieth century when most middle-class families had ceased to employ actual domestic servants, metaphorical servants were close at hand on packages of cereal, rice, and pancake mix. Such images served as what Lears calls "folk icons," allowing "the adepts of progress to have it both ways: to assert that traditional values survived even as modernization whirled ahead at full tilt" (385).

Even as those "traditional values" were associated with the white middle class, the language of advertising engaged in midcentury debates about the nature of the domestic by presenting homemakers as servants who ministered to their families' needs or as ladies of leisure. In "Selling the Mechanized Household," Bonnie J. Fox reports that during 1949–50, only 20 percent of ads for household consumer products in *Ladies' Home Journal* emphasized a reduction of time and effort spent on housework, whereas nearly twice that many promised the consumer that the product would make her a better housekeeper. After 1940, Fox asserts, ads increasingly featured a "labor of love" theme; they affirmed "to housewives and the general public that there was real and important work being done in the home"; "by the

1950s the women pictured in the ads were indistinguishable from the domestic servants pictured earlier—especially since they were often seen waiting on their families" (30, 32–33). Yet the rhetoric of many advertisements suggested that products assumed the function of servants, allowing the homemaker more time for other activities. A 1946 ad for pressure cookers claimed that the product "gives you more time for *living.*" A 1942 ad for Windex pictures a woman playing tennis with the caption, "And where is our Louisa? She's out having fun!" And in 1948 General Electric offered the homemaker an "automatic rotary ironer" that "lets you *sit down* to iron!" Articles in the magazines similarly proposed that products were the servants of women, with titles such as "More Small Appliances That Work for You," "Put Your Steam Iron to Work," and "Modern Machines Make Sewing Easy"; a regular feature in *Woman's Home Companion* in the 1950s was titled "Help for Your House." But as Fox's research affirms, if products were now servants to the homemaker, she in turn was to serve her family. Mingled with the promises of free time and reduced labor was the rhetoric of pleasing the family. Using the Wear-Ever pressure cooker gains for the housewife her husband's praise for her cooking; Ballard refrigerated biscuits will put a "purr-ty smile on your family's faces."

Paradoxically, just as women were encouraged to buy products to better serve their families, many of America's leaders saw postwar consumerism as a way to create a classless society—at least among white Americans. In *Homeward Bound,* Elaine Tyler May characterizes Richard Nixon's vision in the 1959 Kitchen Debate with Soviet Premier Nikita Khrushchev as one in which the suburban home "obliterated class distinctions and accentuated gender distinctions": "In Nixon's vision, the suburban ideal of home ownership would diffuse two potentially disruptive forces: women and workers. In appliance-laden homes across the country, working-class as well as business-class breadwinners could fulfill the new work-to-consume ethic; home ownership would lessen class consciousness among workers, who would set their sights toward the middle-class ideal. The family home would be the place where a man could display his success through the accumulation of consumer goods. Women, in turn, would reap rewards for domesticity by surrounding themselves with commodities. Presumably, they would remain content as housewives because appliances would ease their burdens. For both men and women, home ownership would reinforce aspirations for upward mobility and diffuse the potential for social unrest" (162, 164). In the context of the Cold War, consumption was a patriotic activity, reinforcing capitalism as an ideology in opposition to the evils of communism. And just as the women's magazines had supported America's goals during World War II by instructing women to plant victory gardens, preserve food, and do volunteer work, postwar magazines advised readers on how to buy and use everything from cake mixes to vacuum cleaners. Most of the magazines published regular columns designed to bring new products to the attention of readers. *Woman's Home Companion* featured the "Shopper's Companion," *Good Housekeeping* ran "Strictly as a Customer," and *American Home* touted products in "Market Place." The upscale fashion magazines published similar guides to consumption, focused on fashion accessories and beauty products—for example, *Harper's Bazaar*'s "Shopping Bazaar" and a feature in *Mademoiselle* by "Mlle Wearybones."

Aside from such overt encouragement to purchase consumer goods, the magazines' editorial content frequently constituted thinly veiled endorsements of household appliances and other products. Not long after the end of the war, as factories were being converted to peacetime production, the June 1946 *Good Housekeeping* told readers, "If you don't own an electric beater, our advice is to put it at the top of your list of new-equipment purchases." The January 1950 *Good Housekeeping* pronounced electric mixers "strong right arms" for the homemaker, and the article's author, Helen W. Kendall, noted that in the magazine's test kitchens "we're so accustomed to letting mixers do the work, we wonder why a woman tries to do without one." In the April issue, Kendall advised brides organizing their first kitchens, encouraging the installation of electrical outlets for the "electric mixer, waffle iron, toaster, etc." that she assumes brides own. In November of the same year, *American Home* encouraged the reader to begin her "Christmas hinting" to "papa or the kids" about an array of products that included an electric egg cooker, an electric bean pot, and a clock radio that could turn appliances on and off at preset times. As new convenience foods became available, the magazines regularly reported on them as well. As early as the January 1941 issue of *Parents' Magazine,* noted food writer Clementine Paddleford hailed the food manufacturer as the "busy woman's best friend," enthusiastically describing instant mashed potatoes, canned chow mein, precooked pork sausage, and ice cream mixes. A writer in the October 1957

Seventeen waxed lyrical over frozen dinners, cake mixes packaged with their own baking pans, and cheese in squeezable tubes.

Such messages about consumer goods were tied directly to both the woman's performance of her household responsibilities and to advancements in social status. Owning the proper equipment was often equated with possessing certain skills; thus, in advising brides on organizing their kitchens, Kendall made a leap to brides' expertise in cooking: "No wonder this bride can bake a perfect lemon pie!" In September 1950, Kendall's article was titled "It Takes a Good Range to Make a Good Cook!" A similarly paradoxical ploy was to suggest that using a labor-saving product was tantamount to possessing the skills that the product rendered unnecessary. A writer describing postwar innovations in the January 1946 *Redbook* quoted the directions for preparing a cake from frozen batter and then asked, "with a start like this, what timorous newlywed couldn't do a handsome baking job?" Poppy Cannon's food column in the February 1950 issue of *Mademoiselle* opened with the observation that "a continental observer holds that no woman is a real woman unless she can put a fine meal in front of her man" and then proposed how easy doing so was with a new brand of canned soup and some brown-and-serve rolls. An article about garbage disposals in the January 1960 issue of *McCall's* attempted to make such a convenience seem the norm of American life by noting that one was "installed in more than half a million sinks each year," and the rhetoric of the article reinforced social-class ideals first by freeing the woman from servitude—"if you're still handmaiden to an outrageously disagreeable garbage receptacle—consider acquiring an electric food-waste disposer"—and then by appealing to her aesthetic sense by enabling her to keep "[her] kitchen and [her] yard and [her] street free of mess, smells, and insects."

Thus, while the magazines' ideal middle-class woman served her family, the purchase of certain products and appliances promised to keep her from lower-class drudgery—not to mention smells and insects—and allow her the leisure of a "lady." One among many evidences that magazine readers received these messages was a report in the January 1959 issue of *McCall's* on that magazine's "Second Congress on Better Living," an event attended by 103 women, most of whom had been competitors in *McCall's* home remodeling contests. The article noted that the women's median age was thirty-two, their median family income was $8,500, and their average number of children was 2.4. Although the author stated that these women's "dream homes are down-to-earth," they believed the minimum size to be eight rooms, with two and a half bathrooms, a family room, and "appliances with recognized brand names."[8] "On the whole," the author stated, "they are in love with their appliances," and most participants endorsed the installment purchase of appliances, furniture, and cars. For all of its emphasis on new and improved houses and products, the article concluded on a curiously nostalgic note that suggests that there was a price to be paid for the rush to upward mobility that these women represented at the end of the 1950s. The author noted that most participants in the conference "look back with longing to the parlor, the front halls, the homely comfort of Grandmother's day," and one woman was quoted as yearning for a domestic ideal that might well have been the creation of the women's magazines several decades earlier: "I love that old-fashioned idea of the family with a big round table with a lamp in the middle and everyone sitting around, doing homework or conversing."

Whether or not this grandmotherly scenario had been a part of these women's family histories, in 1959 such families were likely to be living in suburban tract houses. House plans had been a popular feature in the magazines during the war years, when many Americans lived in temporary housing near defense plants or had been driven by the Depression to live with relatives, dreaming about eventual home ownership. For many, the dream was deferred for a good while after the war. As Kenneth T. Jackson points out in *Crabgrass Frontier,* the housing industry had been almost dormant since the early 1930s, and it took time for the country to turn from war production to the needs of peace. The number of single-family housing starts was 114,000 in 1944, rising to 937,000 in 1946, 1,183,000 in 1948, and 1,692,000 in 1950 (232–33). The vast majority of houses built in the postwar years were erected in the suburbs of medium to large cities, and Jackson identifies four characteristics of these developments in addition to their peripheral location: about 97 percent were detached houses with their own land around them, they tended to look alike, they were affordable for the middle class, and the suburbs were economically and racially homogeneous (238–41). House plans appearing in the women's magazines after the war stressed such values as affordability, privacy, and family living. A modest two-bedroom house in the August 1949 *Good Housekeeping* featured a combined living-dining room and substituted bookcases for a wall between the parents' bedroom and the living room. In March of the same year, *Ladies' Home Journal* showed several plans for houses that included "sitting rooms" for "the quieter pleasures." Both magazines assumed a family with two children; the *Good Housekeeping* plan showed two beds in a room marked "small fry," and the more spacious *Ladies' Home Journal* houses had separate bedrooms labeled "boy" and "girl," thus representing the composition of the ideal family.

Just as suburban housing development was in large part spurred by the baby boom of the war years, so the suburbs were widely understood to be the best places to raise children. A June 1952 article in *Mademoiselle*, titled "Suburbia . . . for you?" created a hypothetical "Priscilla" who was happy living in the city until the birth of her child, whereupon the family moved to a suburban house. The article outlined the pros and cons of suburban living, attempting to calm fears about conformity and social climbing while at the same time acknowledging their presence in suburbia. "It is not hard to keep up with the Joneses," the author wrote, "because the Joneses are not very far up." One can go barefoot in the summer if one doesn't mind "a few stares"; it is fine to prefer Picasso to Millet or John Donne to Longfellow "if you're not bothered by being labeled a mild eccentric." The author was forced to admit that "gossip *does* rank high among the forms of entertainment" in the suburbs, but she advised readers on how to avoid being its target. She also acknowledged that suburban home ownership encouraged the purchase of certain products: "[Your husband] will probably acquire a workbench and a power saw and offer to equip the house with all sorts of marvelous gadgets." The same link between home ownership and consumerism was made even more forcefully two years later in a *Life* magazine article titled "The new American domesticated male: A boon to the household and a boom for industry." The article noted that men were marrying and having children earlier than in some unspecified past and were immediately buying houses rather than renting apartments. While the women's magazines were instructing women on the purchase of electric mixers and clothing, *Life* reported that men had become increasingly important as household consumers: whereas Americans had spent $6 million on portable power tools in 1947, they spent $150 million in 1953, and sales of power lawn mowers had increased from 10,000 in 1945 to 1.4 million in 1953. The *Life* article appeared at about the same time that *McCall's* magazine began calling itself "the magazine of togetherness," stressing that it was intended for the entire family, including a husband who was much more involved in the household than in previous years, including improving the family's standard of living.

By the early 1950s, then, the spending of money had become not merely the implicit message of magazine advertising but also a topic to be dealt with in the editorial content. And on this as on so many issues, the magazines' messages were decidedly ambivalent. A January 1952 *Redbook* article advised readers, "Don't Be Afraid of Credit!" The author chided those who resisted borrowing money and buying items on credit, emphasizing the importance of establishing a good credit rating to make emergency loans possible: "an individual without a credit rating of some kind is like an ocean-going vessel without lifeboats." While the article cautioned that not everyone could handle credit—"credit is like alcohol"—and that people must take care to deal with reputable banks and stores, the piece's central purpose is to advocate the use of credit as a boon to everyone, central to the American way of life. "Few buyers," the author wrote, "pay cash for such items as furniture, refrigerators, television and radios." Instead, they used the installment plan, "an economic instrument that has brought more good things to more people than any other instrument in all history." The same view was endorsed by the vice president of the Radio Corporation of America, whom the author quotes as saying that the installment plan is "one of the foundation stones of the American economy," a comment that once again ties family life to national interests. A writer in the November 1950 issue of *Good Housekeeping*, in contrast, counseled families to learn to say without shame, "sorry, we can't afford it," when confronted by the consumer culture. Acknowledging that the size of the "family purse" governed much of family life, the author nonetheless wrote, "we would like to think that something far more intangible and valuable than mere money dictates our lives."

Social critic Margaret Halsey took a middle path in the consumerism debate in her March 1953 *Mademoiselle* article, "Do You Put Money in Its Place?" Halsey acknowledged to her relatively affluent readers that "we live in a money society." She also accepted the fact that women were the primary consumers: "we have a sort of rough division of labor in which the men earn and the women spend." Halsey advised the young women who were *Mademoiselle*'s primary readers to consider carefully how they defined "getting ahead": "Does getting ahead mean abandoning self-respect and idealism to climb over other people's dead bodies? Does it mean jettisoning some real and deeply personal talent—like music or schoolteaching or scientific aptitude—in order to do something superficial, impersonal and uncreative? Such as writing advertisements for a product one does not believe in?" Yet even as Halsey urged her young readers to resist the advertising messages that tell them they " 'need' an electric mixer or a new hat or better-looking luggage or a larger apartment," her argument was at odds with the pages of the magazine in which it appeared. Occupying part of the page on which Halsey's article begins is the list of prices for the fashions pictured on the facing page—including a $59.95 silk dress and a $16.95 pair of sandals—and flanking the remaining columns of her text are advertisements for hosiery, underwear, jewelry, shoes, and makeup. Less visually arresting but even more ironic is the fact that the conclusion of Halsey's article, in which she quotes Henry David Thoreau's statement, "The cost of a thing is the amount of what I will call life which is required to be exchanged for it, immediately or in the long run," appeared on the same page as part of an article on investing in which the author referred to "living money" as that used to purchase "entertainment, vacation, car and whatever you're latching on to on the easy-payment plan."

Although, with the exception of *Vogue, Harper's Bazaar,* and, to some extent, *Mademoiselle,* the magazines continued to uphold middle-class ideals for their middle-class readers, by the 1950s various elements of the magazines' content promoted a more upscale image, with the woman even more a lady of leisure. An advertisement for Frigidaire stoves in the December 1958 *McCall's,* for example, pictures a woman wearing a crown beneath a text that begins "Now feel like a queen!" The easy-to-clean oven promises to "end that slavery forever," elevating the woman from servant to royalty. A 1953 advertisement for kitchen flooring suggests that any homeowner could share with the most affluent this "mark of a luxury home": "The finest families in your town, and the wealthiest, have one thing in common . . . the care they lavish on their homes." The text of the ad equates the choice of kitchen flooring with the choice of sterling silver flatware and paintings and is peppered with the words *rich, luxury,* and *taste.* Product endorsements by celebrities and people with high social ranking also contributed to the sense of elevated status. Film actress Maureen O'Sullivan touted the whitening effects of Snowy bleach; Pond's Vanishing Cream was endorsed by the Mar-

\

chioness of Queensberry; and Herbert Tareyton cigarettes, which "discriminating people" were said to prefer, featured various members of the upper class in its magazine ads, including "Miss Dorothea McGill Scott, attractive young member of Richmond, Virginia, society," pictured on a tennis court.

The October 1960 issue of *McCall's* contains numerous elements suggesting aspiration to high social status. The cover photograph shows a blonde, blue-eyed baby staring directly at the viewer as its equally blonde mother hovers protectively. The advertisement inside the front cover is for Cannon "Royal Family" towels, and other ads in the issue promote Schick "Crown Jewel" electric razors, the "Princess" telephone, Gerber foods for "social butterfly" babies, and Lane furniture with a caption that reads "How rich should you be to own this table?" One of the short stories in the issue begins with the heroine musing that "if you have to go, it's better to go to rich people's parties. They always have thick carpets and hot canapes—and other rich people." Another piece tells the rags-to-riches story of a struggling law student who ends up owning an expensive restaurant and a thriving law practice. The issue's featured article describes the increase in the number of debutante balls in the United States, beginning, "Society is having a revival, 1960 style. For reasons both economic and sociological, countless Americans are returning to a class system that seemed doomed a generation ago. They are following the traditions developed by the Old Guard of an earlier era, but with a difference. The top rung of the social ladder is now the goal of the many rather than the few. Social position today can be earned; whereas formerly it could be achieved only by birth." The article concludes by noting that the possession of "money, a swimming pool, and a sports car no longer guarantees prestige," so that more and more Americans were seeking to launch their daughters into "society." In contrast to the 1923 *Ladies' Home Journal* article on American society cited in chapter 1, the author of the 1960 article is not dismayed by the fact that money rather than birth can afford entry into the highest social ranks. Instead, she provides a virtual how-to manual of the proper schools, dancing classes, and wardrobes. "[I]n the past fifteen years," she concludes, "the desire for status has reached new proportions."

Yet there is evidence to suggest that all readers did not receive uncritically the magazines' messages about status, acquisition, and high standards for women's appearance and homemaking skills. Letters to the editors taking the magazines to task about the values they promoted appeared with some frequency, and three letters in the "Pats and Pans" section of the May 1960 issue of *McCall's*, taken together, address all of these issues. A Dayton, Ohio, reader wants more down-to-earth cooking advice: "About your tartlets: Who's got the time, patience, ambition, and 125 tartlet pans to make them? Give us some plain old hamburger recipes for four." An Idaho reader took issue with the advice on consumption given in a question-and-answer column for newlyweds: "I was much upset with a recent column of 'The First Year.' A reader was actually advised to buy both a Hi-Fi set and some furniture on time payments rather than to make a choice of one. I consider this very poor advice in *any* case—extremely poor for many people. Some of the answers in that column appear to me to be flippant rather than of help to the people who have written." A third reader, from Connecticut, was concerned with *McCall's* articles on physical appearance: "With your advice on make-up and clothes, you are not appealing to the average American woman but to the eccentric, egocentric woman who has nothing on her mind but money and how best to put it on her back. Why must you show the glamorous and surface things in life? I don't think women really want this." Such responses were no doubt shared by other readers who did not take the trouble to write to the magazine.[9]

Beyond the Middle Class

Just as the *Journal's* "How America Lives" series advocated a consistent set of moral values no matter what socioeconomic level its subjects represented, so, in presenting readers with models of ever-higher social aspirations, the magazines insisted on standards of behavior that could be associated with the family, especially with the woman who was its affective center: duty, self-sacrifice, hard work, consideration for others. *McCall's* "togetherness" theme was not the only evidence that the magazines were intended for the whole of domestic existence; features for children aimed to bring younger readers into the magazines' orbit, and an increased emphasis on manners and etiquette simultaneously reinforced the home as the school for proper behavior and prepared readers to deal comfortably with new social settings. Fiction as well as articles and advertisements attempted to negotiate be-tween social aspiration and basic values such as honesty and decency, suggesting that both were necessary to the promised fulfillment of the postwar years.

Well before the 1960 *McCall's* article reported an increased interest in debutante balls, a feature for female adolescent readers of *Ladies' Home Journal* suggested that every young girl was a potential debutante. "The Sub-Deb," which ran in the *Journal* from 1928 until 1956, offered advice on dating, appearance, health, and social behavior to girls who would one day look to the magazine to solve their adult problems. That the "sub-deb" the magazine addressed was relatively privileged is evident in the articles' references to parties and stylish clothing, but it is equally important that she learn to behave in a manner commensurate with her social class. In December 1953, for example, the young reader was reminded that "a Sub-Deb does unto others, especially when her heart is full of Christmas," and this reminder was followed by a holiday wish for a spirit of noblesse oblige: "We wish you many chances to meet people who differ from you, and the understanding to accept those differences. We wish you a heart that scorns mere pity for those less fortunate and feels the joy of helping." The January 1955 "Sub-Deb" article offers fairly straightforward advice on how to carry on conversations in a variety of social settings, but a sidebar article suggested how the messages of American popular culture were being conveyed to adolescent girls in other countries: asked by a representative of the United Nations Children's Fund what film would be "helpful in their cultural development," a group of Pakistani teenagers, none of whom had ever seen a movie, unanimously chose "How to Marry a Millionaire." And in April of the same year, the sub-deb was instructed in the etiquette of introductions, table manners, and correspondence, with the reminder that social behavior was an index of class standing: "She doesn't need a penthouse or a black satin skirt to prove that she knows what to do when."

Magazine features for children and adolescents do more than remind us that women's magazines were family publications, intended for readers of all ages. In their emphasis on proper behavior, such articles reinforce the idea that girls, like their mothers, had to be taught to perform their roles in society and suggest that these girls will be observed and judged. Even more significantly, such features announce social class aspirations by emphasizing the manners and behaviors of the "lady." Indeed, the April 1955 "Sub-Deb" article was titled "That Sophisticated Lady": it assumes that the adolescent to whom it is addressed pays weekend visits to the families of friends and that she may one day travel to Spain and need to know that it is perfectly proper to drink the garlic sauce from snail shells. The "Sub-Deb" series thus suggests in its content as well as its title that the young reader may one day surpass the class status of her parents.

In addition to conveying messages about social class, the magazines' features for young people also signaled uncertainty about the woman's role in an expanded concept of domestic life. Margaret B. McDowell has suggested that magazine features for younger female readers have appeared during periods when anxieties about women's roles have provoked editors to adopt conservative stances regarding women's domestic responsibilities. Arguing that editors of women's magazines "have perceived women as grownup girls and little girls as miniature mothers" (36), McDowell focuses on *The Delineator* in the first decade of the twentieth century and *McCall's* in the 1950s to suggest that articles for children reinforced the woman's role as mother and forecast girls' future lives as homemakers. Under the editorship of Theodore Dreiser beginning in 1906, *The Delineator* featured strictly gender-segregated columns for boys and girls, instructing the former, the "Boy Knights of the Round Table," in how to build things, play sports, and earn money, while the female "Jenny Wrens" learned how to sew clothes for their dolls and thus prepare for an adulthood in which they would clothe their families. The "Betsy McCall" feature that began in *McCall's* in the mid-1950s similarly emphasized feminine apparel and appearance, but whereas the Jenny Wrens were taught the skill of sewing, readers of the *McCall's* feature were encouraged to be consumers: the articles included information on where to purchase Betsy McCall dolls, dollhouses, and clothing. And, like the *Journal's* "Sub-Deb" feature, the Betsy McCall series emphasized proper behavior; Betsy is a model six-year-old whose manners mark her social-class standing. McDowell argues convincingly that Betsy McCall is the embodiment of the editors' perceptions of adult women: "one finds in Betsy's preoccupation with clothes and good behavior a documentation of the anxiety felt by women who grew up in the depression, who matured and married during wartime, and who were trying to be perfect and beautiful wives and mothers in a decade of burgeoning birth rates. The commercialization of the feature reflects the era of suburban homebuilding, overdressing, and status-seeking" (49).

The emphasis in both editorial content and advertising on the woman as the "lady," with its implications for class status, provoked Thompson, in her June 1955 *Ladies' Home Journal* column, to explore the question "Can Women be Ladies?" The impetus for Thompson's remarks was an advertisement for a "foundation garment" whose text promised the wearer "the only *fashionable* look, the only *possible* look . . . the ladylike look." Expressing consternation at the fact that "the ideal of the lady [was] about to be revived" by the wearing of the undergarment, Thompson reviewed the history of the terms *lady* and *gentleman,* acknowledging that women have always appeared in "a dual light"—either much worse or much better than men but in either case possessing power not found in "the pale image of a lady." Yet the description of ideal "women" with which Thompson concluded her column could have been taken from nineteenth-century advice to "ladies": "They will wear shiningly washed hair, simply dressed; they will throw out the musky perfumes and return to mignonette and Parma violets; they will enhance their charms by the most subtle concealment of them; they will lower their voices; they will retreat from advances; they will assume a mien of gentle pride, mind their manners, and be known for their sexual morality and their good works." In short, Thompson gave women the same behavioral advice that was given to "that sophisticated lady," the sub-deb.

In 1957 the *Journal* editors were sufficiently concerned about proper American social behavior to convene a group of "writers, wits and practical observers of life," including etiquette expert Emily Post, to discuss the subject. In the resulting November article, "Are Good Manners Important Today?" the participants reported their agreement that manners remained important, although most of the panel insisted that true manners had more to do with kindness and dignity than with knowing which fork to use. As the decidedly privileged group—which included a former diplomat and a former editor of the British periodical *Punch*—conversed, it became clear that many were anxious about democracy's effect on social manners, fearing that people equated manners with snobbery and class distinctions. At the same time, however, the roundtable participants deplored what they perceived as a coarsening of American manners. Humorist Ogden Nash referred disdainfully to a "deliberately cultivated oafishness which takes pleasure in sneering at anything more civilized than a beer commercial," and *Journal* editor Bruce Gould concurred, citing the example of Marlon Brando, "an extraordinarily capable actor, [who] has become one of our most popular heroes by personifying bad manners—by coarsening the human emotions." As the members of this group thus betrayed their own social-class biases, they also betrayed anxiety about 1950s youth culture; as the talk turned to clothing, Nash erupted about "the damnable blue jeans, leather jackets and dirty white shoes we see on young people," concluding that "sloppy dress is part of a general breakdown of social morale." Any doubt that this panel of experts on modern manners believed in the linkage of manners and social-class standing was dispelled by an exchange between Gould and former *Punch* editor Malcolm Muggeridge that also reflected a Cold War mentality. After Gould reported witnessing bad table manners during a visit to Russia, Muggeridge stated, "In Russia people *try* to belong to the lower classes," to which Gould responded, "And very successfully, it seems to me."

The fiction the magazines published also reflected certain assumptions about behavior and social status. Those most knowledgeable about magazine requirements for acceptable stories were the freelance writers who regularly sold fiction to the magazines and who, in turn, offered advice to other aspiring authors. In a 1955 article in *The Writer*, Sheila Sibley, who had contributed stories to *Good Housekeeping, Cosmopolitan, Ladies' Home Journal,* and *Woman's Home Companion,* offered the following counsel to writers: "The heroine has got to be a nice girl, high-spirited, if you will, but no vice in her, or if there *is* vice, you've got to work yourself to the bone to justify it. If she's acting awfully strange, it's because of that neglected childhood or that fractured romance" (45). In describing her own background, Sibley acknowledged a link between fiction and advertising when she touted writing advertising copy as good preparation for writing popular fiction: "Advertising teaches you the most direct way to communicate with your audience" (44). Faith Baldwin, one of the most prolific fiction writers of the twentieth century, who published nearly one hundred romance novels and scores of short stories in women's magazines from the 1920s to the 1970s, advised would-be writers on the proper socioeconomic status for fictional characters. Believing that one should avoid writing about the "hideously rich," Baldwin nonetheless favored an element of class aspiration: "I differ with the idea that the forty-five dollar a week worker isn't interested in the doings of the rich. These make for glamour and escape. True, she likes to read about other forty-five-dollar-a-weekers, but sometimes it's fun to drink champagne instead of a less bubbly brew. Also, it astonishes her to read that even upper brackets have problems . . . if not the one problem which is of utmost concern when you don't get the raise" (77). Baldwin referred to a different link between fiction and magazine advertising when she wrote about how editors assessed their subscribers' reading tastes: "This yardstick is arrived at in several ways, including letters from readers, polls—although I have never understood how these work—and circulation figures, and all seem to be tied up with advertising" (79). Gertrude Schweitzer, also a successful author of magazine fiction, claimed in 1951 that the periodicals had matured to the point that there were "precious few genuine taboos" regarding stories: "You cannot . . . sell a story of miscegenation, nor may you allow immorality or wrong-doing to emerge victorious, nor, since magazines go through the mails and are subject to postal restrictions, may you use obscenity" (326). But Schweitzer agreed with Sibley that bad behavior must be traced to some root cause: "Perhaps she was always hungry as a child, so that now she will do anything for security—or maybe she was jilted by the first man she ever loved, and she is trying to revenge herself through other men" (329). For Schweitzer, women's magazine fiction is a reflection of "life as it is lived by millions of people all over the United States—an average people, concerned with the ordinary business of living" (329).

Yet the fiction the women's magazines published in the 1940s and 1950s suggests that "average" and "ordinary" meant people of at least middle-class means living in urban or suburban settings. As would be true also in television soap operas, central characters frequently have careers in the professions: men are commonly doctors, lawyers, or businessmen, and women often have careers as well, although in typically female areas. In "Clem Joins the Station Wagon Set" (*Ladies' Home Journal*, August 1946), the central female character runs a preschool and has served as adviser to a manual on parenting; in "Two in One" (*Women's Home Companion*, August 1948), the heroine quits her job as chief advertising designer for a department store to become an artist; in "The Urge" (*Good Housekeeping*, December 1949), the woman is a writer on a book tour; and in "Woman Power" (*Woman's Home Companion*, January 1942), she is a successful actress, a single parent, who visits her son at boarding school. As the title suggests, the central character in "Princess Penelope" (*Good Housekeeping*, July 1959) is royalty; "Brunette and Seventeen" (*Good Housekeeping*, November 1949) deals with sisters vacationing with their mother in Mexico. Some stories concern households with servants: "Now and Forever Just" (*Ladies' Home Journal,* October 1946) deals with Mrs. Sayres and her live-in black maid, and "I Met Edmund Lowe" (*Harper's Bazaar,* October 1950) begins, "Soon after our maid Hannah's departure in the year of the Great Depression Mother decided to give her room a thorough cleaning."

When a character was intended to be truly "average," authors sometimes went to great lengths to establish this fact. In "One Day Late" (*Good Housekeeping,* December 1939), for example, Dorothy Canfield described her heroine as "a woman so much like you—like me, like all of us—that [the story] might have happened to us." The woman and her family lived in a house that was "medium size, smaller than the ones some of us live in, but larger than many, in a small large town, or a large small town, whichever way you like to put it." When her character made a common grammatical error, Canfield commented, "you can see from her grammar that she hadn't as much schooling as some of us. But at that, she'd had more than many." Even more common than insisting on a character's representative nature was an author's tendency to show a character making a choice between high aspirations and middle-class values and behavior, as two stories from 1942 issues of *Woman's Home Companion* demonstrate. "Prescription for Success," in the May issue, concerns an aging small-town doctor who realizes that rather than being a failure, he has been morally right all along in treating the town's working-class citizens instead of seeking patients among its small upper class. In "Rainbow Chase," in the February issue, a Maine farm woman who enters a contest for a trip to Bermuda has so much fun learning to swim and ride a bicycle in preparation for her trip that, when she wins, she decides to take the prize in cash instead and enjoy staying with her family.

The magazines' messages about social class were thus as complex and contradictory as were those about marriage, work, and motherhood. Advertising encouraged the purchase of products for personal and household use, promising alternatively freedom from homemaking servitude and the opportunity to better meet the needs of home and family. Articles often endorsed categories of products and promoted the latest technological developments, from canned "oven-ready" biscuits to kitchen cabinetry. At the same time, however, the magazines' editorial content encouraged the thrifty use of both time and money, printing quick recipes and instructions for extending the life of fabrics and appliances. If the *Journal*'s "How America Lives" series explored economic diversity and household budgeting, the profiles of famous people that most of the magazines published offered glimpses of glamour and power, as did some of the fiction they published. On the matter of proper social and moral behavior, though, the magazines' message was unambiguous: anyone could learn the manners and values that represented acceptable class status. If intelligence was assumed to be genetically determined and transmitted, behavior—whether good or bad—was purely a product of nurture rather than nature. Schweitzer reflected the influence of midcentury popular psychology when she advised aspiring fiction writers that "in this psychiatric age, nobody is really bad. All villainy, even in the pages of the women's magazines, stems from something in the past, such as a drunken father, the rejection of playmates, or the over-indulgence of one of Philip Wylie's insufferable 'moms' " (329).[10] With innate flaws and evil out of the question, in other words, everyone could improve morally—and, by implication, materially.

CHAPTER 5

"How To..."

The Experts Speak

Michael Kammen's analysis in *American Culture, American Tastes* of the transition from cultural authority, vested in individuals acknowledged and trained to set aesthetic standards, to cultural power, manifested in corporate structures that disseminated products and media messages, is paralleled almost precisely by the shift, beginning in the 1940s, from the advice women's magazines offered readers in the prewar period, provided by experienced homemakers and credentialed experts such as university professors, to that provided by representatives of various "bureaus" and "institutes" in fields such as psychology, sociology, nutrition, and child care as well as by corporations through product advertising. Just as intellectual and aesthetic authority became undermined by a "free market" attitude in which any individual's opinion was as valid as any other's, so the urgency of the debates about the domestic world allowed an array of different people to be presented as "experts" on domestic life. If a college president and the director of the Federal Bureau of Investigation could speak as "authorities" on motherhood during World War II, the way was clearly open for numerous voices to articulate— and often disagree about—the shape and significance of the domestic experience. Kammen notes that cultural observers such as David Riesman and Vance Packard, who by the 1950s warned Americans about increasing conformity, pointed to corporations and their advertising as particularly culpable (157), and nowhere could their influence be seen more clearly than in the women's magazines.

Thus, while product advertising—often abetted by the editorial content of the magazines—urged upward class mobility and a certain material conformity through the purchase of consumer goods, the domestic world itself was both enlarged and contested. While the magazines continued their traditional role of providing advice on accomplishing specific tasks, such as cooking, sewing, and entertaining, a variety of "experts" addressed marital harmony, social adjustment, and even the role of the home in national security. Although at all the social-class levels the magazines addressed, marriage and motherhood were assumed to be central to the adult woman's experience, there was little agreement on how she was properly to fulfill either role, and magazine advertising ran the gamut from presenting her as a lady of leisure and privilege to suggesting that she existed to serve her family and, by implication, the well-being of the nation as a whole. Technological advancements, especially those affecting the preparation of food, created particularly contradictory messages. Whereas cooking had previously involved a set of skills to be learned, the introduction of convenience foods and new appliances after the war challenged the very definition of cooking: if opening cans and turning knobs could produce a meal, was the homemaker a dedicated cook or merely a technician? On a larger scale, debate about the nature and position of woman, represented by such influential works as *Modern Woman: The Lost Sex*, *The Second Sex*, *The Natural Superiority of Women*, and *Male and Female* not only were reflected in the magazines' contents but also were part of the discussion about the domestic that concerned both men and women, just as *McCall's* "togetherness" campaign stressed the entire family unit, not just the woman.

Advising the "Second Sex"

The November 1959 issue of *Good Housekeeping* includes a short story titled "The Golden Age," in which a woman is inspired by a guest speaker at her women's club to prepare meals that would introduce to her family the foods—and something of the culture—of other countries.[1] Parts of the story—certainly to a reader in the 1990s—read like a parody of the magazine culture of experts that by the late 1950s advised women on everything from the use of pressure cookers to mental health. The lecturer's title is "The Hand That Rocks the Cradle Rules the World," and the heroine's husband, who grew up with the speaker, comments, "That's Lydia Izara for you. She never rocked a cradle in her life, but I'll guarantee she thinks she knows more about the subject than the old woman who lived in a shoe." The speaker's rhetoric embodies Cold War exhortations—for example, "Bring our citizens of tomorrow understanding of the peoples of the world. With understanding comes brotherhood!"—that seem comically overblown, and the heroine's children are far more interested in watching a television Western than in learning the culinary customs of Hawaii, which she has selected for the family's first cultural excursion. But the heroine, who has read Lydia Izara Mattison's books—"*Female, the Superior Sex; The Obsolete Man; The Masculine Myth; Man and Superwoman*"[2]—is happy to have her guidance, as she says without irony, "It takes someone like Lydia Izara Mattison to show us what's wrong with our husbands, our children, our marriages." And just when readers may be at the point of believing that Mattison's advice and that of others like her has been debunked, the heroine's husband (who, the story has established, routinely orders ham and eggs in a Chinese restaurant) announces his enthusiasm for the program of weekly exotic dinners, not because the children will benefit from them but because they remind him of the couple's courtship. The story thus wavers between parody and seriousness. The hyperbole of Mattison's rhetoric and book titles is finally undercut by the successful application of her advice. If the heroine is unable to teach her children about other cultures, she is able to restore romance to her marriage; global concerns are transformed into domestic ones.

Whether or not it was intended as parodic, the *Good Housekeeping* story brings together several important messages of the postwar women's magazines. The family is the most effective defense in the Cold War, and it is the woman's responsibility to bring education and culture into the home. Woman as consumer is here as well: the heroine shops for unusual ingredients for Hawaiian and Thai cuisine and at the end of the story is about to purchase—on credit—a second television set, for the children. Most importantly for my purposes in this chapter, the story underscores the idea that women need external advisers to inform them about their responsibilities as homemakers. The story's heroine describes the women's club speaker as "formidable-looking and very self-assured" and comments that when she began to speak, "you knew you were listening to the world's greatest authority on marriage, children, and husbands." Although Mattison is a character in a work of fiction, she is interchangeable with the hundreds of writers of nonfiction articles and advertising scenarios that helped to fulfill the magazines' role as teachers and testified to deep anxiety about women's household performance at midcentury—an anxiety that the magazines in part created even as their panel of experts worked to alleviate it.

A brief survey of the 1948 volume of *Good Housekeeping* will serve to indicate the range of tasks and behaviors on which readers were given advice in the years immediately following the war and the forms that such advice took. An article in the January issue advised on the purchase and use of automatic washing machines, which were newly available following wartime shortages of metal. Helen Kendall, writing for the Good Housekeeping Institute, reminded readers that washers advertised in the magazine had been tested by engineers and "experienced home economists" and found to be reliable. In addition to hints on how to wash various fabrics, readers were advised to wash sheets and towels on Thursday or Friday to have them "fresh and clean, all ready for the weekend." In the April issue, a series of photographs instructed women on how to make a "perfect pincurl," and another article, "How to save pennies and food," provided tips on budget-conscious food shopping and preparation. Some articles mixed straightforward instruction with attempts to alleviate social anxiety. An article about the proper preparation of artichokes in the April *Good Housekeeping,* for example, was subtitled, "are you self-conscious about eating them?" and offered "a special but simple technique" for doing so. Other articles directly addressed proper social behavior. "Don't be a knitwit," in the January issue, advised women not to become so obsessed with knitting that they bored or annoyed others with the craft; the verse that comprises the text concludes, "Hardly any girl bewitches / When she's always counting stitches." In the February issue, teenagers were advised to read more of a daily newspaper than the "funnies" so that they could participate intelligently in conversations: "Maybe it's time you grew up and started reading *all* the paper."

Indeed, the wide range of topics on which the magazines provided advice indicates both the complexity that the domestic arena had assumed by midcentury and the magazines' function as all-purpose advisers. In the years just before and during World War II, readers were often addressed as citizens. An article in the December 1940 *Good Housekeeping* instructed them on "How to Understand the News," an article offering basic, practical advice on distinguishing fact from propaganda, choosing a morning or an evening newspaper, and understanding the function of headlines. While some of the article's points seem today extremely condescending—women are encouraged to read only those columnists with whom they agree to save "nervous wear and tear"—the overall tone of the article is patriotic, extolling the virtues of a free press. A somewhat more active citizen role was suggested in "When and What to Report to the F.B.I.," which appeared in the August 1942 *Good Housekeeping*. Beneath a photograph of a woman peering out the window of her house, the article began, "The enemy is at work in this country," and went on to advise the reader on how to be "vigilant" without being "a vigilante." In a similarly nationalistic spirit was Dorothy Thompson's "A Primer on the 'Cold War' " in the August 1950 *Ladies' Home Journal*. Using a question-and-answer format, Thompson began with a basic definition of the term and answered such questions as "Can we win the cold war?" before departing from the "primer" format to advise that "America should be strong, but not bellicose or provocative." At the other end of the scale were articles that advised on personal and familial lives. In April 1951 *Harper's Bazaar* announced the availability of its guide to private and professional schools, and the December 1956 *Bazaar* offered "How to Mend a Broken Heart," which concluded that the only real way to do so was to fall in love with someone else.

Magazine advertisements, of course, implicitly advised readers to buy one brand of a product rather than another, but they frequently intensified this message by showing women actively seeking help from a variety of authority figures. An ad for Chicken of the Sea canned tuna in the January 1948 *Good Housekeeping* casts a young woman's mother in that role as "Sue" phones her mother to announce that she is "frantic" because her husband "thinks he doesn't like fish." After "Mom" assures Sue that her own father thought the same thing until she served him "he-man tuna dishes," the text of the ad suggests ways to prepare canned tuna that will please "that important 'He' in your life." Husbands themselves are sometimes the source of advice, as when a young mother is at her "wit's end" about how to get her children to eat enough vegetables and her husband recommends V-8 vegetable juice. Friends often serve as product advisers in advertising copy. Typical is the woman who introduces her friend Jane to the features of the Frigidaire electric range in the July 1940 *Good Housekeeping*, admonishing Jane to "believe me, darling, a Frigidaire Range is the surest way to a cooking reputation." Far more intimidating in tone is the Wesson Oil ad in the July

1942 *Good Housekeeping* in which a woman is pictured being accused in a courtroom of serving boring salad dressings.

"Scientific studies" were frequently invoked in advertisements for household appliances. In the April 1948 *Good Housekeeping*, an ad for Eureka vacuum cleaners promised that the Eureka removed 183 percent more dirt than cleaning by hand, introducing Elaine Knowles Weaver, Ph.D., "formerly Home Economics Dept. Columbia University," as the researcher responsible for this statistic. While home economics was not truly a science, the citing of degrees and university affiliations was intended to lend authority to such pronouncements. The most telling word in Weaver's credentials was *formerly:* her role in 1948 was as intermediary between corporate America and domestic consumption. As Barbara Ehrenreich and Deirdre English point out in *For Her Own Good*, by the mid–twentieth century, "the home economist was an accepted part of the corporate team—not only helping to develop product lines, but participating directly in marketing and advertising" (180).[3] Ehrenreich and English cite a 1959 article in the marketing journal *Sales Management* that pointed to the key role the female home economist was thought to play in the marketing of products: "It takes one to know one—could be said of women, too! Certainly only the bravest, or most foolhardy, of the stronger sex claims to grasp the workings of the female mind . . . hence the growing importance of the home economist in marketing. . . . She has the touch of the sociologist, a creative temperament, a background in natural sciences—and the vaunted female touch. She is the Home Economist in marketing . . . a woman to convince women" (180).

Not only real women served as the "female touch" for product manufacturers. A number of fictional women, created by advertising agencies and departments, came to embody certain consumer goods. While General Mills's Betty Crocker was the best known of these personae—created in 1921 and by 1945 recognized by 91 percent of American housewives—many companies had similar icons. Karal Ann Marling, in *As Seen on TV*, lists others who were inspired by the success of Betty Crocker, including Ann Pillsbury for General Mills's competitor, Pillsbury Flour, Aunt Jenny for Spry shortening, Kay Kellogg for Kellogg's cereals, and Martha Logan for Swift meats. Nor, Marling notes, were such female images used only in the food industry: "Airlines and manufacturers of ranges and television sets also adorned their advertisements with head-and-shoulders cameos of crisp professional women endorsing the wares offered for sale. Monsanto Plastics identified the 'Marion Palmer' whose signature was affixed to ads for vinyl floor coverings and easy-wash TV trays as a 'modern living consultant.' Modern living had something to do with the proliferation of female experts, both real and make-believe, and the use of their pictures to soften the image of corporate America" (206–07). Yet if women were best suited to convince other women to trust and purchase certain products, ads often depicted members of the "stronger sex" coming to women's rescue. Thus, the April 1948 *Good Housekeeping* issue featured an ad in which a knight in shining armor came to the assistance of a homemaker with Old English floor wax, promising "A coat of shining armor for your floors . . . my lady."

By the mid-1950s, the magazines' reliance on credentialed experts had, if anything, increased, reflecting both a continuing professionalization of the role of the homemaker and a national faith in scientific advancement to improve domestic life and help to wage the Cold War. Technological advancement was promoted as the way not merely to more efficient housekeeping but also to improved class status and general domestic happiness. An advertisement in the April 1957 *McCall's* asked the reader, "How does *your* kitchen rate on the electrical living scale?" and provided a checklist of thirty-three electrical appliances—from toaster to clothes dryer—so that readers could determine whether their possessions entitled them to view their lives as "roughing it," "bearable," "enjoyable," or "just wonderful." The text promised that ownership of these "electric servants" enabled the homemaker to have "more time and energy for [her] self and [her] family," which made the ad fit perfectly into the magazine's emphasis on family solidarity; beginning in 1954, *McCall's* billed itself as "The Magazine of Togetherness." Lest readers have an imperfect sense of what that cozy term meant, *McCall's* commissioned a monthly definition from an "expert." In April 1957, for example, Norman Vincent Peale appeared on the contents page to define *togetherness* as that which made a husband and wife a "team," sharing work, play, and "faith in the church and the community as well as in the home." In June of the same year, Walt Disney also stressed teamwork, compared the members of a family to the variety of talents that came together to produce his television programs and films, and ended his version of "What togetherness means to me" with a statement that attempted to forge unity from diversity in the national interest: "The more diversified our labors and interests have become in the modern world, the more surely we need to integrate our efforts to justify our individual selves and our civilization."

The 1957 volume of *McCall's* reveals both an emphasis on the advice of specialists and strong indications that despite the rhetoric of teamwork and togetherness, it was the woman who had to make adjustments and submit to male authority to create the ideal domestic environment. Each issue included at least two articles by medical doctors, including a monthly feature titled "The Doctor Talks About . . . ," with topics including frigidity, "postnatal blues," and miscarriage. The *McCall's* editors noted that this series was "prepared under the supervision of a distinguished group of doctors who serve as McCall's Board of Medical Advisors," and each article featured an "eminent specialist." Pediatricians and child psychologists appeared in the "Children" section of the magazine to advise on temper tantrums, shyness, and allergies. In the June issue, Harrison Salisbury, then specialist on Soviet affairs for the *New York Times*, reported on "What Americans *don't* know about Russia," and a collection of soup recipes in the May issue (many of them using canned condensed soup as a base) was accompanied by a testimonial to soup's nutritiousness by two members of the Harvard School of Public Health's department of nutrition. Other articles advised on how to shop for fresh fruits and vegetables, how to stay on a diet, and how to keep peace with one's neighbors. While some of the articles were not overtly gendered in terms of readership, others made clear that women were particularly in need of expert advice. An article in the March 1957 issue advised young couples on setting up and decorating a small apartment, but the heart of the article was the "editor's open letter to a bride," which, despite an admonition to make her husband a "partner" in the "exciting arts and joys of homemaking," advised her to study her husband's "habits and hobbies" and arrange the furniture to "accommodate" him. Involving her husband in cooking would require more subtle skills, as the bride is advised to, "without his knowing it," interest her husband in making a salad dressing and "let him discover his special talent for broiling a steak." When the relationship was between doctor and patient, the woman's submission could be even more dramatic. In "The Doctor Talks About Miscarriage," in the March issue, readers were presented with the case study of "Mrs. W——," who had suffered six miscarriages without apparent medical reasons. Diagnosing the problem as emotional, the doctor described his cultivation of the woman's complete trust in him as the remedy; priding himself on this successful treatment, he quotes Mrs. W—— as saying, "If you weren't here, I'd still miscarry."

The most basic and comprehensive kind of advice the women's magazines provided, of course, dealt not with specific tasks or purchases but with how to be a woman. Marjorie Ferguson's observation in *Forever Feminine* about women's magazines addressing the "totality" of women's experience (2) is curiously paralleled by Simone de Beauvoir in her introduction to *The Second Sex* (published in France in 1949 and in America in 1952). Although de Beauvoir does not refer specifically to periodicals, she points to the cultural assumption—which she has observed in both France and the United States—that women must be instructed in womanhood. "We are exhorted," de Beauvoir writes, "to be women, remain women, become women." She continues in a tone of considerable irony: "It would appear, then, that every female human being is not necessarily a woman; to be so considered she must share in that mysterious and threatened reality known as femininity. Is this attribute something secreted by the ovaries? Or is it a Platonic essence, a product of the philosophic imagination? Is a rustling petticoat enough to bring it down to earth? Although some women try zealously to incarnate this essence, it is hardly patentable. It is frequently described in vague and dazzling terms that seem to have been borrowed from the vocabulary of the seers" (ix). With regard to her own project of writing *The Second Sex*, de Beauvoir echoes Virginia Woolf's *A Room of One's Own* when she asserts that being male does not present the same set of problems: "A man would never get the notion of writing a book on the peculiar situation of the human male" (xxi).

The Second Sex was one of three books published in the late 1940s and early 1950s that were particularly influential in the midcentury debates about womanhood reflected in the women's magazines. The first and in some ways the most controversial of these books was *Modern Woman: The Lost Sex* (1947), by sociologist Ferdinand Lundberg and psychiatrist Marynia F. Farnham. Described by de Beauvoir as "irritating," *Modern Woman* posited that women were "lost" because both social and technological revolutions had unmoored them from any certainty about their fundamental role in society. Confronted with too many choices and options, argued the authors, women had become "maladjusted," and their consequent unhappiness had caused "mass unhappiness and uneasiness in our time, in periods of peace as well as war" (20). Although men and children participated in this general malaise, "women are the principal transmitting media of the disordered emotions that today are so widely spread throughout the world and are reflected in the statistics of social disorder" (23). In Lundberg and Farnham's essentialist view, men had access to spheres of influence that enabled them to be psychically "normal": "men have appropriate means to social adjustment: economic and political power, scientific power and athletic prowess" (24). Women, in contrast, have had their primary site of power removed by what the authors termed "the destruction of the home," a rather amorphous phenomenon the authors traced to the Industrial Revolution and the French Revolution. While both movements emphasized freedom—the former materially, the latter intellectually—their combined effect had been destructive, these authors asserted: "like a bull in a china shop [man] destroyed the matrix of his feelings of psychic well-being: his worldly childhood home" (90). By Lundberg and Farnham's somewhat convoluted logic, the removal of manufacturing from the home to the factory and the rise of democratic political institutions had a pernicious effect not only on women but on Western society in general: "The home was the place in which women, much more than men, had since the start of civilization made their chief emotional and material investments. The destruction of the home as a result of man's economic and technological exploits has bred deep unhappiness—not only in women but in society as a whole. The stage, indeed, has been set for general chaos and confusion, which we are reaping today. The result of what happened to the home is neurosis on a wider scale than was seen before" (93). While Lundberg and Farnham acknowledged that the modern home might be cleaner and more efficient than the home of the preindustrial past, they asserted that women had lost their sense of "self-importance" and declared—without offering any evidence to substantiate this assertion—that "medieval home life, whatever else it was, seldom failed to be stimulating and emotionally sustaining" (103).

While de Beauvoir would have agreed with the authors of *Modern Woman: The Lost Sex* that woman's lot was not particularly happy, her *Second Sex* located the cause not in woman's removal from her position of importance in the home but instead in her cultural position as the "other." De Beauvoir described a world in which the male was the norm and the female was secondary, and she interpreted history quite differently than did Lundberg and Farnham. Rather than being the source of women's power, the home had been the site of her secondary status, and the various emancipatory movements of the eighteenth century did not destroy the home but instead placed women more firmly within it: "woman was ordered back into the home the more harshly as her emancipation became a real menace" (xxix). Whereas the sociologist Lundberg and particularly the psychiatrist Farnham did not hesitate to diagnose modern woman's unhappiness, philosopher de Beauvoir found such assessments questionable: "Are not the women of the harem more happy than women voters? Is not the housekeeper happier than the working woman? It is not too clear just what the word *happy* really means and still less what true values it may mask. There is no possibility of measuring the happiness of others, and it is always easy to describe as happy the situation in which one wishes to place them" (xxxiv). One of de Beauvoir's central projects in *The Second Sex* was to free discussions of women and men from the "rut" of oppositional thought: she took issue with those who "have tirelessly sought to prove that woman is superior, inferior, or equal to man" and wanted to "start afresh" without such preconceptions (xxxiii).

In the same year that *The Second Sex* was published in English, Ashley Montagu's *The Natural Superiority of Women* was published in book form, portions having been published in the *Saturday Review* and *Saturday Evening Post* in 1945. Despite his title, Montagu declared in the book's foreword that he wished to "bring the sexes closer together, not to set them apart by placing one above the other" (xv). Montagu also did not wish completely to reorder social arrangements; early on, he pointed out that he did not predict that women would eclipse men in artistic and scientific achievements, "because the motivations and aspirations of most women will continue to be directed elsewhere" (3). An anthropologist, Montagu wrote as a student of human social behavior, noting, for example, that man's greater size and physical strength had commonly led to destructive actions ranging from bullying to waging wars, whereas women's biological makeup lent itself to peaceful nurturance. Women's superiority was also demonstrated, Montagu believed, by their resistance to disease and greater longevity, their tendency to be more spiritual and idealistic, and their better performance on intelligence tests. In the concluding chapters of his book, Montagu pointed to the steady increase of married women working outside the home, proposing that the workday for everyone be shortened to four hours so that men and women could spend more time with their children and with each other. While thus arguing for equality and shared responsibility, Montagu was as much an essentialist as were Lundberg and Farnham, believing that women were uniquely fitted to exert a humanizing and civilizing influence; women's "great evolutionary mission" was to "keep human beings true to themselves, to keep them from doing violence to their inner nature, to help them to realize their potentialities for being loving and cooperative" (250).

Montagu's *Natural Superiority of Women* prompted Thompson's article "What is Wrong With American Women?" in the August 1953 *Ladies' Home Journal*. Thompson rejected Montagu's essentialist view of the sexes, noting that "every generalization or abstraction reduces the individual to one of a certain number of types." She was far more sympathetic to de Beauvoir's *The Second Sex*, which Thompson described as a "monumental masterpiece." Although Thompson expressed weariness with the category of book into which both Montagu's and de Beauvoir's books fell—"no effort has been spared by biologists, sociologists, psychologists, historians, novelists, dramatists, and poets to describe, dissect, analyze and interpret 'woman' to herself and the other half of humanity"—Thompson preferred de Beauvoir's emphasis on "cultural forces" to Montagu's analysis of "natural" sexual differences. Having asserted that the answer to the question posed by her title was that "*nothing's* wrong with them," Thompson nonetheless analyzed two different problems affecting American women of the early 1950s. One was women's tendency to dominate men in all matters domestic, including house decor, the spending of money, and an insistence on marital sexual fidelity. With regard to the last of these phenomena, Thompson preferred European women's tolerance of their husbands' occasional affairs: married love "is much more than 'sex,' which is one of the more common commodities." The second problem Thompson addressed was women feeling torn between their duties as mothers and homemakers and a desire for a working life outside the home. After proposing several solutions to this problem, such as daycare centers in workplaces, Thompson ended on a note that prefigured Betty Friedan's *The Feminine Mystique* ten years later: "That psychiatrists flourish in America from the pockets of women patients, as they do nowhere else, shows that whether or not there's anything wrong with American women, their environment is not yet adjusted to their needs."

In 1957, when *McCall's* magazine interviewed thirteen prominent women for the article "Why I Like Being a Woman," Thompson was the only one who refused to acknowledge significant differences between the sexes, stating that "the highest satisfactions are happily open to persons of both sexes, provided they have the instinct, will and a yearning greater than mere 'ambition' to seek and find them." Almost all of the other interviewees, who included actresses, writers, and anthropologist Margaret Mead, testified to enjoying creativity, motherhood, and nurturance. By using the remarks of women whose names would have been familiar to mid-1950s readers, the article was both testimonial and admonitory in effect. If actress Arlene Dahl expressed her pleasure in transforming "a drab place into a haven of delight," and Mead justified her career on the grounds that she was studying children, the article reinforced the domestic as the source of women's satisfaction despite the highly public nature of these women's working lives. Even Mildred McAfee Horton, who had served as both president of Wellesley College and director of the WAVES during World War II, attributed her career opportunities to the graciousness of men and declared that she primarily enjoyed being her husband's wife. Betty MacDonald sounded the one note of protest in the article, but her use of humor allowed her message to be trivialized.[4] Describing what she termed "truly womanly things," MacDonald noted with considerable sarcasm that she felt "almost overcome with my good fortune in being born a female" when she had to clean up the kitchen after a dinner party. Despite MacDonald's sarcasm and Thompson's refusal to accede to rigid gender distinctions, the tenor of the article is that even famous women find their greatest satisfaction in domestic activities; the clear implication is that the reader should do so as well. And yet the fact that *McCall's* placed before its readers more than a dozen women with national and even international reputations conveys quite a different message about female achievement.

While the women's magazines offered "expert" testimonials to the rewards of womanhood, the social scientists who studied American life during the period focused attention on the lives of white middle-class men, emphasizing their adjustment to an increasingly corporate, bureaucratized, consumer-oriented culture. As Wini Breines points out in *Young, White, and*

Miserable: Growing Up Female in the Fifties, such works as David Riesman's *The Lonely Crowd* (1950), William H. Whyte Jr.'s *The Organization Man* (1956), and John Seeley's *Crestwood Heights* (1956) expressed both anxiety and optimism about a culture that promoted conformity and peer pressure but also invited everyone to join the middle class and created greater equality between men and women. Breines stresses the wide currency of these sociological analyses: "These narratives were not merely academic. They were duplicated throughout American society in the schools, by family experts, the mass media, and the families in which girls grew up" (27). While these experts, using as their starting point the corporate male employee, did not overtly analyze gender differences, their studies had significant implications for women's lives. Riesman's well-known description of the "other-directed" personality, for example, which constantly measured its behavior and values against those of the group, was actually more feminine than masculine, as Breines points out: "Being attuned to others, worrying about their opinions and feelings, being adaptable and avoiding conflict—precisely the traits and skills demanded by the corporations and white-collar occupations—are all traditional feminine personality characteristics. . . . The sex role 'convergence' [the sociologists] noticed was toward the feminine" (31). The resulting anxiety about masculinity made even more urgent a definition of womanhood that emphasized passivity and dependence and that located the woman in the domestic arena.

"Here Are the Main Rules to Guide You"

By the time the United States entered World War II in 1941, the magazines' role as a conduit for dispensing certain kinds of advice to women was well established. Wartime conditions, however, created new issues about which such advice could be deemed necessary, and the role of government agencies in regulating various aspects of Americans' daily lives to support the war effort lent a tone of authority to much of this advice that paved the way for the authority of experts in areas such as marriage, child care, and medicine after the war. Put another way, the chatty, convivial tone of much prewar advice about cooking, cleaning, and raising children, seeming to arise from a women's culture of mutual support, was supplanted by the voices of writers, often male, who were identified by professional titles and degrees and represented various agencies, institutes, bureaus, and universities. Before the war, the magazines tended to interact with readers in ways that largely disappeared during the 1940s. During the 1920s, for example, *McCall's* featured "Mrs. Wilcox's Answers to Women," which offered advice on relationships similar to that offered today by Ann Landers. Rather than posing as a singular expert, however, Winona Wilcox invited readers to share in problem solving: "Your opinion, experience or observation of woman's emotional dilemmas will help to determine the best ways of solving old puzzles." The August 1929 *Ladies' Home Journal* printed readers' recipes for summer dishes, identifying the readers by initials and hometowns. Even an article on how to clean house in the February 1932 *Woman's Home Companion* was written in a tone suggesting that the author participated with the reader in finding ways to accomplish the task. About drying windows after washing them, she reported, "I have tried various methods."

The character of wartime advice articles can be seen in Jonathan Wake's "The Censor Reads Your Letters," which appeared in the November 1942 issue of *Good Housekeeping*. Wake adopted the position of standing between the presumably female reader and the anonymous male government censor charged with editing out of her letters to servicemen any information that could jeopardize the Allied cause. Between the title and the text of the article appeared the following explanatory statements: "He is lenient with what you write to men overseas, but he has to be careful. Here are the main rules to guide you." Most of the article detailed the kind of information that writers should withhold from letters, including the location of war manufacturing plants, the precise locations of military units, and comments critical of the U.S. government or the military. Toward the end of the article, Wake shifted position to stand between the letter writer and the serviceman overseas, advising women that men wanted to read about the people at home: "school friends, brother Elks, the gang at the office and the shop." A regular wartime feature of *Better Homes and Gardens* was the question-and-answer column "Late Tips on Wartime Living," which offered a grab bag of hints for coping with shortages and rationing. In the September 1943 issue, readers were advised to conserve electricity, press unused bicycles into service, hang their own wallpaper, and keep their families healthy because of a shortage of doctors. Another article in the same issue seemed designed to assist with the last of these cautions and reflected a new concern with vitamins in light of the fact that large numbers of military draftees were found to have nutritional deficiencies (Levenstein 65).[5] Cast in the form of a quiz (the correct answers to which were provided on another page), the article asked readers to answer a series of questions including "Do vitamins make you fat?" and "Do vitamins in themselves make up for rationed food shortages?"

The most common wartime advice article addressed doing without such familiar commodities as leather, metal, nylon, and sugar, and typical was "5 Ways to do More with Less" in the July 1942 *Good Housekeeping*. Readers were admonished to take good care of any currently irreplaceable rubber items they might own, to save leftover tea in the refrigerator, and to send to the superintendent of documents and the Bureau of Home Economics for booklets on how to can and dry food at home. Advertisements similarly stressed the economical management of resources. An ad for Sunbeam electric mixers in the September 1942 *Good Housekeeping* included a "victory recipe" for a meat pie to serve six. Social-class differences were clear in wartime advice on food preparation. An article in the January 1943 *Harper's Bazaar* mentioned "the servant problem" along with shortages and rationing and encouraged readers to eat in restaurants to collect ideas for cooking at home. The menus included in the article featured kidneys in red wine (the cook was advised to stock up on "native wine" to lend "cachet" to her meals) and risotto with chicken livers. Other advice articles during the war period were more tangential to the war itself but dealt with general social malaise. A case in point is "Tomorrow's Worries Today" in the July 1942 *Good Housekeeping*. Written by Philip Wylie, whose book *Generation of Vipers*, accusing women of coddling their sons, was published the same year, the article advised women to avoid worrying about things they could not control and to be satisfied with their social status rather than yearning for material wealth.[6] Wylie's concern about proper maternal behavior, as articulated in *Generation of Vipers*, was part of a larger national debate about parenthood at a time when the war disrupted the nuclear family so revered by the magazines, leaving thousands of women to be single parents at least temporarily. Not surprisingly, wartime advice articles began increasingly to focus on motherhood in a difficult time.

If, as I discussed in chapter 3, authorities such as FBI Director J. Edgar Hoover could claim one kind of expertise on motherhood, a second category of such expertise was part of the structure and function of the magazines themselves. Representing this group was Gladys Denny Shultz of the *Better Homes and Gardens* "Child Care and Training Department," whose article "If Daddy's Gone to War" appeared in October 1943. Articles written by staff members representing various magazine "bureaus" and "departments" tended to have a far more chummy, between-us-girls tone than did those of external authorities such as Hoover. Shultz, for example, posited that her article was written in response to readers' pleas for assistance in raising children in the absence of husbands, and throughout the article she referred to her own experience as a mother. Yet Shultz sounded a number of the same alarms as did Hoover, stating that the mother's "main job" was "raising the next generation" and encouraging those with young children not to work outside the home out of "any misguided ideas of patriotism, or of financial advantage." She cited the "tragedy" of a mother who went to work in a defense plant, whereupon her seventeen-year-old son "got in with the wrong kind of companions and landed in jail." At the same time, Shultz echoed Wylie when she warned that motherly care could easily tip over into coddling: "The worst fault we modern mothers have as a class is to overindulge and spoil our children," and the tendency to do so only increased when "Daddy's saving presence is removed."

Amid the advice the American woman was given during wartime—to be a good mother, to save tin cans for recycling, to follow "Uncle Sam's Recommendations for Nutritious Meals" (*Good Housekeeping*, December 1942)— was the unspoken assumption that with peace would come ideal marriage and family life. As Stephanie Coontz has demonstrated in *The Way We Never Were*, Americans looking back on the postwar period from the 1970s and 1980s tended to think, nostalgically and erroneously, that such an ideal had been achieved during the period. But a look at postwar women's magazines reveals that even for the white, middle-class readers who were the primary audience, marriage was filled with problems. If doctors were the most ubiquitous experts in the pages of the magazines, marriage counselors were a close second, and many others, from clergymen to fiction writers, offered advice on this troublesome relationship. Given the numerous functions that domestic life was expected to perform—as primary emotional and sexual relationship, haven from the outside world, training ground for the young, social unit in the community, and bulwark of the democratic way of life—it is not surprising that it frequently fell short of expectations. Even before the war, articles such as Andre Maurois's "The Art of Marriage," which appeared in the April 1940 *Ladies' Home Journal*, pointed both to the centrality and the difficulty of marriage in human life. Bearing the marks of Freudian psychology, Maurois's article argued that marriage was necessary to curb the potentially dangerous egotism of self-preservation by bringing it into conflict with "other equally strong instincts"—the sexual and the maternal. In Maurois's view, marriage could succeed only if male and female retain what he posited as their essential natures: "the man is happy when he can invent some device with which to transform the universe; the woman is happy when she can devote herself, in the tranquillity [*sic*] of her own house, to some simple task." Yet these differences, necessary for human balance, also required constant negotiation of values and priorities. Similar sentiments were expressed by the 1950s sociologists whom Breines cites in *Young, White, and Miserable:* "The marital relationship had been presented as the link that held the family together, the one enduring human relationship in society, based as it was on growing equality and companionship. But at the same time, the factors separating husbands and wives were shown to be substantial indeed" (39).

The fact that articles advising on the marital relationship appeared in magazines intended for female readers suggests both that women had the most at stake in preserving marriage and that they were responsible for making most of the adjustments necessary for improving marital happiness. Indeed, the authors of articles about marriage were sometimes overt about women's greater interest in marriage. In the April 1947 issue of *Woman's Home Companion*, Clifford R. Adams, who conducted the *Companion*'s regular "Marriage Clinic," both posited and analyzed this disparity: "Women in general are more likely to worry about their marriages—and become dissatisfied with them—than men. The fact shows up in all surveys. This is so partly because women are more introspective than men, partly because marriage looms larger in their lives. The woman who becomes dissatisfied with her marriage becomes dissatisfied with her whole life. The husband who becomes dissatisfied can sometimes shrug it off." The fact that heterosexual marriage was the only culturally approved status for the adult female was underscored by David L. Cohn's scathing analysis of women's magazines in his 1943 book *Love in America*. Referring particularly to magazine fiction, Cohn commented, "If marriage isn't in sight the editors want to know why, and meanwhile anything goes so long as it is going toward wedlock" (193). While Cohn's sarcasm reflects his criticism of this monolithic stance, writers for the magazines were quite serious in their endorsement of marriage as "normal." In 1935, Paul Popenoe, who in the 1940s became the author of *Ladies' Home Journal*'s long-running feature "Can This Marriage Be Saved?" was already warning women in the *New York Times* that the pursuit of education and careers lowered their matrimonial chances. Clearly alarmed at the prospect of numerous unhappy single women who did not know where they had gone wrong, Popenoe concluded his article with some straightforward advice: "They must take the problem more practically, prepare themselves for marriage and parenthood, associate with somewhat older men as well as with their own contemporaries, and plan to marry in their early twenties" (14). Nearly twenty years later, in the spring of 1954, *Ladies' Home Journal* ran a four-part series titled "How to be Marriageable," drawing on the experience of the counselors in the "Marriage Readiness" program of the American Institute of Family Relations, a Los Angeles organization headed by Popenoe. When Popenoe published a collection of his "Can This Marriage Be Saved?" articles in 1960, Joan Didion used the occasion to analyze the marriage counseling offered by women's magazines. In Didion's view, advice on improving marriage differed little from any other advice on running a household, having as its essence a "marital know-how": "The real trick, be not deceived, is . . . *savoir-faire.* Good management. Handling" (90). In short, marital problems, like meal preparation or dealing with unruly children, merely required women to develop certain skills.

Midcentury marital advice dealt with wide variety of topics, from arguments about money or in-laws to sexual matters, and such a variety reflects both the professionalization of marriage counseling and an increased awareness of the number of factors that impinged on the marital relationship. In contrast, in the February 1932 issue of *Ladies' Home Journal,* advice columnist Dorothy Dix had placed the whole burden of marital happiness on the woman's attractiveness. In "And So You Are Married!" Dix cautioned, "Well, whether your marriage is a success or failure depends upon you, little bride. . . . For marriage is not only a woman's vocation, it is her avocation. It is her meal ticket as well as her romance. . . . So it is not only good ethics but good business for a young wife deliberately to set about keeping her husband in love with her." In February 1940, an article emanating from the *Good*

Housekeeping "School for Brides" struck much the same note in its emphasis on the young woman's physical appearance; the article asserted that to continue to be the "leading lady of his life," the bride must "play [her] role beautifully." But as advice on marriage became increasingly the province of psychologists in the 1940s, such simplistic formulas were replaced by recognition that marriage was a complex interaction requiring professional counsel. As Francesca Cancian and Steven Gordon have pointed out, emphasis shifted to a "focus on internal feelings and expectations," and readers were encouraged to be more "realistic" about marriage. Cancian and Gordon cite in particular a 1947 *Ladies' Home Journal* article that encouraged readers not to expect perfection in marriage, so that frustrated expectations would not lead to hasty divorce (315–16).

Magazine articles tended to view divorce with alarm, and as the divorce rate increased after the war, articles analyzing its causes increased in frequency. The April 1948 issue of *Ladies' Home Journal* included "What Sends People to Reno?" written by Dr. James F. Bender, director of the National Institute for Human Relations. In the postwar spirit of expert problem solving, Bender announced that "psychologists, sociologists, [and] human-relations counselors . . . have been busy making a scientific study of the problem," discovering the "hard, cold facts of what causes happiness and unhappiness in marriage." Among the factors these researchers found to have a negligible effect on marital success were adultery, disputes about money, and living with relatives, while marital difficulty could be traced to marrying too young, sexual intercourse before marriage, childlessness, and poor cooking. A year earlier, in the March 1947 issue, Mary Fisher Langmuir, a professor of child study at Vassar College, reported similar conclusions: while adultery and desertion might be named as the reasons for divorce, the true cause lay in the couple's failure to adjust to each others' differences. Children were necessary for a good marriage: "without children . . . marriage is incomplete and unfulfilled." Langmuir concluded on a typical Cold War note: "We know that the welfare of our nation depends on the integrity and strength of our homes. Our goal is to have sound, happy, stable and democratic marriages." With sufficient advice and counseling, the experts agreed, almost any marriage could be "fixed." Bender attributed the rising divorce rate to a "general conviction that women and men have a right to happiness in marriage." Five years later, popular Catholic clergyman

Fulton J. Sheen agreed that people had unrealistic expectations of marriage. In "How to Stay Married Though Unhappy," in the February 1953 *Good Housekeeping*, Sheen challenged the idea that happiness was a right, positing that "the purpose of life is not pleasure" but rather serving God, which might include putting up with a less than perfect marriage. In the magazines, marriage counseling seldom failed, and when it did the result was viewed as tragic. In a rare departure from the success stories of *Ladies' Home Journal*'s series "Can This Marriage Be Saved?" the author of "This Marriage Could *Not* be Saved" (September 1954) expressed great frustration when reporting that Dena and Kevin's marriage had ended in divorce: "So far as I can see, nobody has profited. Everybody has suffered."

Even as readers of women's magazines were told that marriage was not perfect, they were given a constant stream of advice about how to improve or "save" it. As with other areas of advice, articles by staff members or free-lance writers continued to adopt a lighter, less authoritarian tone than did those written by psychologists and marriage counselors and tended to ac-knowledge that both husbands and wives bore responsibility for marital suc-cess. The October 1958 issue of *McCall's* featured "84 Ways to Make Your Marriage More Exciting," based on a brainstorming session the magazine had arranged with a group of people that included advertising executives, a minister, an actress, a songwriter, and the producer of the radio program "Right to Happiness." The list of suggestions for men was primarily phrased in positive terms—for example, "Kiss the back of your wife's neck once a day," "Buy her sexy perfume"—while the list for women included a number of behaviors to avoid, including "Don't tell him your problems until you've fed him," and "No pincurls when he's in sight." Ideas for the couple were largely directed at keeping the romance in marriage, although there was also an emphasis on family activities, including the blunt directive, "Have a large family." The 1950s *Good Housekeeping* series "Man Talk/Back Talk," how-ever, provided a dialogic structure that suggested there might not be easy solutions to marital conflict. "Man Talk," subtitled "The intelligent woman's monthly guide to a reasonably happy marriage," written by Samuel Grafton, was followed immediately by Felicia Quist's "Back Talk," which often called into question the effectiveness of Grafton's advice. In the March 1954 pair of articles, for example, Grafton advised a wife whose husband stayed out late with friends to simply go to bed and thus avoid a conversation that he will assume is full of recrimination; Quist, in turn, reported trying this strategy only to have her husband accuse her of not being concerned about him.

So intent were magazine editors on positing marriage and family life as the normal adult condition that they offered parents advice on ensuring the eventual marital happiness of their children. An article in the April 1948 *Woman's Home Companion* asked "Will Your Child Have a Happy Marriage?" and the statement below the title sounded a note of warning: "Start preparing him for it the moment he's born or you may be too late." The text of the article, written by the editor of the *Companion's* "Our Children" section, encouraged parents to raise well-adjusted children who had healthy attitudes toward sexuality and a firm sense of their future roles—boys to be instructed in the "manly virtues" and girls prepared to be "a real wife and mother." Ten years later, *Parents' Magazine* worried about an increase in teenage marriage, and the author of "Why They Can't Wait to Wed" consulted experts that included marriage counselors, the dean of freshmen at Williams College, and anthropologist Margaret Mead to diagnose and offer solutions to the problem. Asserting that young people lacked the heroes, ideals, and causes of their parents' generation, the experts concluded that young people sought in marriage the sense of identity lacking in the larger culture and, often failing to find it, resorted to divorce. The solutions reflected the culture of experts that existed by the late 1950s: parents should support the "marriage education" courses offered in schools and should encourage married teenagers to seek professional marriage counseling.

When marriage counselors, psychologists, and other professionals wrote for the women's magazines, they employed the medical model of diagnosis and remedy, a strategy suggested by such feature titles as *Woman's Home Companion's* "Marriage Clinic" and *Ladies' Home Journal's* "Making Marriage Work" and "Can This Marriage Be Saved?" The authors used survey results and case studies of "typical" marital problems to assure readers both that these approaches had scientific validity and that readers' own problems were shared by others. In the April 1947 "Marriage Clinic," Clifford R. Adams reported that his interviews with one hundred "truly dissatisfied wives" revealed the basic cause of trouble to be the lack of a "genuine partnership," whether intellectual, spiritual, or sexual. Readers who felt such a lack in their own relationships were advised to meet the problem head on by discussing it with their husbands in "a calm and helpful spirit." Adams admonished readers to "do *more* than your share" to address the problem. In the January 1948 "Making Marriage Work," Adams used the case of the unhappy "Alice Rand" to advise women to take positive action to meet their own basic needs for love, approval, and belonging. The unhappy wife had not "adjusted to her environment," which suggested that the environment was normal and that happiness awaited the woman who changed to fit her surroundings. That normality and happiness could be measured and tested was further suggested by the quiz that readers could take to discover whether their marriages were happy; answering fifteen or more of the questions correctly proved that it was, a score of eleven to thirteen was "average," and if the score was less than ten, the reader was urged to "analyze your answers with your husband to see how conditions can be improved."

The fact that some readers found such advice columns and their accompanying quizzes silly or even damaging surfaced occasionally in letters to the editor. A letter from an Illinois man published in the October 1951 *Ladies' Home Journal,* for example, revealed that whereas his wife took such articles seriously, he found them misguided. Having read the August installment of "Making Marriage Work," she wondered whether she was a "creative wife" as measured by the following questions: "Bought a little gift for your husband? Served a new dish that he liked? Tried a new dinner arrangement? Given him several unexpected compliments? Told him how much you love him?" At the end of his letter, the man expostulated, "Ye gods! If there is anything wrong with the American housewife today it is because her mind has become distorted by the rot she reads in magazine articles and fiction. No doubt Doctor Adams has the most honorable intentions, but some of us would prefer to muddle along in our old-fashioned way."

While some experts dismissed money as a major source of marital discord, others believed that marital happiness involved economic as well as emotional components. Adams's marital quiz asked whether couples disagreed about money and whether they were "free from debt and financial stress." Marital problems were sometimes traced to a woman's spending habits, even as magazine advertising encouraged increased consumption. And while the percentage of married women in paid employment continued to increase during the postwar years, the magazines generally assumed that the husband was the sole financial support of the family and that the wife played a key role in his ability to do so well. This role is the focus of Mrs. Dale Carnegie's

"How to Help Your Husband Get Ahead" in the January 1954 issue of *Coronet*. For men intent on successful careers, Mrs. Carnegie advised, wives must "stand by as bodyguards, nurses and morale-builders, gritting our teeth silently." The wife of a man who spent a great deal of time on business pursuits was encouraged to spend her time going to art galleries and concerts, doing volunteer work, or taking night courses. If a career of her own conflicted with the husband's advancement, she was urged to give it up—"If not, you are more interested in promoting yourself than promoting your husband." The worst thing a woman could do, according to Mrs. Carnegie, was to interfere in any way in her husband's career, including phoning him at work, belittling his coworkers, and, above all, nagging, which Mrs. Carnegie called "a devastating emotional disease." Yet some forms of nagging were clearly necessary to help a husband succeed. Near the end of the article, Mrs. Carnegie insisted that wives put overweight husbands on diets, arrange for regular medical checkups, and urge their spouses to get enough rest. Above all, the wife must "keep his home life happy."

Although Mrs. Carnegie did not overtly mention sexual relations as part of the "happy home life," the magazines offered plenty of advice on this aspect of marriage, especially in the 1950s. In *Homeward Bound,* Elaine Tyler May notes that for all the midcentury taboos against premarital sexual experience, sexual satisfaction within marriage was widely expected by both men and women. "Sexual satisfaction would presumably safeguard marriage against unhealthy developments that would weaken the family from within" (116). The family was touted as the answer to all of its members' emotional needs, and sexually frustrated couples could not claim such fulfillment. More specifically, a sexually unfulfilled wife might transfer too much of her attention to her children, spoiling them and making sissies of her sons. In the popular imagination, May writes, "healthy families were built upon the bedrock of good sex" (134). Yet prohibitions against sexual intercourse during an increasingly long period of dating during adolescence and young adulthood—whether or not such prohibitions were obeyed—created problems of emotional repression and guilt that meant that "this ideal often worked better in theory than in practice. The tension surrounding premarital sex, combined with highly inflated expectations for sublime marital sex, often led to disappointment and difficulty" (136). In her study of twentieth-century courtship, *From Front Porch to Back Seat,* Beth L. Bailey notes that even as polls conducted from the 1930s through the 1950s suggested that most young people condoned some level of premarital sexual activity, authorities ranging from etiquette books to popular magazines sought to contain such practices; one expert writing for *Parents' Magazine* in the 1930s even counseled parents who did not want their daughter to become a "petter" to avoid showing her too much affection lest she become "hungry for physical demonstrations of affection" (Bailey 81–83).

Few people at the time were willing publicly to concede that restricting sex to marriage could make marital sex problematic. An exception was Mead, who viewed American sexual mores with considerable alarm. In an excerpt from her book *Male and Female* (*Ladies' Home Journal*, September 1949), Mead presented a clear-eyed analysis of the paradoxes of American sexual rules: "During adolescence, the male learns to let his direct potency be checked by a girl who learns not to be moved beyond the point of control. Then in marriage they are faced with the demand that he be simply and directly potent, and that she experience climactic satisfaction from his simple, unelaborated potency. The wife feels inadequate if she is not swept away—after years of learning not to be swept away. Yet the complete, total relaxation of feminine surrender . . . is hardly available to women who have had to live through years of bridling their every impulse to yield and surrender."

Despite the publication of Mead's study, the women's magazines continued to reinforce the containment of sexuality in marriage and to offer advice on improving it within that context alone. The inability to "surrender" that Mead saw as a natural outgrowth of women's prolonged emotional control was popularly understood as "frigidity" in the postwar years—a dreaded condition that sent women to physicians and psychiatrists and prompted numerous reassuring articles. Typical was "The Doctor Talks about Frigidity" in the April 1957 issue of *McCall's*, in which an unnamed psychiatrist assured readers that true frigidity was quite rare and that temporary sexual disinterest or unresponsiveness usually resulted from unresolved marital issues quite apart from sexuality. Using the case study of "Roger" and "Mary," the psychiatrist pointed out that the pressures of his career and a growing family made Roger preoccupied and tired and that Mary's consequent fear that he had lost interest in her had made her unresponsive. As was usually the case, the burden of adjustment fell on Mary, who needed to understand the stress her husband felt. The article concluded on a note of admonition: "Her insistence . . . on keeping their marriage up to absolute sexual standards was the worst thing she could have done for him. What he needed more than anything else was the assurance of her trust and love instead of added pressure." Paul H. Landis, a sociologist who wrote "What is 'Normal' Married Love?" for the October 1957 *Coronet*, agreed that couples had unrealistically high expectations for marital sexuality. Landis's answer to the question posed in his title was that there is no norm to which people— especially women—should aspire. The "modern" understanding that women should be able to find pleasure in sexual intercourse had led, Landis believed, to a false mandate that they must do so, and "the sooner [women] who share this misconception realize that it is a *false* standard, the better it will be for their marriages."

If sexuality in marriage was assumed to present problems for women, the one area in which they could find complete fulfillment was motherhood. As May notes, "through children, men and women could set aside the difficulties of their sexual relationship and celebrate the procreative results" (136). Especially during the postwar baby boom, marriage was equated with children, and having children to care for defined women as domestic in ways that sexuality and even housekeeping could not. Maternal love was widely touted as a female "instinct," particularly by midcentury psychoanalysts, and women who ignored or resisted it were at risk. As Ehrenreich and English observe, such theories reinforced the home as the "natural" place for women: "The psychoanalysts discovered the maternal instinct in much the same spirit as if they had isolated a new chemical element to be found only in women. Obviously, love is the only ingredient of child raising which cannot be mechanized, merchandized, or farmed out to outside institutions. It is the intangible core of the mother-child relationship, the glue which alone could hold the mother to the child and the woman to the home. Psychoanalysis now took up the project which nineteenth-century gynecology had attempted earlier: To anchor female domesticity in the bedrock of female *biology*" (220–21). In cover art, articles, and fiction, women's magazines routinely defined *family* as including children. Reporting on the 1958 Kinsey Institute report *Pregnancy, Birth, and Abortion*, an April 1958 *McCall's* article reminded readers that the fears of "race suicide" because of declining birth rates in the 1920s and 1930s were, happily, a thing of the past: "The 'baby boom' that accompanied World War II," wrote Ernest Havemann, "has relieved any fear that the race may be dying out; indeed, the United States is currently undergoing the greatest population explosion in its history." The average woman had three pregnancies, according to the Kinsey report, and the author concluded with approval that "there can be no question that today's young wives are the most eager for motherhood of any our nation has seen in years."

Yet a woman faced the greatest challenges, ran the most risks of failing, and needed the most—and the most contradictory—advice in her role as a mother. By the late 1940s, the concept of instinctual motherhood had been modified to include the possibility—indeed, the likelihood—that a woman's instinctual behavior as a mother might be destructive, resulting in "two broad categories of bad mother—the rejecting mother and the overprotecting mother—mirror images and equally malevolent" (Ehrenreich and English 227). The insistence on the importance of maternal caregiving, which was heightened by the anxieties about women working outside the home during the war, also meant that a child's physical or emotional problems could be traced directly to his mother. In 1944 J. Edgar Hoover declared in the pages of *Woman's Home Companion* that mothers were "our only hope" in preventing juvenile delinquency, and a few months later Alfred Toombs, in "War Babies," pointed to the lack of adequate day care for women engaged in war work, but in the years following the war the experts' advice on motherhood suggested that the presence of the mother could be more dangerous to a child than her absence unless she found precisely the right balance between neglecting and coddling. One of the earliest expressions of these twin dangers was Amram Scheinfeld's "Are American Moms a Menace?" in the November 1945 *Ladies' Home Journal*. Citing the opinions of psychiatrist Edward A. Strecker, who had helped with the psychological screening of armed services inductees during the war, Scheinfeld described the two kinds of bad moms: "sweet, doting and self-sacrificing, or . . . stern, capable and domineering." Strecker believed that for both of these types of mother, child care was compensation for what was lacking elsewhere in their lives: "both these moms are busily engaged finding in their children satisfactions for life's thwartings and frustrations. . . . [T]hey exact in payment the emotional lives of their children." Scheinfeld's article concluded with ten

"Don'ts for Doting Mothers," warning about breast-feeding too long, "mouth" kissing, and raising a boy in an all-female environment.

The foremost exponent of what came to be known as "Momism" was Wylie, whose 1942 book, *Generation of Vipers*, charged that mother worship had allowed women to assume inordinate and dangerous power. Articles in the women's magazines seldom featured the angry, sarcastic tone of Wylie's best-selling book—the magazines had no interest in alienating their readers—but the debates about motherhood in the magazines' pages, like the debates about other areas of domestic life, reflected concerns about women's perceived power. During the 1940s *Ladies' Home Journal* adopted the slogan "Never underestimate the power of a woman," which can now be understood to refer most directly to her power as a consumer but which was left deliberately vague. Furthermore, although people such as Strecker and Wylie professed concern about mothers' influence on their sons, it seems clear that this concern masked fears that adult men were somehow losing power to women. Articles published shortly before the end of World War II advised women on how to make their returning soldier-husbands feel important in the household. A writer in *Parents' Magazine* in January 1945 cautioned women to shift their attention from their children to their husbands: "Don't tie Junior to your apron strings. . . . You can't be a good wife if you let Junior overshadow his father in your mind, if not your heart." Even before the war, the title of an article in the July 1941 *Better Homes and Gardens* signaled a similar concern. In "Are Good Mothers Unfaithful Wives?" Wainwright Evans cautioned women not to get so caught up in motherhood that they neglected their husbands. Evans begins his article with the exemplary tale of a sensible woman who had put her two children in nursery school part of each day because she realized they were becoming an "obsession": "I was becoming 99 and 44/100 percent mother," she confessed, and her husband had become "a part of the furniture." While commending this woman for being sufficiently perceptive to see that she had become "unfaithful" to her husband, Evans warned women who might not be so wise: "For in a very real sense she 'philanders'—and is fully supported by society and the conventions in so doing, because she is being a Good Mother." And he pointed out that husbands neglected by "Good Mothers" sometimes responded with marital infidelity, a form of being unfaithful that was not sanctioned by society, but, he warns, "this does happen."

Anxiety about the power and abuses of motherhood were also reflected in articles about fatherhood. And here, too, the experts offered conflicting advice. In "Fathers Are Parents Too," in the June 1953 *Woman's Home Companion*, David R. Mace, a professor of human relations at Drew University, argued for fathers becoming more involved in their children's lives, and the argument turned on the assumption that women belonged to the domestic sphere but might wield too much power within it. The father, Mace wrote, could serve as "interpreter and guide" to "the big mysterious world outside—the place where tremendous things happen and important people move around." But just as importantly, interaction between father and child served as a check on the mother's authority. Mace acknowledged that the 1950s father often helped his wife with "domestic chores," but the author viewed this phenomenon as dangerous, because "this auxiliary role may only strengthen the child's impression that it is Mother who is really in charge." Further, while "nature" made a woman a mother, women had to teach men how to be fathers, and Mace believed that some women would be reluctant to do so because they risked relinquishing some of their power: "Dare I say that I have met wives who were too jealous or distrustful of their husbands as potential fathers to let the poor men really discover the joys of parenthood?" Three years later, in the October 1956 issue of *Parents'*, Bruno Bettelheim was more alarmed at the blurring of men's and women's roles in the home. Although the title of his article, "Fathers Shouldn't Try to Be Mothers," suggested that he disagrees with Mace's support of men's parental involvement, the bases of his argument were essentially the same. Nostalgic for a time when men's and women's roles were clearly and separately defined, Bettelheim warned that when a father came home to a "request to do things around the house," the child might get the impression that his father "has been more or less loafing all day and Mother now expects him to start on the serious tasks." Thus, his "importance as a breadwinner is undermined." Like Mace, Bettelheim believed that parenting came naturally to women but not to men, but whereas Mace wanted men to be taught to be good parents, Bettelheim insisted that fathers maintain a proper distance from their children to underscore their authority. When fathers became "play companions" with their children, they relinquished the opportunity "to teach the child what it means to be a man." The child in Bettelheim's formulation was consistently a boy, and without the firm guidance of an unmistakably masculine presence, he was vulnerable to the influence of "mom."

If the male experts believed that women were fulfilled—even if dangerously or perversely—by motherhood, women who read parenting advice in magazines by no means uniformly agreed. Two letters to the editor in the October 1951 *Ladies' Home Journal* took issue in different ways with the experts' pronouncements. An Arizona reader responded sarcastically to cautions about the first and last children in a family—warnings that the oldest could suffer from parental inexperience and the youngest could be spoiled. The first of the reader's "two rules for successful family living" was simply not to have a first or last child; the second proposed that each child needed three parents: "one to earn a living, one to run the house, and one to attend to the physical and mental needs of the child." The second reader was angry rather than sarcastic as she refuted the notion that women took naturally to motherhood. "It is a bitter quirk of fate," she writes, "that, since Mother Nature decided women were to bear children, she didn't include in all of us the maternal urge or the urge to become slaves." This reader describes the routines of child care as "boredom, complete and overpowering boredom." In a midcentury issue of *Redbook*, Jane Whitbread and Vivian Cadden spoofed the plethora of advice women were offered on how to be mothers by creating the character of "Mrs. P.," who had been admitted to a mental hospital after being driven mad by conflicting instructions on caring for her baby. "Mrs. P. soon discovered that she, the mother of this Steven, was the only person unqualified to rear him. She was an amateur among pros, a mother of one among a host of experts." Whitbread and Cadden comically lamented the fact that the adage "mother knows best" had been supplanted by "nursery-school teachers, educators, pediatricians, lady magazine writers and authors of books called 'Baby Knows Best.'" Implicit in the article, of course, was the authors' own advice that mothers believe in themselves.

The most influential child-rearing expert of the second half of the twentieth century, Dr. Benjamin Spock, gave precisely the same advice. One of the first sentences in *The Common Sense Book of Baby and Child Care*, first published in 1945, is "You know more than you think you do" (3). Aware, as were Whitbread and Cadden, that advice on parenting emanated from multiple sources, Spock acknowledged that such advice could be confusing: "You hear that a baby must be handled as little as possible, and that a baby must be cuddled plenty; that spinach is the most valuable vegetable, that spinach is a worthless vegetable; that fairy tales make children nervous, and that fairy tales are a wholesome outlet. . . . Don't be overawed by what the experts say" (3). In his autobiography, Spock noted the change from his mother's generation, which "never had a moment's doubt" about how to raise a child, to the twentieth-century theories that held parents responsible for a child's every behavior trait. He attributed the "oversimplified notion that when there were behavior disturbances in children, it was always the result of parents' mistakes in handling them" to "those who were mobilizing up support for the mental hygiene and child guidance movements" (Spock and Morgan 134–35).

It is ironic that despite Spock's admonition that parents not be cowed by "articles by experts in the magazines and newspapers," he became one of these experts himself, not only through the best-selling *Baby and Child Care* (the last edition of which was published in March 1998, on his ninety-fifth birthday), but also in a regular column for *Ladies' Home Journal,* beginning in July 1954. In a sidebar accompanying this first monthly column, Spock explained why his feature would not answer letters from readers: first, letters might deal with "unusual or severe medical or psychological problem[s]" that could not be dealt with in a column; second, readers might not raise issues such as legislation affecting children, which "I will be bursting with opinions about." Spock thus announced that he would feel free to address political and psychological issues as well as medical ones, expanding his range of expertise beyond his training as a pediatrician. Some of Spock's articles dealt with medical concerns, such as when a child's symptoms warranted a call to the doctor (October 1954), fussy eaters (October 1955), and breast-feeding (March 1957), but just as frequently they addressed issues of psychological development and family dynamics. In July 1955, for example, Spock dealt with the teenager's simultaneous needs for freedom and parental rules, and in May 1957 he counseled young mothers on how to cope with mothers-in-law who interfered in child raising.[7]

Whereas *Baby and Child Care* is directed to both parents, opening with "A Letter to the Mother and Father" and including chapters on the special problems of parents who separate and working mothers, Spock's *Journal* feature was titled "Dr. Spock Talks with Mothers." Such a focus was, of course, appropriate for a magazine such as the *Journal,* whose readers not only were far more likely to be mothers than fathers but also were the purchasers of the baby food, strollers, diapers, and other products whose ads routinely appeared on the same pages as Spock's articles. But addressing a female reader also seems to have led Spock to speculate about differences between the sexes. In January 1957, for example, writing about boys and men who teased and bullied young children, Spock announced his belief that males were innately more aggressive than females, and in advocating breast-feeding in March 1957, he emphasized the natural bond it fosters between mother and child. Such essentialist notions of gender were widespread in the 1940s and 1950s, a fact that Spock used in his own defense in his 1989 autobiography. "In the forties," he wrote, "I was a sexist like almost everybody else" (Spock and Morgan 247). Recalling an attack by Gloria Steinem during his 1972 bid for the presidency, Spock wrote with chagrin, "Some things in *Baby and Child Care* were obviously sexist. When I wrote that a father's influence on his daughter is no less important than his influence on his son, I gave two examples: that he should compliment his little daughter on the pretty dress she is wearing or on the cookies she has baked. I couldn't have picked worse examples!" (248).

By the end of the 1950s, Benjamin Spock was a household name, and, at the same time, expert theories of child raising were so ubiquitous in the popular media as to be the object of satiric treatment, even in the same magazines that published the experts' sober advice. The January 1959 *Ladies' Home Journal* included B. M. Atkinson Jr.'s "What Dr. Spock Didn't Tell Us!" Atkinson reported dutifully purchasing a book on "the care and maintenance of babies"—which the article title implied was Spock's *Baby and Child Care*—only to discover that it failed to address such afflictions as "Goat Mouth," in which babies chewed on lamp cords, coffee grounds, and dogs' ears, and "Potty Arm," which caused two-year-olds to throw a variety of objects into the toilet. When the hapless father asked a friend why such conditions were not addressed in the book, he was told that "if those experts told *everything* about children, there wouldn't *be* any more children and without any more children there wouldn't be any more books about children." In the May 1959 *Journal,* humorist Jean Kerr pointed out that children needed their own etiquette book so that they would learn not to use forks to poke holes in the tablecloth or push each other down stairs. With such articles the women's magazines acknowledged that the ideal family life they in many ways promoted was in fact illusory.

Cooking, Consumption, and Class

Less threatening and certainly less controversial than advice on marriage and motherhood was the advice the magazines offered women on cooking for their families and guests. Yet a careful study of the constant stream of articles on the purchase, preparation, and serving of food reveals that this apparently straightforward and even mundane aspect of the magazines' content served as the locus of myriad concerns expressed more overtly in the other parts of the publications. While the dailiness of meal preparation would seem to render such articles ideologically neutral—mere road maps for cooking a roast or baking a pie—the magazines' food advice is deeply implicated in larger midcentury issues. Such articles reflected the increasingly scientific nature of food preparation and in this and other ways reinforced the woman's role as family nurturer, with serious consequences for marriage and parenthood. Meal planning and cooking also reflected social-class aspirations and levels of consumption, represented, for example, by the relative sophistication of ingredients and recipes and the appliances used in their preparation. And the competition among women that was implicit in articles about fashion and physical appearance was equally present in magazine pages devoted to culinary mastery. Indeed, precisely because the preparation and serving of food was for most women a daily activity in the decades before the widespread availability of frozen dinners and fast food, it seems likely that cooking constituted the most constant marker of a woman's skill and status as a homemaker.

Articles on cooking were, of course, a staple of the contents of women's magazines long before World War II. Recipe exchanges constituted one of the earliest forms of reader contributions to the pages of the service magazines, and the turn-of-the century domestic science movement quickly came to center on food preparation because it provided such a clear demonstration of the principles of chemistry. As Laura Shapiro points out in *Perfection Salad*, food provided a point of access for those who wished to make the home conform to the scientific model that was becoming standard in the workplace: "The women who founded and led the domestic science movement were deeply interested in food, not because they admitted to any particularly intense appetite for it, but because it offered the easiest and most immediate access to the homes of the nation. If they could reform American eating habits, they could reform Americans; and so, with the zeal so often found in educated, middle-class women born with more brains and energy than they were supposed to possess, they set about changing what Americans ate and why they ate it" (5). The founding of schools such as the Boston Cooking School (1879) and the development of cookbooks that emphasized the precise measurement of ingredients in cups and teaspoons instead of the trial-and-error estimations of generations of home cooks opened up a whole new area of advice literature for homemakers, and women's magazines responded by setting up test kitchens to verify the accuracy and hence the success of the recipes they printed. As late as the 1940s, magazine recipes reflected the cooking-school era, complete with its ladies'-luncheon fussiness. *Woman's Home Companion*'s monthly "Food Calendar" feature detailed the eating habits of the fictional Taylor family. The entry for 18 July 1941 recorded that "cooking school memories prompt Mrs. T. to have broiled liver sausage slices for lunch. With them, thick slices of tomato on toast rounds, each topped with 2 small stewed okra pods sprinkled with grated cheese and then broiled." On 23 July, "Sis" made a "stunning salad" composed of strips of canned pineapple spread with orange cream cheese, each topped with three strawberries, "pointed end up." Such precise combinations, along with vegetables in white sauce served in pastry shells, recall the advice given by *American Cookery* magazine in 1923 regarding serving vegetables at a luncheon buffet; stressing that they should not "look messy on the plate," the publication recommended "baked beans in dainty individual ramekins with a garnish of fried apple balls and cress, or toasted marshmallows, stuffed with raisins" (Shapiro 3).[8]

But World War II introduced new considerations into the magazines' advice on food preparation. One of these was a renewed emphasis on proper nutrition sparked by horror stories of malnourished young men attempting to enter the armed services. At the same time, however, food rationing was perceived as a threat to a healthful diet, so the magazines had to chart a course between these crises in advising the homemaker. Typical was "Making the Meat Go Farther" in the May 1944 *Good Housekeeping*, which provided recipes for a ham pie using canned "pork and ham loaf" (Spam), chili made with ground chuck and soybeans, and a stew made with diced bologna and potatoes. The January 1944 *Good Housekeeping* offered hints on substitutes for butter, including lemon-mustard sauce for vegetables, bacon drippings on mashed potatoes, and lard in pie crust. The meat industry, meanwhile, was quick to remind readers of the nutritional value of its rationed product. In its 1943 advertising, the American Meat Institute stressed that meat contained "proteins of the highest biologic value" as well as essential B vitamins and minerals. Titled "The Proteins of Meat . . . and Women at War," the ad boasted of the "substantial meat meals" the armed services furnished for "the girls of Uncle Sam" and advised those at home to "get all the good from the food we have."[9] Indeed, Harvey Levenstein notes in *Paradox of Plenty* that while the average civilian male in 1942 consumed 125 pounds of meat, the average American soldier received 360 pounds (89), a fact that created expectations for the postwar American diet.

In preparing food, the homemaker was required to meet multiple criteria. Food was to be economical, attractive, tasty, and nutritious. During the 1940s, the food editors of the middle-class magazines frequently featured articles such as *Good Housekeeping*'s "$2 Dinners That Serve Four," which boasted that a home economist for the Good Housekeeping Institute had planned, shopped for, prepared, and served the seven meals described in the article. Eggs, beans, and lunch meat were the main protein sources, and the housewife was instructed to serve "enriched" bread and "high-protein" chocolate milk. An advertisement for Heinz products in the July 1942 *American Home* featured egg dishes made with Heinz vinegar, chili sauce, and salad dressing and was headed "Eat an Egg a Day . . . The experts Say!" In January 1944 Dr. Carl P. Sherwin, director of the Good Housekeeping Bureau, answered questions about food values, assuring readers that both honey and cane sugar were easily digested and that the small amount of oxalic acid in chocolate and the coloring agent used to make margarine yellow were both perfectly harmless, and providing the caloric values of apple butter and potato chips. Recipes in *American Home* and other magazines routinely provided the number of calories per serving and noted the major vitamins each dish contained. Even those who cooked only for themselves were encouraged to be attentive to nutrition. An article in the August 1949 *Good Housekeeping* offered assistance with "Good Meals and Thrifty any *Business Girl* Can Make." The article began with hints from "career girl cooks": one declared her allegiance to the "Basic 7" foods, while others suggested sharing food with other single people and keeping a good stock of canned goods on hand.

While food articles emphasized nutrition, economy, and aesthetics, such pieces frequently also urged the purchase of certain products and thus participated in creating the desire for upward social mobility that was particularly apparent after the war. One of the "career girls" quoted in the 1949 *Good Housekeeping* article credited her pressure cooker for quick, tasty meals. The role of the home economist as intermediary between manufacturer and magazine reader was nowhere more apparent than in articles about food preparation. One of the home economist's roles was to design recipes using certain foods or appliances; even when she was not mentioned or named, her presence could be inferred from the credits provided in the article. A page of recipes in the September 1942 *American Home*, for example, noted that the recipes, though "tested in the American Home Kitchen," are "courtesy of" Campbell Soup, Swift, Armour, and Standard Brands. Such articles were thus interchangeable with ads for products such as Knox Gelatine, Wesson Oil, Cheez Whiz, and Spam, which regularly included recipes.

Articles advocating the use of kitchen appliances typically did not include brand names, although accompanying photographs and descriptions of special features would have allowed easy brand identification. Electrical appliances were touted as enabling women to prepare better meals while saving time; the articles' featured menus and recipes, however, suggest that the more elaborate meals the appliances made possible would at least have made up for any time saved with simpler meals. Shortly before World War II put a near stop to the manufacturing of electric cooking stoves, an article in the July 1941 *Woman's Home Companion* promised with "With Good Planning and a Modern Range Anybody Can Serve Easy Week-end Meals" and provided a timetable and menus for a family of four requiring "only 2¾ hours" in the kitchen. The menus, which included two homemade desserts, were designed for the special features of the stove, including a "well cooker," a broiler for cooking bacon and French toast, and timers for each feature. If the homemaker could work quickly according to the timetable, she was, at 4:44 on Saturday, rewarded with "time out for fun until 5:55 and supper," and to have five and a half hours of "fun" between dinner and supper on Sunday, she was advised, "Don't do the [dinner] dishes!"

As the manufacturing of domestic goods resumed following the war, the women's magazines busily encouraged the purchase of an increasing range of electrical appliances. In June 1946, a *Good Housekeeping* article on the use of electric mixers was straightforward in its message to readers: "If you don't own an electric beater, our advice is to put it at the top of your list of new-equipment purchases. No appliance is more versatile, more time- and work-saving." In March 1948, the Good Housekeeping Institute reported on the latest developments in toasters, waffle irons, and coffeemakers, noting the careful testing each product had received: coffee tasting was "not confined to our home economists. Our engineers taste the coffee, too, for their opinion of the finished product is just as important as their determinations on a coffee-maker's design and construction." A number of articles made explicit the link between the latest innovations in appliances and high standards for cooking performance. "It takes a good range to make a good cook," in the September 1950 *Good Housekeeping*, for example, began, "If young American girls don't make this a nation of the world's best cooks, it won't be because they can't have good ranges." Features such as automatic timers, "waist-high, swing-out broilers," and two-oven ranges meant that "even the busiest housekeepers find time to bake." The August issue featured freezers, recommending that they be stocked with a variety of foods to facilitate the preparation of "attractive main dishes." At the end of the article, the reader was advised to "try to keep one superb dessert in your freezer," offering a recipe for a frozen lime pie.

The link between appliances and standards of cooking excellence was not limited to the magazines but appeared in other media as well, including cookbooks and, increasingly, television. Gladys Taber, whose column "Diary of Domesticity" chronicled New England country living in *Ladies' Home Journal* in the 1940s and 1950s, also published several cookbooks, among which the *Stillmeadow Cook Book* (first published in 1947) was the most popular. In the introduction, Taber enthusiastically endorsed cooking appliances, writing that "today's homemakers have almost everything from self-defrosting refrigerators to automatic coffee makers," a statement she then qualified by adding, "or they can look forward to possessing them as soon as the budget allows." Taber was particularly fond of her electric skillet, electric knife, and pressure cooker. But even with all this assistance, she admitted to being somewhat flustered before guests arrived for dinner: "I wonder about those women I read of in the magazines who greet their guests feeling relaxed and casual. Even should they have help in the kitchen, does the current never go off as the rolls go in?" (12, 14). One person who always seemed perfectly relaxed in the kitchen was Betty Furness, an actress who demonstrated Westinghouse appliances on television beginning in May 1949 and who therefore appeared to be an expert in the kitchen. One way in which manufacturers advertised their appliances was to publish cookbooks featuring their use, and so, in 1954 Simon and Schuster published *The Betty Furness Westinghouse Cook Book,* dedicated to "You, a busy homemaker who gladly prepares three meals a day for your family, and who delights in doing it." In the book's preface, Furness admitted that she was "not the worst cook on my block, but I'm afraid I'm not the best either," and she acknowledged the assistance of Julia Kiene, director of the Westinghouse Home Economics Institute, whose "knowledge" was combined with Furness's "enthusiasm" to create the book (n.p.).[10]

If kitchen appliances constituted one form of assistance in becoming the perfect cook, convenience foods, from canned soups and cake mixes to brown-and-serve rolls, were a less expensive aid in the postwar years. The 1950 *Good Housekeeping* article on electric ranges attributed the modern homemaker's fondness for baking in part to "all kinds of cakes, cookies, muffins, and rolls coming from the grocer's shelves just one step removed from the oven," and Taber, although she expressed reservations about frozen dinners, wrote admiringly of "frozen meats, fish, fowl, vegetables, and fruits along with the good packaged mixes" (13). But the mass-circulation women's magazines were not content that the middle-class homemaker merely heated up canned soup and followed the instructions for adding water to a cake mix. In both articles and advertisements, convenience foods were regarded not merely as food but as ingredients in more complex dishes. Thus canned soups were used to make casseroles, Spam was to be layered with pineapple slices and baked, and brown-and-serve rolls should at least be sprinkled with Parmesan cheese or sesame seeds before browning. While the magazines routinely reported on new developments in convenience foods, it was still the homemaker's job to cook, not merely to open cans and boxes. As the author of the January 1959 *McCall's* article "Head Start on Dinner" put it,

"On this and the following pages *McCall's* illustrates how well you and your family can eat when prepared and precooked and ready-to-eat foods are used *imaginatively.*"

Immediately after World War II, the magazines expressed great enthusiasm for convenience foods, some of which had been made possible by technologies and processes developed for feeding American servicemen. The January 1946 *Redbook,* for example, featured "Better Meals With Less Work," which promised a wide range of canned, frozen, and dehydrated foods, along with such items as an angel-food cake that was baked in the container in which it was sold. "With a start like this," the author asked, "what timorous newlywed couldn't do a handsome baking job?" But the magazines for middle-class women quickly retreated from endorsing products that made actual cooking the job of the manufacturer rather than the homemaker, instead recommending ways to make casseroles that added several ingredients to canned tamales and to create such delicacies as "Mexican gumbo" by combining canned chicken gumbo and pepper-pot soups. While the women's magazines seldom overtly expressed fears that reliance on labor-saving products would render the homemaker obsolete, these anxieties were articulated in the introduction to a cookbook compiled in 1949 from recipes submitted by readers of *Time* magazine:

> There seems to be a whole school of social scientists who have been trying to scare us lately with predictions that, if woman goes on turning more and more household chores over to the machines, she will soon cease to function except as an ornament, and will be doomed like the dodo.
>
> All such could well be answered with a present of this book. It is a happy tribute to this age of electric kitchens and frozen foods and freedom from drudgery . . . and it's the best testimony I've seen that the theorists' dread forecast is cockeyed. (Arfmann 3)

While most of the recipes in the collection were contributed by women for whom the publication of this book was the closest they came to national recognition, a small number came from well-known authors, actresses, and even the *Joy of Cooking* creator, Irma Rombauer, all of whom were presented as dedicated homemakers. Actress Rosalind Russell, for example, was identified as "in private life . . . Mrs. Fred Brisson," the mother of "a husky six-year-old," and a woman who "manages to supervise the family meals" (21).

The magazines that appealed to upper-middle-class readers, or, like *Mademoiselle* and *Seventeen,* that were essentially devoted to the social lives of young, unmarried women, took two different approaches to food advice, both of them different from the canned-soup and cake-mix emphasis of the service magazines and both of them suggesting social-class distinctions. The 1946 *Redbook* article that touted convenience foods began by noting the ultimate in convenience: complete frozen dinners shipped from fine restaurants to be heated for one's dinner guests. The *Redbook* author acknowledged that for most readers such luxuries would seem the stuff of fantasy—"Sounds like something out of Hollywood, doesn't it?"—but the upscale and young women's magazines of the period matter-of-factly endorsed prepared foods that made possible elegant meals with very little work in the kitchen. The author of "Cutting a Cook's Corner," in the January 1948 issue of *Seventeen,* stated that convenience foods were not a substitute for the "older or start-with-the-basic-ingredients plan" but subsequently recommended a pantry stocked with canned pâté, dehydrated soups, biscuit mix, and canned roast chicken. Poppy Cannon's regular "Food for Fun and Fitness" column in the February 1950 *Mademoiselle* was titled "Cooking Is No Job." Cannon recommended a new brand of canned soup that included cream of artichoke and "Cordon Bleu Vichyssoise" and the ubiquitous brown-and-serve rolls with "home-baked fragrance." In "Sauces from the Source," in the October 1955 *Harper's Bazaar,* the reader was introduced to frozen versions of classic French sauces, made in the United States under the supervision of chefs from Maxim's restaurant in Paris; these sauces, the author concluded, could serve as "the scaffolding on which to build a reputation as a gourmet cook."

When not engaged in recommending such "scaffolding," the upscale magazines promoted classic European cooking by suggesting cookbooks and publishing complicated recipes that eschewed convenience foods altogether. In the July 1949 *Harper's Bazaar,* Sheila Hibben defended American cooking against those who preferred minestrone and borscht to clam chowder, but the recipes in the article include poached (not fried) chicken and shortbread "from the English Lake Country." Food articles in the *Bazaar* frequently focused on specific cultural cuisines: "Tropical Cookery," in the August 1956 issue, featured recipes from the Caribbean, one of which permitted the use of canned beef bouillon "if you have no stockpot," although references to "my cook, Malvina" suggested that the author had a stockpot but did not use it herself. In the October 1956 *Bazaar*, James Beard presented a culinary journey through England and Europe with recipes featuring beer. In May 1961, *Mademoiselle* visited Greece for "A Taste of Resin." While magazines such as *Harper's Bazaar* and *Mademoiselle* alternated between touting prepared foods—preferably those with some approximation to French cuisine and especially for young career women—and encouraging the creation of authentic international dishes, the middle-class women's magazines advised homemakers on how to borrow from both worlds to create meals that mimicked the tables of their more affluent neighbors without great expenditure of either time or money. Sylvia Lovegren points out in *Fashionable Food* that while Americans became increasingly interested in European—especially French—cuisine during the 1950s, the typical homemaker who ventured into such cooking was likely to have a repertoire of recipes limited to such dishes as onion soup, Boeuf bourguignon, poulet marengo, and Swedish meatballs (198–205). The popular dessert baked Alaska, Lovegren notes, has no clear French pedigree and was easy to prepare if one could beat egg whites and work quickly (200–201). In both articles and advertisements, the magazines encouraged readers to make "French" onion soup using canned beef bouillon. The March 1952 *Good Housekeeping* offered a recipe for an "Old-Dutch Style" entree made from canned luncheon meat, canned apple slices, lemon juice, nutmeg, and onion; the "French Peasant Supper" featured in the February 1950 *Good Housekeeping* includes a "French Potage"—split pea–spinach soup with sliced frankfurters. Perhaps the most ironic convergence of the elegant and the easy was embodied in the 1950 publication of *Betty Crocker's Picture Cook Book*. Published by the General Mills Corporation, which manufactured the popular Betty Crocker cake mixes, the best-selling book featured page after page of illustrated instructions for baking homemade cakes, which, as Marling suggests, only served to increase the sales of cake mixes: "By depicting exquisite homemade cakes, the cookbook established an ideal—an ideal of lush, moist, decorated cakeness—that could be approximated in a variety of other, easier ways, including the use of a mix. . . . The *Picture Cook Book* was the best possible advertisement for the brightly colored boxes of cake mix stacked high on the grocer's shelves" (231).

When Marling comments that convenience foods such as cake mixes offered homemakers a combination of "novelty and prestige" (222), she hints at the social-class aspirations embodied in the magazines' food advice. Poppy Cannon was also the author of the *Can-Opener Cook Book* (1951), in which she wrote, "I become the artist-cook. . . . It is easy to cook like a gourmet though you are only a beginner" (qtd. in Hess and Hess 154). The texts of cookbooks and magazines thus increasingly challenged women to aspire to standards for meal preparation that had more to do with social reputation than with nutrition or economy. Writing in the *American Mercury* in 1949, Ann Griffith took the magazines to task for promoting impossibly high standards of housewifely performance in several areas, one of which she identified as "competitive cookery" (273). Griffith noted that whereas the advertising in the magazines offered "every modern device and potion that gets the little woman out of the kitchen faster," the articles had a "tendency to send her right back to the kitchen again" with elaborate menus and recipes (276). It seems no coincidence that the year in which Griffith's article appeared also saw the beginning of the best-known national cooking competition, the Pillsbury Bake-Off. While state and county fairs had for many years sponsored contests for the best pickles, preserves, pies, and cakes, the Bake-Off was qualitatively different: it received national media attention, featured the use of convenience foods, and, as Marling observes, "put home cooking on an equal footing with televised sports" (212).[11]

Humor Mixes the Message

As earnestly as the women's magazines advised readers about their various domestic responsibilities, their editors nevertheless felt compelled to recognize the growing genre of domestic humor that began with MacDonald's 1945 best-seller, *The Egg and I*, and that, by the mid-1950s, included popular works by Phyllis McGinley, Jean Kerr, Shirley Jackson, Margaret Halsey, and Elinor Goulding Smith, all of whom also published work in the leading women's magazines. These writers and others satirized the very standards of perfection promulgated by magazine articles and advertisements; heroines were beset by falling souffles, naughty children, malfunctioning appliances, and husbands who had never heard of "togetherness." A close reading of such works as Kerr's *Please Don't Eat the Daisies* (1957), Jackson's *Life among the Savages* (1953), and Halsey's *This Demi-Paradise* (1960) makes clear that such failures are not to be attributed to ineptitude on the part of the homemaker but instead to the impossibility of the standards for perform-ance. In her introduction to *The I Hate to Cook Book* (1960), for example, Peg Bracken specifically referred to magazine cooking articles when she pointed out the intimidation of "those ubiquitous full-color double-page spreads picturing what to serve on those little evenings when you want to take it easy": "You're flabbergasted. You wouldn't cook that much food for a combination Thanksgiving and Irish wake. (Equally discouraging is the way the china always matches the food. You wonder what you're doing wrong; because whether you're serving fried oysters or baked beans, your plates always have the same old blue rims!)" (viii).

Perhaps the most comprehensive spoof of perfectionism in the arts of homemaking was Elinor Goulding Smith's *The Complete Book of Absolutely Perfect Housekeeping* (1956), lengthy segments of which occupied fifteen pages of the March 1956 *Ladies' Home Journal*.[12] After describing house-keeping as "a job that is satisfying, meaningful, varied and perfectly loath-some," Smith listed the homemaker's responsibilities: "All you have to do, actually, is cook and serve three meals a day, do the marketing, the laundry and ironing, clean the house and make the beds, do the sewing and mending, painting and papering, a little simple plumbing and wiring, a bit of carpen-try, some bookkeeping and gardening, and be relaxed, charming and well groomed at all times. Isn't it laughably simple? Now let's all sit down and have a good laugh over it." Of the many household tasks that Smith ad-dressed in the *Journal* excerpts from her book, the section on cooking seems most directly referential to magazine advice articles. "Each meal," she wrote, "must be balanced in its nutritional elements, attractive in color, varied in texture, and as different as possible from the previous meal. It should make use of the butcher's specials, and it should not include too many complicated dishes or require too many serving plates." In response to the repeated ad-vice that housewives carefully plan their shopping, Smith noted that she would keep a notepad handy to write down her list, "but I can't because the children use it for their really important memoranda like addresses for send-ins on cereal boxes." Smith echoed Bracken in referring to the magazines' idealized table settings. For a winter roast beef dinner, Smith mused, "a dark red velvet cloth would be a happy choice, and for a centerpiece an old silver christening basin (any old silver christening basin you find around the house) heaped with white roses would be a nice touch." Yet even as such satiric pieces tacitly acknowledged that the magazines' advice was susceptible to mockery, the messages that readers received remained complex and contradictory: the *Ladies' Home Journal* pages on which Smith's satire appeared also carried advertisements for hosiery, perfume, china, floor coverings, floor cleaner, sewing machines, and children's clothes, all with illustrations promising domestic harmony and bliss.

The inclusion of articles that made fun of the messages conveyed not only increased the magazines' multivocal nature by the mid-1950s but also signaled that the domestic could be critiqued as well as constructed. In this way the magazines participated in the decade's cultural self-criticism, showing that while corporate America presented the "good life" in terms of uniform material aspiration, those people who were the primary targets of domestic advertising could articulate resistance to the implied perfectionism. In November 1955 *Ladies' Home Journal's* "How America Lives" series, which for more than fifteen years had implicitly or explicitly advocated an ideal domestic life by stressing such values as family solidarity, frugality, and homemaking efficiency, featured Jean Kerr and her husband, Walter, who had recently bought a large, fancifully designed house on Long Island Sound. Not only were the Kerrs a dual-career couple who often collaborated on theatrical productions, but Jean, who wrote the article's text, was wildly irreverent about her role as mother and homemaker. Instead of keeping her dining room rug clean, she looked for one "the color of mashed potatoes, Russian dressing, and butter-pecan ice cream." Rather than subscribing to "any of the more advanced methods of child psychology," she adhered to the philosophy that "we're bigger than they are, and it's our house." As sociologists warned about the dangers of increased conformity, such voices as those of Kerr and Smith, along with experts' mixed advice, invited resistance to a monolithic vision of domestic perfection.

CHAPTER 6

Cold Wars

Jell-O and Sputnik

In the short story "Sputnik," published in the 8 September 1997 issue of *The New Yorker*, Don DeLillo constructs a middle-class suburban family in 1957, the year the Soviet Republic launched the world's first artificial satellite. The three-page story captures the tension between the Demings' apparently complacent lives in a split-level house complete with picture window, breezeway, and "bright siding" and the Cold War challenge represented by Sputnik. As Erica Deming makes a Jell-O chicken mousse to put into her "Bermuda pink and dawn gray" Kelvinator refrigerator and Rick Deming simonizes the family's new two-tone Ford Fairlane convertible, both are aware of the Soviet satellite somewhere in the sky above them—"theirs, not ours," Erica muses: "were there other surprises coming, things we haven't been told about them?" Yet DeLillo makes clear that disruption of the Demings' suburban peace is much closer to home than a distant nuclear threat. As the elder Demings go about their ritual domestic tasks, their teenaged son, Eric, masturbates in his room, gazing at a photograph of Jayne Mansfield, whose breasts remind him of "the bumper bullets on a Cadillac." The activities in which Erica and Rick engage are vaguely haunted as well. Despite her delight in concocting molded meals, Erica thinks of one gelatine mold she never uses because, "sort of guided-missile-like," it "made her feel uneasy somehow"; Rick thinks about his Ford that "beneath the routine family applications was the crouched power of the machine, top down, eating up the landscape." When Eric opens the door of the Kelvinator, he is disoriented by the parfait glasses his mother has propped against the walls to create slanted layers: "It was as if a science-fiction force had entered the house and made some things askew while sparing others." Erica Deming is smug about "having something others did not," such as a vegetable crisper in her Kelvinator: "There were people out there on the Old Farm Road, where the front porches sag badly and the grass goes unmowed and the Duck River Baptists worship in a squat building that sits in the weeds on the way to the dump, who didn't know what a crisper was, who had iceboxes instead of refrigerators, or who had refrigerators that lacked crispers, or who had crispers in their refrigerators but didn't know what they were for or what they were called, who put tubs of butter in the crisper instead of lettuce, or eggs instead of carrots." But her sense of middle-class security must be constantly bolstered by reciting a litany of "words to believe in and live by," all of which refer to her late-1950s suburban surroundings:

> Breezeway
> Crisper
> Sectional
> Car pools
> Bridge parties
> Broadloom.

DeLillo's story insists on the manufactured quality of 1950s middle-class life, reminding us of both the media presentation of consumer goods and the political construction of the middle-class home as the bastion of democracy. The Demings' way of life is as fragile as a molded Jell-O salad. Erica Deming is the ideal domestic consumer, learning from advertisements the proper use of a vegetable crisper and striving for the ideal of cleanliness that Ann Griffith had ridiculed in her 1949 *American Mercury* article; before loading her automatic dishwasher, Erica dons "rubberoid" gloves and washes the dishes, "because if you don't get every smidge of organic muck off the fork tines and out of the pans before you run the dishwasher, it could come back to haunt you in the morning." Yet these lessons offer her family no protection against the threat represented by Sputnik or against her son's emerging sexuality, of which she is dimly aware but which she avoids confronting directly. At the end of the story, as Erica makes yet another molded Jell-O salad, she awaits "the reassuring sound of her men coming home, car doors closing in the breezeway, the solid clunk of well-made parts swinging firmly shut."

Erica Deming's sense that her domestic space is protected by "her men" and the "well-made parts" of postwar American technology while an alien satellite spins overhead reflects the dual consciousness evident in the women's magazines as the Cold War years advanced: the domestic arena was, more than ever, presented as the object of all desires and the site of the most fundamental satisfactions, while a consciousness of impending danger provided a countervailing anxiety. As early as January 1946, Dorothy Thompson's regular column in *Ladies' Home Journal* took the form of a letter from "Mary Doe" to the United Nations Security Council. Mary Doe represented all women whose profession was "housekeeper, homemaker, wife, mother": she appealed to the men of the Security Council, on behalf of home and family, to do whatever was necessary to prevent even the possibility of another armed conflict, especially with the atomic bomb a reality. Just as Thompson and others had argued in 1940 and 1941 that women's moral suasion could prevent the United States from becoming engaged in World War II, so Thompson's 1946 article appealed to the "gentlemen" of the Security Council as men who were once little boys raised by mothers who taught them to be "good boys." While the woman in DeLillo's story feels protected by "her men," Thompson was not reassured by world leaders who proposed maintaining peace by amassing weapons: "Your peace seems almost more terrible to us than was the war. For beyond the war we saw the rainbow of peace, but beyond your peace we see the lightning flashes heralding the thunders of war."

Several years after Thompson addressed world leaders on behalf of motherhood, another writer offered concrete, practical advice to women on preserving peace and democracy. Lucy Madeira Wing, headmistress of the elite Madeira School for girls in Falls Church, Virginia, addressed the alumnae of that school in a letter excerpted in the letters-to-the-editor column of the September 1951 *Ladies' Home Journal*. Although Wing advised participation in the political process through voting as one way to secure democracy against communism, the heart of her admonition to her readers emphasized the creation of a happy home life as the means to "demonstrate a democratic society": "I am urging you all to have gardens: to work in them with your own hands, to grow the food you will eat; then to become excellent cooks and have what I like to call deep family life. By deep family life, I mean enjoying one another by reading aloud as a family; playing games together; hearing good music every day, and bringing in friends. Family life is the richest thing in this world." The fostering of such a "deep, rich" family life was one of the central purposes of the midcentury women's magazines. The pastoral image of growing one's own food represents a dramatically different antidote to the possibility of nuclear destruction than does the technology that provides Kelvinators and Ford Fairlanes, but the magazines' contents promoted both the affective and the material to create the domestic democratic bulwark. By instructing women on their housekeeping and parenting skills, presenting idealized images of domestic harmony and—to use McCall's term—"togetherness," and even in suggesting, through both advertisements and editorial content, appliances and furnishings to enhance the home, the magazines implicitly participated in fighting the Cold War in the terms in which many Americans understood that fight. The August 1957 issue of McCall's featured plans for a suburban kitchen with laundry facilities and the furnace located in adjacent closets so that "doing three things at once becomes three times as easy." The woman who inhabited this space was actually described as doing four things at once: "laundry can be washed, flowers arranged for the table, and children supervised at play outside, all while dinner is being readied." The passive voice suggests rhetorically that these tasks are being accomplished without human intervention, while the title of the feature, "Heart of the House," proposes a metaphorical link between the room and the homemaker who provides the family's affective stability in an uncertain world.

The political implications of such magazine content, while subtle, were not accidental. Just as service—including planting victory gardens and recycling tin cans—was promoted as patriotic during World War II, the consumption of household goods was a sign of the democratic spirit after the war. In As Seen on TV, Karal Ann Marling points to the popularity in the 1950s of photographs of American families surrounded by all the groceries they would use in a typical year; the apotheosis of this trend was the 1959 Life magazine picture essay about a couple who spent their honeymoon in a bomb shelter stocked with packaged food and other amenities. Marling notes the correspondence between such displays of abundance and the Cold War: "Like the endless shots taken in well-stocked supermarkets, such photos celebrated abundance, insisted on its reality, and served to ward off whatever threatened America's kitchens of tomorrow, crammed with instant mashed potatoes and ready-to-heat-'n-eat, homestyle, frozen Salisbury steaks. Life's underground kitchen was America's symbolic front line of defense against the bombs concealed in Russian satellites" (250–51). While the underground honeymoon was a publicity stunt devised by a building contractor, the promotion of American capitalism was at times official U.S. government policy. In *Fables of Abundance*, Jackson Lears points out that in the mid-1950s, the U.S. Information Agency promoted overseas the concept of "People's Capitalism," which presented the American economic system as "a deus ex machina which erased class lines, transformed workers into capitalists, and eliminated all forms of drudgery." Such an alliance between government and advertising was ideally suited to the Cold War period, as Lears explains: "The effort to ally advertising with the American Way of Life, begun in the dark days of the Great Depression, came to full fruition in the ideologically charged atmosphere of the Cold War. Advertising apologists mixed all the old rhetorical strategies with renewed fervor and added a few new ones as well. Advertising was not only necessary commercial information, they claimed, it was the basis of free speech, as it provided the economic foundation for mass-circulation newspapers and magazines. And advertising was fun, the ebullient expression of a triumphant, spirited people" (250–51).

More than any other mass-circulation periodicals, the women's magazines promoted the American way of life, from menus for Fourth of July picnics to advertisements for washing machines. With the kitchen and its female inhabitant the "heart of the home," women were implicitly on the front lines of the battle against Soviet aggression. A poem occupying a full page in the December 1959 *McCall's* offered striking evidence of this sentiment. "Modern Christmas," by Christie Lund Coles, prayerfully requested a "reconciliation" between the star that shone on the birth of Christ and the man-made "star" now occupying the same sky.[1] Yet readers were not presented only with wishful holiday sentiments. In the same month, Thompson's article in *Ladies' Home Journal* took issue with the notion that the battle lines of the Cold War were drawn between communism and capitalism. In "The Challenge from Russia Is Not Communism," Thompson argued that it is a mistake to see the conflict as one between two economic systems, when in fact in both the United States and the Soviet Union, "an increasing proportion of the national wealth is invested and expended by the state . . . used to maintain the apparatus of the state." Further, she pointed out, the Soviet Union was by no means a "classless" society in which everyone shared equally but instead was ruled by a "governing elite" that held the reins of power. The true challenge from Russia, Thompson believed, was its dedication to the belief that "the world of the future belong[s] to the Slavs," while in America she detected "alarming signs of physical, moral and intellectual decadence." Implicit in Thompson's article was the message that the emphasis on the glories of capitalism had made Americans soft rather than tough. Ironically, the *Journal* editors chose to illustrate the first page of Thompson's article with a reproduction of one of Grant Wood's midwestern farm scenes, which, the caption notes, depicts "the fruits of [the farmer's] labors" and thus reinforces the rewards of individual hard work—in other words, capitalism.

While articles on Cold War politics such as those by Thompson were relatively rare in the magazines, and the relationship between the purchase of frozen dinners and the democratic way of life remained implicit rather than explicit, articles about the American educational system, which were numerous in the postwar years, were openly inspired by a climate of international competition and conflict. Immediately after the war, such articles reflected the screening of hundreds of thousands of young people for military service. Just as this process had revealed widespread malnutrition that prompted intense national interest in vitamins and calories, so it had shown that large numbers of draft-age American had derived little benefit from the educational system. Writing in the April 1946 *Ladies' Home Journal,* Robert Maynard Hutchins, then the chancellor of the University of Chicago, argued for programs of adult education—not vocational training, but education in the liberal arts—to create thoughtful citizens capable of solving problems. Citing statistics showing that the U.S. Army inducted 150,000 illiterates during one year of World War II and that Selective Service had, by September 1943, rejected more than 300,000 people on the grounds of "lack of educational accomplishment," and predicting that the average work week would soon be reduced to thirty hours, Hutchins proposed that adults occupy some of their leisure time with study. Although Hutchins's title, "Learning to Live" and his emphasis on reading classic works could suggest that he was advocating a humanistic education to enhance the quality of everyday life, much of the article's rhetoric made clear that he was instead concerned with the survival of American democracy and even the survival of the human race: "We have found," he wrote, "in atomic energy, the means of wiping ourselves off the earth. We know that the adult generation of today may have to save us if we can still be saved." After suggesting several models for the adult education he had in mind, Hutchins concluded on a similarly urgent note: "As [liberal education] was the only education that made intelligible the age of the slingshot, so it is the only education that will make intelligible the age of the atom."

By the mid-1950s, America's public schools were the focus of intense debate on two fronts: school desegregation as mandated by the 1954 Supreme Court decision in the *Brown v. Board of Education* case, and concern about the quality and rigor of the educational curriculum. The former issue rarely surfaced in the women's magazines, while article after article explored what a May 1956 *Good Housekeeping* article termed the "soft curriculum." The fact that school desegregation, with its immediate and far-reaching impact on the lives of millions of Americans, received little attention in the magazines while the more abstract issue of educational quality was a common topic suggests two different perceptions of the magazines' nature and that of their readers. One of these perceptions, which I discussed in chapter 4, was that race was a divisive issue, sure to alienate many readers, whereas the Cold War served to unite Americans in common cause, just as the family was to be united against external threat. The second perception concerns the proper role of the woman as activist. While active involvement in the civil rights movement would be viewed as an abandonment of the domestic arena, acting as a parent to ensure the quality of one's child's education was merely an extension of the nurturing role that had long been sanctioned for women. Although many women, both white and black, were actively engaged in civil rights in the 1950s, the stance of mass-circulation periodicals remained traditional. As Susan M. Hartmann puts it, "national leaders as well as popular culture proclaimed that women's role in the international crisis was to strengthen the family and raise new citizens emotionally and mentally fit to win the Cold War" ("Women's Employment" 85).

"The Soft Curriculum," written by educator Arthur Bestor, placed curricular concerns firmly in the context of the national interest and urged parental action to lobby for more substantial public education. Bestor began by proposing that "brain power, not mere rocket fuel, put the first man-made satellites into their orbits." The "life-and-death contest" in which the United States was engaged was, fundamentally, "a contest to produce the best-trained minds." Bestor cited such high school courses as "beauty culture," "radio speaking and broadcasting," and "girls' science" as the sort that must be eradicated in favor of traditional subjects and proposed a direct link between the welfare of the child and the welfare of the nation when he claimed that "other nations care more for their security—yes, and care more for their children—than to tolerate a system like ours." Although these "other nations" are unspecified, when Bestor spoke of the need to require four high school years of a foreign language, he noted parenthetically that Russian schools required five years. Two years later, in the November 1958 *McCall's*, Milton Senn, director of the Yale Child Study Center, took readers on a tour of Russian culture and the Russian educational system, proposing that "The Russians' Secret Weapon," as the article was titled, was a love of learning. Senn described the citizens of Moscow engaged in reading, attending the theater, and pursuing formal education and then recounted his observation of Russian schools. In addition to the fact that Russian students attended classes six days a week and often did several hours of homework, Senn was most struck by the seriousness with which students approached their studies, not afraid of being called "bookworms." In comparing such seriousness with the attitudes of American students, Senn noted the American emphasis on social skills: "Too many children grow up with a contempt for book learning, having been taught that a pleasing personality and a good golf game will sell a lot more insurance policies than a knowledge of calculus."

And, in fact, despite repeated calls for greater academic rigor, many American parents in the 1950s were at least as concerned with their children's social skills as with their intellectual achievements. As Wini Breines notes in *Young, White, and Miserable*, the key word in parental aspirations for their children was *normal:* "One of the striking themes of the fifties mothers is how academically unambitious they seemed for their children, or rather, how much they wanted their children to be 'normal' and 'average.' Many stated that they were not 'pushy' about educational achievement but wanted their children to get along well with others. The desire for normal children, defined as cooperative, congenial, and well-adjusted children, was characteristic of 1950s childrearing goals" (68). Although such aspirations for "normal" children applied to both boys and girls, traditional concepts of women's lesser intellectual abilities, coupled with an intense emphasis on marriage and childbearing, caused parents—and society generally—to have even less intellectual ambition for girls. Although the proportion of female college students increased steadily in the postwar years, neither intellectual development nor career preparation was the expressed goal. In *American Women Since 1945*, Rochelle Gatlin reports that in the mid-1950s, women received 28 percent of bachelor's of arts degrees from universities and 62 percent of degrees from teachers' colleges. Many more women enrolled in colleges and universities than these percentages indicate. Cultural pressure to consider marriage a more important goal than a degree caused many young women to withdraw from college once they became engaged. Nonetheless, between 1950 and 1974, while enrollment of men in higher education increased by 234 percent, for women the increase was 456 percent (Gatlin 43, 47). As Breines comments, "even if it was assumed that girls would go to college, they were often discouraged from serious educational pursuits and careers in the name of marriage and family. It is not uncommon for girls who grew up in the 1950s to talk of the stigma of being 'too smart' " (73). College curricula were sometimes complicit in steering young women to domestic lives rather than careers outside the home. In an article deploring the fact that universities were abandoning traditional curricula to become "not a community of scholars, but an enormous agglomerate service station," Hutchins cited the example of an unspecified California university that offered "Hope Chest 61A and 61B," a two-semester, six-hour course designed to "prepare students in the specialized homemaking field." The catalog description specified that "the college has on its campus a modern practice home. Sophomore girls can experience various phases of home living and learning. Included in the course is instruction about buying silverware, appliances, linens, etc." ("Our Basic Problems and Our Educational Program," *McCall's*, May 1960). The fact that the women's magazines had no single, monolithic message is manifest in the fact that the article containing this indictment of such courses appeared in a periodical which in many ways offered just such instruction itself.

So pressing were concerns about American higher education that in 1959 *Ladies' Home Journal* editors Bruce and Beatrice Gould organized a forum on the subject and published an edited version of the conversation in the October issue. Although the editors claimed that they had been concerned about educational quality well before Sputnik, citing previous forums on the issue in 1954 and 1956, it is also the case that fears about the educational system did not originate with the launch of the Soviet satellite but had been present since the start of the Cold War. Further, the headline that precedes the text of "Is College Education a Right or a Privilege?" reads, "The *immediate* future of your child, the *ultimate* future of this civilization depend upon how well this question is answered . . ." The forum participants, which included the chancellor of the University of Nebraska, the dean of admissions at Amherst College, the president of the Carnegie Corporation, a labor leader, a Texas homemaker, cartoonist Al Capp, and singer Marian Anderson, in fact presented no definitive answer but seemed to agree that students attended college more for status and career purposes than for intellectual growth and that while all Americans deserved to develop their talents, college was not the appropriate means of doing so for everyone. While most of the conversation seemed implicitly to concern white, middle-class male students, issues of gender, race, and class did enter briefly. The Texas housewife and mother of four was not challenged when she stated that "we want our daughters to be good wives, mothers, good citizens and community leaders, but I don't think they are helped to accomplish all this merely by courses in home economics and marital relations." It fell to Marian Anderson, the only African American on the panel, to raise the socioeconomic and racial aspects of the debate. "I wanted very desperately to go to college," she said, "but there wasn't money for it." She later reminded the others that life ambitions were partly a matter of racial privilege, remarking, "Children of my race often go from kindergarten through high school, or until they can quit, without any reason why they should study becoming apparent to them." One can only wonder how Anderson reacted when she saw that one of the most prominent advertisements flanking the columns of the published article was for Aunt Jemima corn bread mix.

"Any Moron Can Do It . . ."

Thus, one cultural tension reflected in the women's magazines of the 1950s was that between domestic order and prosperity on the one hand and, on the other, palpable threats to this ideal in the form of nuclear danger and an educational system incapable of deterring it. A second, somewhat more subtle tension called into question the magazines' historic role as domestic guides and handbooks. As increasing numbers of married women—including those with children—participated in the paid workforce,[2] the magazines were forced to confront readers' aspirations that went well beyond new tricks with cake mixes. This is not to suggest that the magazines actively promoted careers outside the home or ceased to offer advice on homemaking. Indeed, they continued to mirror the reality that even a woman with a full-time paid job still had primary responsibility for cooking, cleaning, child care, and entertaining. But as technological developments allowed some of these jobs to be accomplished with less time, the magazines were quick to bring these advances to readers' attention. Coupled with this increased reliance on convenience and speed—which represented greater household expenditure—was an implicit recognition that the two-income household allowed a higher standard of living. Consequently, the magazines increasingly emphasized what might be called the good life: stylishness in home decor, travel, the arts, and a generally more upscale presentation of the domestic life than had been the case during the 1930s and 1940s. At the same time, articles on women's education, jobs, the role of the homemaker, and women's mental and emotional health reflected significant anxieties about women's lives a decade before the publication of *The Feminine Mystique*.[3]

The fact that in the popular imagination many middle-class men and women were less certain that they had been a decade earlier of what the culture expected of them is amply demonstrated in magazine content. While advertising continued to depict aproned and high-heeled women joyously busy at domestic tasks, and magazine fiction tended to follow the happily-ever-after formula, a number of articles expressed uncertainty and confusion about gender roles. Despite the forces of conformity, there is ample evidence that it was no longer so clear—if, indeed, it ever had been—just what "normal" roles and behavior were. Throughout the 1950s, sociologists analyzed the plight of the "man in the gray flannel suit," the "organization man," and other manifestations of corporate culture. For Louis Lyndon, writing for the November 1956 *Woman's Home Companion*, the dilemma was that an increasingly domesticated male had lost the opportunity to be a hero. "Uncertain Hero: The Paradox of the American Male" began with a stark image of the man as a kind of domestic prisoner: "Visit any suburb on a Sunday afternoon—from Levittown, Long Island, to Lakewood, California—and you can view the captive male. . . . [T]he women . . . look like keepers of a prosperous zoo and the men like so many domesticated animals inside it." The greatest challenge men faced, according to Lyndon, was catching the commuter train to and from work, and when they came home they faced "the leaky roof, . . . the rampant crabgrass," and wives who greeted them "with a sack of charcoal and orders . . . to cook the steak." The corporate world might stifle his individualism by day, but the suburban world of evenings and weekends likewise offered no scope for his masculinity. The article concluded by accusing women of practicing a form of "Momism" on their husbands, even to the point of "adult toilet-training": "insisting that he wash his hands and hang up his towels and dispose of his razor blades at the same time, in the same way, in the same place." More than a decade after the end of World War II, Lyndon reminded women that their husbands had served in a military setting that permitted "certain deep and perfectly normal masculine drives" that were not permitted in the suburban backyard; stifle them completely, he warned, and "the man in the gray flannel suit will stop being a man."

If Lyndon was nostalgic for the male American hero "who moves like a shadow in our daydreams," Phyllis McGinley, in "The Honor of Being a Woman" in the September 1959 *Ladies' Home Journal*, was nostalgic for his counterpart: the woman who was honored for her "natural accomplishments." McGinley, a regular contributor of light verse and prose to midcentury women's magazines, was regarded as a defender of women's traditionally domestic role.[4] In this article, she expressed confusion about what women were to be rewarded for: "We are urged to take our rightful place in the world of affairs. We are also commanded to stay at home and mind the hearth. We are lauded for our stamina and pitied for our lack of it. If we run to large families, we are told we are overpopulating the earth. If we are childless, we are damned for not fulfilling our functions. We are goaded into jobs and careers, then warned that our competition with men is unsettling both sexes." McGinley primarily blamed education for this confusion; young women, she posited, become "cog[s] in an enormous system which was designed originally for boys" and thus are led to have aspirations for which the culture will not reward them. Most women will marry and will also have false expectations of that institution. "Marriage is *not* a 'partnership' in the usual sense of that word," McGinley wrote. "It is an institution invented to do woman homage; it was contrived for her protection." She envied women of earlier generations, who "did not have electric dryers or the vote" but "knew what was expected of them. And they were aware what honor was due them." The nostalgia that both Lyndon and McGinley expressed for an era of clear, fixed gender roles emerged from a sense that such certainty had disappeared; it is therefore ironic that people of later decades recalled the period during which these articles appeared as one of just such domestic stability.

Evidence that many women felt confined and dissatisfied in the homemaker's role can be found in articles that attempted to professionalize this role. One of the most comprehensive of these attempts was an installment of "How Young America Lives" in the September 1953 *Ladies' Home Journal*. Titled "Meet Mrs. $10,000 Executive in the Home," the article profiled a New Jersey couple who lived on the husband's earnings of $6,000 per year but "saved" more than $3,000 per year because of the wife's household jobs. The article was prefaced by an imaginary conversation with a woman who, in filling out a form, refused to use the term *housewife*, claiming instead to be a dietician, interior decorator, clothing manufacturer, chef, custodian, tutor, purchasing agent, and official hostess. A list at the end of the preface detailed what her husband would have to pay for skilled help with these duties as well as television repair and bookkeeping, for a total of $263.25 per month. Although the article described Nita McCloskey as a skilled and efficient homemaker, it also suggested that were her work not valued as a real financial contribution to the family, she would find it entirely unrewarding. McCloskey was quoted as saying, "About housework itself I have only one theory. . . . Any moron can do it—so get it over with. . . . When I feel real rebellious about housework I sit down and read magazine stories for a few hours or call up a girl friend and talk it out." And the article's author commented that McCloskey's schedule "might be branded slavery by someone paid in cash alone," so she had to give herself "psychic boosts": "I don't like to discourage myself, so I don't set my work standards too high." Despite her tone of rebelliousness about housework, McCloskey was the ideal *Ladies' Home Journal* reader: not only did she read magazine fiction as an escape, but she acknowledged that her mother taught her little about homemaking, thereby suggesting that the magazine had provided her instruction.

Articles about mental health suggested that without the "psychic boosts" that women such as McCloskey provided for themselves, women suffered from—or feared suffering from—depression, nervousness, or mental breakdowns. If parents wanted their children to be normal and well-adjusted, they wanted those conditions for themselves as well, and a woman who found herself yelling at her children might develop anxieties not only about the psychic effects on the children but also about her own "normalcy," to use one of the decade's buzzwords. Such, at least, was the thesis of articles such as "Are You Afraid You're Going Crazy?" by Dr. Walter C. Alvarez in the August 1957 *Good Housekeeping*. As in most such articles, Alvarez (then an emeritus consultant to the Mayo Clinic) adopted a reassuring tone, implicitly answering his title question with "probably not" and pointing out that only a sane person could consciously fear that she is going insane. Alvarez pointed to the stigma attached to mental illness when he stated that the woman who doubted that she was normal usually suffered "in utter loneliness, unable or unwilling to confide in her husband, her mother, or even her doctor." For the woman who tended to go into what Alvarez termed a "tizzy," he advised a physical examination to rule out physical causes, tranquilizers, a psychiatrist for truly stubborn cases, and for milder cases a twentieth-century version of S. Weir Mitchell's well-known nineteenth-century "rest cure": "Many a woman, as nervous as a witch, and on the edge of a nervous breakdown, could be straightened out if, for six weeks, she would only go back to bed in the morning after the family has had breakfast and has gone for the day." Dr. Murray Banks, writing in the March 1960 *McCall's*, even denied that nervous breakdowns existed and stressed the need to adjust to life's challenges: "The nerves never, never break down. What are weak are not your nerves, but your habits of adjustment." While articles such as these may not have solved what Betty Friedan called the "problem that has no name," they served as indications that by the late 1950s, women were sufficiently concerned about their mental and emotional well-being that their magazines attempted to confront the issue.

Suggestions that women's emotional health was both fragile and very important cropped up in odd places in the magazines. The "Hostess Almanac" in the December 1957 *Good Housekeeping*, which otherwise reads almost like a parody of Martha Stewart, includes occasional hints for maintaining one's balance. The calendar schedules some element of holiday preparation for every day of the month, including gifts, home decor, and menus for entertaining. By 21 December, the hostess was advised, "Don't tense up; alternate sitting and standing jobs; take time to rest a bit." The entry for 27 December asked, "EVERYTHING SET FOR NEW YEAR'S EVE?" But the next entry provided a cautionary reprieve: "Make time for a rest, do-it-yourself beauty treatment. Keep serene. You are your family's disposition barometer." The article acknowledged the paradox of the decade: while the ideal family Christmas can happen only with daily, detailed preparation on the part of the homemaker, there is potentially a psychic toll for such standards of perfection. By the late 1950s, articles such as Dorothy Canfield Fisher's 1941 *Journal* piece "Housekeeping Need Not Be Dull" were as outdated as war bonds and padded shoulders. But rather than a job with intrinsic rewards for mastering certain essential skills, homemaking, when it was not the ticket to a nervous breakdown, was often presented as glamorous, involving making mother-daughter outfits and "gourmet" meals—all accomplished with ease, thanks to new appliances and products. As early as 1953, food writer Poppy Cannon announced a "new epicureanism" that had an "Alice-in-Wonderland aspect": "Even though you may have avoided any connection with matters culinary in your life, now *you can start at the top.* You don't have to do simple dishes first. When you put your dependence upon a chocolate pudding mix, for instance, a *souffle au rhum* is a good deal easier than a regular pie. A miraculously dark, glossy, beer-rich beef *flambe* leaps in less than fifteen minutes from a tin of beef stew and a can of onion soup" ("How to be a Pace-Setting Gourmet," *House Beautiful,* May 1953). It seems no accident that the magazines portrayed the woman's domestic role as a set of professional responsibilities or as magical and effortless just as many women were rejecting full-time homemaking, either in actuality or on the level of emotional commitment. To continue to attract advertisers who depended on the female reader to be the household consumer, editors somehow had to make the job of homemaker attractive. At the same time, they needed to keep readers who felt less allegiance to traditional domesticity.

Articles about higher education and careers for women increased in frequency during the 1950s, even though many such pieces expressed reservations or at least ambivalence about women's suitability for these pursuits and by no means posited women's equality with men outside the home. Such articles were nothing new for *Mademoiselle,* whose primary readership was the college woman, yet even here authors often reflected the era's biases. In "What is College?" in the August 1952 issue, sociologist Russell Lynes (then an editor at *Harper's*) identified the intellectual and social benefits of the college experience but concluded the article with classic gender stereotyp-

ing: "College is many little things. It is the man who believes in the intellectual elite; it is the girl who wants to ask a very intellectual question but
doesn't want to have anyone think she is bright." A few months earlier, in
the May *Mademoiselle,* the author of "Have the Colleges Let Us Down?"
answered in the affirmative. The women who were not being well served,
argues Pamela Taylor, were not "the small minority of girls who are aiming
for a profession and the born scholars" but instead were "the great majority."
The "average college woman," Taylor stated, "is going to make someone a
fine wife; she'll probably be a good mother without making heavy weather
of it and take an active part in community life." This "average" woman
needed courses that linked the theoretical with the practical: economics
should prepare a woman to deal with "personal budgets, insurance and investments"; psychology should stress "better adjustment in human relationships"; and nutrition should be taught without requiring "so much chemistry
first that all but scientific specialists are ruled out." Conversely, Taylor recommended courses in women's history so that female graduates would be
equipped with "a more philosophical and intelligent appraisal of the status
of [their] sex." The January 1953 *Mademoiselle* article "Can You Afford Not
to Go to College?" attempted to speak to young women with a variety of
aspirations. One of the benefits of a college degree, the article pointed out,
was the ability to get a job and "turn it into a career," and the author listed
careers in scientific research and advertising as well as the more traditional
fields of teaching and sales. Yet when enumerating the skills a college education could provide, the author offered "domestic" as well as career applications. Skill in writing could be put to use in "field reports" and "theses for
advanced degrees" but also in "love letters." Given *Mademoiselle's* upper-
middle-class audience, it is not surprising that college was also presented as
a means of enhancing social prestige: it could get the graduate invited to
"plushier parties, swankier clubs."

   If *Mademoiselle* actively promoted the social and personal as much as the
intellectual benefits of attending college, an article in the May 1957 *Ladies'
Home Journal* soberly analyzed the effect of 1950s culture on female college
students. Based on a study of Vassar students conducted by Nevitt Sanford,
a University of California psychologist, "Is College Education Wasted on
Women?" began by addressing young women's reasons for going to college
in terms that seem almost a direct response to the 1953 *Mademoiselle* article:

"They go . . . because it is 'the thing to do'; because not to have gone will be a social handicap. They go to make friends, to 'learn how to get along with others.' They go to meet eligible young men." Rather than being judgmental about these motivations, Sanford attributed them to a culture that decreed that "the best way for a girl to show that she is healthy, wholesome, mature, well adjusted and the like is to get married and have children. We should not be surprised if many girls have drawn the conclusion that the sooner this is accomplished, the better." Sanford succinctly and accurately summarized the effect of Cold War culture on middle-class women's aspirations: "In the time of the Cold War the crisis has not been great enough to require that all hands pitch in and do useful work. But it has been great enough to place accent on the 'manly virtues' in men and traditional virtues in women. Not only is feminism dead; we have passed into a phase of antifeminism. Clever writers berate women for exercising their new-found rights and privileges. Psychologists and psychiatrists issue grave warnings about mothers' responsibilities to their young children. Thus it is that we have an upsurge of the attitude that one must not appear too bright or too competent, lest this threaten one's ability to take traditional female roles." Sanford's 1957 analysis is remarkably similar to that offered by cultural historians in the 1980s and 1990s, and its appearance in one of America's largest-circulation magazines is evidence that awareness of the cultural pressures on women is not a matter of hindsight but was available to millions of 1950s readers. Dorothy Thompson's regular feature in the May 1960 *Journal* similarly provided a cogent discussion of women's education and goals. Acknowledging the debate about whether women should obtain college educations when only a small percentage used them to pursue careers, Thompson first put forth the well-worn argument that education is never wasted and that the college-educated homemaker would be better at her domestic tasks. But toward the end of the article, Thompson turned her attention to the fact that in the absence of adequate tax deductibility for child-care expenses, many women could not afford to work outside the home. Noting that in 1960 the maximum deduction for such expenses was $600 per year and that families earning more than $4,500 per year could claim no deduction at all, Thompson urged her readers to take political action to change these policies. In a closing exhortation that has a remarkably contemporary ring, Thompson wrote, "Women have had the vote for over forty years and their organizations lobby in Washington for all sorts of causes but why, why, why don't they take up their *own* causes and obvious needs?" Even earlier, in the September 1952 *Journal,* Thompson had acknowledged a different problem for the woman who worked outside the home. In "The Employed Woman and Her Household," Thompson pointed to the absurdity of the "employed woman" also being responsible for all housework: "Our society is still organized on the assumption that the conduct of the home is every woman's natural function, [but] no one has expected men to work from nine to five in an office and then come home and cook a dinner for four or five people; or get up hours before time to go to work in order to sweep, dust, make beds and prepare breakfast."

Although articles such as those by Sanford and Thompson did not have the galvanizing effect of a book such as *The Feminine Mystique,* they serve as striking evidence that during the 1950s there was widespread acknowledgment in the popular press that economic and cultural forces—and not the lack of desire or innate ability—prevented many women from pursuing intellectual accomplishment and careers. Part of the reason, of course, why such articles did not provoke social change was that they shared space in the magazines with dozens of other messages. The most striking visual element of *Mademoiselle,* for example, remained pictures of fashionable clothing for the college woman, and even the most probing article in one of the general-purpose magazines was flanked by advertisements for convenience foods, deodorant, household appliances, and women's underwear. A look at the table of contents of the 1957 issues of *Good Housekeeping* reveals just how varied and even contradictory the magazines' messages could be. In the July issue, Charles Goren explained why women made the best bridge partners, and the life of Golda Meir was profiled, while another article presented the pros and cons of large and small weddings, and the two articles for teenagers focused on appearance and dating. The August issue featured an article on jobs for women as postmasters, but the fashion section was devoted to what girls should wear to start school in the fall. In the October issue, readers could learn from AFL-CIO president George Meany about careers for women in labor, while the fashion section told them "How to Dress the Part of the Executive's Wife." Similarly, the February 1960 issue of *McCall's* presented portions of the memoirs of Anthony Eden as well as patterns for clothing worn by Miss America.

Thus, rather than conforming to a single concept of what middle-class women wanted to know or should aspire to, as they had tended to in the 1940s, women's magazines of the 1950s and early 1960s recognized that changes were taking place, and the 1957 demise of *Woman's Home Companion* sent a signal to the other leading service magazines that definitions of "home" and the "domestic" had to be more flexible and inclusive. *Good Housekeeping*'s "Jobs for Women" feature, for example, conveyed the message that while housekeeping might be one of a woman's jobs, it might not necessarily be the only one. Monthly articles advised on career opportunities ranging from public stenographer to working for the Federal Bureau of Investigation, although the article made clear that women could not become agents but worked as clerical or technical support staff. Articles by and about prominent women had been a staple of the magazines for decades, at least tacitly providing role models for readers. In 1944 *Mademoiselle* began giving annual "Mlle Merit Awards" to women who had achieved distinction in their fields; the January 1953 issue profiled that year's winners, who had excelled in dietetics, dance, business, medicine, fashion, sports, theater, and social work; the one housewife of the women featured had been blind for ten years. Each of these women, the editors announced, had "charted a course for others to follow." The service magazines were rarely as overt about providing career inspiration for women and often featured women who had achieved fame in such areas of popular culture as film and television. The one exception was politics; beginning with Thompson's monthly *Ladies' Home Journal* column in 1937, most of the magazines had featured regular articles by women involved in politics and/or journalism, although Eleanor Roosevelt's "If You Ask Me," in the *Journal* during the 1940s and in *McCall's* in the 1950s, addressed readers' questions about etiquette or Roosevelt's personal life at least as often as it concerned political issues. In January 1960 *McCall's* announced that the following month Clare Boothe Luce would become a regular contributor, joining Roosevelt, so that the magazine would have "the nation's two most distinguished women on its roster." In her first *McCall's* "Without Portfolio" column, Luce addressed the issue of whether a woman could be nominated for U.S. president or vice president. Luce's answer was that while legally there was nothing to prevent such a nomination, no woman possessed what she identified as the four basic qualifications that would enable her to be elected and serve effectively: considerable experience in "practical politics," military service, "economic and financial know-how," and a thorough knowledge of international affairs. Luce's suggested solution to this dilemma was to create the office of "2nd Vice-President," to be filled by a woman who could, through serving in this office, acquire the expertise to be elected president.

When she pointed out that most women lacked the qualifications for the presidency because they had spent their young adult years keeping house and raising children, Luce reiterated the norm that the women's magazines in many ways continued to represent. Indeed, even as the magazines began to devote more attention to women's higher education and careers, profiles of well-known women often focused on their domestic lives, although even here the messages are mixed. In 1957, for example, the editors of *Good Housekeeping* asked former child film star Shirley Temple Black to write about her life as she approached age thirty. The mother of three small children, Black wrote for the November issue that she did not "decide" to be a housewife rather than an actress: "when the time came, I just knew. . . . And I have not the slightest doubt where my first interest lies; what I *have* to do is be at home." Although she admitted that she did not enjoy cooking, she did it because "I would rather cook than lessen the intimacy of our household." A reader who went no further than the first page of Black's article would assume that she felt entirely fulfilled by domesticity, but on the third page she revealed that she was a professional interior decorator, "almost always working on a corner of a room or even a whole house for someone, on a professional basis." In addition, she was overseeing the renewed manufacture of the 1930s Shirley Temple dolls to coincide with the rerelease of several of her films: "anything connected with business appeals to me."

Black's article represents the schizophrenia of the women's magazines in the late 1950s. On the one hand, homemaking and motherhood are described as almost a "calling"—"I just knew"—but on the other hand, Black is immersed not only in what could be considered the feminine profession of interior decorating but also in the continued business promotion of her own image as child film star. Articles on food, decorating, and entertaining stressed glamour, luxury, and ease, but other articles showed women resisting identification with the domestic and yearning for professional status. The August 1957 *Good Housekeeping* included in its fashion section articles on

"The Well-Educated Wardrobe," "The Well-Adjusted Wardrobe," and "The Well-Bred Dress." The October 1956 *Woman's Home Companion* proposed that sewing was far more than a utilitarian skill with articles titled "Sewing Brings Out the Artist in You" and "Most Women Are Designers at Heart." A lengthy, statistics-filled article in the same issue proclaimed "The Married Woman Goes Back to Work." Noting that one-third of the paid U.S. labor force was female and that most of these women were married with children, the article announced that "women's hard-won right to work outside the home has developed into a powerful urge to work." At the same time, the magazines continued to exhort women to "work on" their marriages. Clifford R. Adams's regular "Making Marriage Work" column in the December 1959 *Ladies' Home Journal* placed the responsibility for the relationship squarely on the female: "Can Brides Break the Habits That Break Up Marriages?" concluded with a list of questions the young wife should ask herself about her habits and skills, noting that "if she is immature at marriage, it is up to her to accept and fulfill the requirements of her new status as quickly as possible." On the material level, the magazines urged readers to strive for an ever higher standard of living. The house plan featured in the October 1959 *Journal* was titled "How Much Luxury Will $30,000 Build?" and the one-page text describing the five-bedroom house (complete with a "breeze-way") used the term *luxury* eight times.

Magazine advertising—nearly all of it aimed at women as homemakers, mothers, and people concerned about their physical appearance—delivered a similar mixture of messages. Housekeeping was an art, but it was easy to create elegance, not mere coziness. In 1960 Campbell's presented its frozen cream of potato soup as a quick alternative to flying to France for dinner and noted that the soup made an "elegant Vichyssoise" when served cold. Brillo soap pads used "Jeweler's Polish" to make pans shine. Dream Whip made desserts, including "Chocolate Continental," "easily elegant." Hunt's tomato sauce made a meatball recipe "such fun to fix." Vinyl upholstery gave rooms "an air of opulence and an aura of luxury," and "Movie Star" lingerie "[brought] out the actress in you." Tappan's new "Fabulous Debutante 400" oven was as "easy to clean as a china plate," and *McCall's* "Needlework Boutique" offered its patterns for "Midas touches" to make rooms "regal." Simultaneously, however, appeals to tradition reassured the reader that she had not really abandoned her responsibilities. Borden's instant mashed potatoes were "so delicious you can't tell them from homemade." Green Giant canned corn promised "fresh-shucked flavor," and Betty Crocker's devil's food cake mix was part of its "Country Kitchen" series, with "old-fashioned" taste. A full-page General Foods ad in the October 1960 *McCall's* featured a drawing of a young couple holding hands on a couch, and the text, headed "Love Story at 250 Elm," both reinforced woman's domestic role and hinted that it did not fully define her life: "Five P.M., and you're fresh and waiting to hear what's new in your husband's life. These days a woman's world doesn't stop at the kitchen door. Even the busiest schedule must leave time for him. General Foods kitchens is on your side. That's why we try to bring you foods that are long on pride, short on work." A Wool Bureau advertisement in the same issue suggested that skills learned in professional life transferred directly to homemaking and consumerism. Beneath a photo of a woman wearing a wool coat, the text, headed "Alicia knows," read, in part, "her ballet theatre days trained mind and body to single out the beautiful. Sets charity bazaars and P.T.A. dances in motion with the same brilliance she exhibits decorating rambling farmhouse, painting porcelain dolls for her two little girls. She has kept her values, knows what's real and what isn't." The suggestion that Alicia has learned her "values" in her ballet training rather than in the home represents not so much a shift from the domestic to the professional as it does an attempt to appeal to women whose priorities lay in either realm: if "any moron" could perform household tasks, taste and discrimination were necessary to make the home the site of "luxury."

Magazine Wars

In March 1989, popular culture critic Leslie Savan wrote in *The Village Voice* about *Good Housekeeping's* current marketing campaign, which touted what it termed "The New Traditionalism." This oxymoron was described by the Yankelovich market research firm, which claimed to have "discovered" the new traditionalism, as follows: "It's a combination of the best parts of the '40s and '50s—security, safety, and family values—with the '60s and '70s emphasis on personal freedom of choice. It's the first major change in the basic way we want to organize our society since the '60s." While the pronoun *we* in this statement has no clear antecedent, seeming to invoke "we, the people," Savan points out that the advertising campaign to promote *Good*

Housekeeping coincided with the campaign for the 1988 presidential election, and he quotes the creative director of the magazine's advertising agency as saying that when Republican candidate George Bush used the term "new traditionalism," "We said, 'Holy shit.'" The television version of the *Good Housekeeping* ad was timed to coincide with the Bush inauguration, thus riding on the coattails of the "family values" political campaign. What concerns Savan about the alliance between a magazine's self-definition and political rhetoric is the sales motivation of both: "The distasteful thing is that the categorizing, naming, and publicizing of a social trend is colored entirely by the need to sell, whether it's votes for George Bush or ad pages for a women's magazine. When advertisers package social movements, they inevitably tell you *how* to become the thing they're defining, what look, what attitude, what product to buy."

In truth, however, the women's magazines—in both their advertising and their editorial content—had been, in a sense, "selling" social movements for more than a century. The nineteenth-century *Godey's Lady's Book* promoted gentility and social mobility as well as what would later be termed "family values." In 1865 the "Editors' Table" pronounced that "The family is God's institution for human happiness, as well as for the highest moral culture this life affords." In announcing its "American Uplift" series of articles in February 1906, *Woman's Home Companion* promoted the spirit of the Progressive Era. The "Editor's Note" that accompanied the first article in the series reads in part, "The world and the people in it are really growing better. This we believe despite all the talk of corruption and graft in public and private life. . . . The very revelations of the press are in themselves a convincing sign that the public conscience is all right." In the 1920s *McCall's* endorsed the look and the freedom of the "flapper" with page after page of fashion illustrations. With the maturation of the advertising industry in the 1920s, such social and political affiliations could be more cleverly and persuasively packaged, but they were by no means new.

By the late 1950s, however, the women's magazines' traditional reliance on advertising revenue was confronted with the challenge of television, whose potential as an advertising medium was rapidly being realized. In the highly competitive world of the popular magazine, success tends to be measured by two separate figures: circulation, or the number of issues sold by subscription and on newsstands, and the dollar amount of advertising revenue generated. While magazines occasionally touted their circulation figures to testify to their popularity, readers were generally unaware of where a given magazine stood on these numerical scales. Readers of the December 1959 *Ladies' Home Journal*, however, found a half-page ad in which the *Journal* promoted itself as an ideal venue for advertising products. Headed by the familiar *Journal* slogan, "Never Underestimate the Power of a Woman," the copy further claims that "To reach women nowadays, advertisers use the no. 1 magazine for women . . . *no. 1 in circulation *no. 1 in newsstand sales *no. 1 in advertising." Visually, the ad presents an interesting mixture of messages. The two-panel illustration employs the motif of the fairy tale "Rapunzel," as a young man first gazes longingly at a window in a tower and then climbs up the long hair the young woman has let fall from it. Is the woman the *Journal*, helping the advertiser of a product? Does the "power" of a woman reside in her physical attributes, such as her hair? The other significant visual element is the typography of the magazine's name: the words "Ladies' Home" appear in tiny print alongside the large word "Journal," as though to minimize the concepts of both *lady* and *home* and emphasize the less value laden term *journal*.

Uncertainty about women's attitudes toward the domestic world the magazines had always promoted, then, was joined by increased competition for readers and dollars to create turbulence in the world—and the pages—of the women's magazines as the 1950s drew to a close. As early as 1952, *Business Week* reported that the women's magazines distributed by supermarket chains—led by *Woman's Day* and *Family Circle*—were drawing dramatically increased advertising revenues and beginning to rival the "big four" magazines in circulation. Both *Woman's Day* and *Family Circle* had begun in the 1930s as small, inexpensive magazines sold only in supermarkets.[5] In March 1951 *Ladies' Home Journal* had a circulation of 4.6 million copies, and *Woman's Day* had more than 4 million. The latter's advertising revenue had increased more than 30 percent between 1950 and 1951, and more than half of its advertisers made products not sold in grocery stores. Ironically, as magazines such as *McCall's* and *Ladies' Home Journal* were beginning to deal with women's changing roles and aspirations in the postwar period, the supermarket magazines were, as the *Business Week* author put it, "primarily 'how to do it' primers. They tell the housewife how to cook economically, how to bring up her children, how to clothe them and herself, how to take care of her house." It is no wonder, then, that *Woman's Day*'s editors felt that "it should not be classified in the food-distribution field at all, but in the same category with the women's service magazines" ("Food-Store Magazines"). By the early 1970s, the "store" magazines proved to be even more of a threat to the older magazines for several reasons, the most obvious being economic: the Postal Service had dramatically increased mailing rates for magazines, a budget item about which publishers of magazines sold at supermarket checkout stands did not have to worry. According to a 1974 article in *New York* magazine, the December 1973 issue of *Family Circle* sold 9.7 million copies—a record for any women's magazine—and *Woman's Day* was not far behind. A second reason, proposed by a veteran of magazine publishing, was that the store magazines, with their down-to-earth advice and low cover prices, appealed to the "blue-collar ladies." He theorized that "the upper-class ladies [were] drifting away from *McCall's* and *The Journal* to *Psychology Today*, *Ms.*, or the Cook Book Club" (Diamond 43–44).

Of the four leading service magazines that had survived two world wars, the Depression, and dramatic demographic changes since the late nineteenth century, *Woman's Home Companion* was the only one that did not survive the 1950s.[6] In mid-December 1956, the directors of the Crowell-Collier Publishing Company decided to cease publication of both the *Companion* and *Collier's* with the January 1957 issues. Each magazine had a circulation of 4 million, and as Theodore Peterson put it in *Magazines in the Twentieth Century*, "their passing made publishers, advertisers, and indeed the general public uncomfortably aware of magazine mortality" (129). While the reasons for the demise of *Woman's Home Companion* are complex, one contemporary commentator attributed it to a lack of editorial freedom: "Things often were done editorially solely to attract advertising" (Peterson 130). Such was certainly not the case when Gertrude Battles Lane edited the *Companion* from 1912 until her death in 1941. More than most women's magazine editors, Lane was committed to determining and meeting the needs of her readers. In addition to instituting regular features on child health and consumer advice, in the mid-1930s she established a panel of 2,000 subscribers who became "Reader-Advisers" on various issues affecting women's lives. In establishing this close link between the magazine and its audience, Lane drew on earlier magazine features such as the "Help-One-Another Club," which appeared in the magazine during the years she served as household editor, beginning in 1903. In the February 1906 issue, for example, readers—identified by initials and home states—contributed hints on time management, instructions for cleaning felt hats and canaries' feet, and recipes for orange marmalade, molasses candy, and green tomato pie.

By the mid-1950s, such chummy neighborliness would have seemed hopelessly old-fashioned, and there was little in such a feature to attract potential advertisers, whose philosophy was that help came from the purchase of products rather than friendly advice from other readers. In its last year of publication, the contents of *Woman's Home Companion* closely resembled those of its rival service magazines. Each issue included several short stories and sections devoted to cooking, fashion, household equipment, beauty, child care, and advice about marital difficulty. There was a regular column for teenage girls and a section on home decor. The featured articles in each issue included interviews with celebrities, updates on medical research, and seasonal pieces: how to pack for travel (July), how to make use of the fall harvest (October), how to choose appropriate gifts (November). When the *Companion* was so abruptly discontinued, it came as no surprise that *McCall's* and *Ladies' Home Journal* each announced that it anticipated adding nearly 400,000 former *Companion* subscribers to its own list (Peterson 140).

The ensuing competition between *McCall's* and *Ladies' Home Journal* was concerned with more than vying for the *Companion* subscriber list. The *Journal* wanted to maintain its position as the leading women's magazine, and *McCall's* wanted to occupy that position—which it managed to do in 1960, when it could claim a slightly larger circulation than the *Journal* and advertising revenues that exceeded it by $2.6 million (Peterson 195). In the process, *McCall's* underwent dramatic changes that had at least as much to do with competing in the "numbers game" of magazine publishing as they did with the needs and interests of American women. The first major alteration had been instigated in 1954 by editor Otis L. Wiese, who declared that the magazine was no longer solely intended for women but was for the entire family. The resultant "togetherness" theme directed attention to the family as a totality—as Peterson put it, "a family's living not as isolated members but as a unit sharing experiences" (204). Whether deliberately or coincidentally, Wiese's decision coincided with the television debut of "Lassie," "Father Knows Best," and "Walt Disney," all of which glorified the family unit. Further changes followed the appointment of Herbert R. Mayes as *McCall's* editor in 1958. Mayes, who until shortly before had edited *Good Housekeeping*, entered with enthusiasm into the competition with the *Journal* and made *McCall's* into the slick, stylish magazine it was when it nosed out the *Journal* in 1960. In his memoir, *The Magazine Maze*, Mayes recalls that the most sweeping changes he initiated did not concern *McCall's* editorial content but rather its visual impact: "It was no stroke of genius to conclude that the transcending thrust had to be visual, certainly in the initial stages—a grand, radiant, opulent, smashing look" (300). Mayes called on the magazine's art department to make it eye-catching, even having the cover sprayed with plastic to make it shine. In terms of editorial content, he increased the magazine's coverage of celebrities and revamped traditional features to give them greater cachet. According to Peterson, Mayes "thought women were bored by cooking, so he glamorized food with pictures and text" (205). One perhaps-unintended result of all of these changes was to give *McCall's* the aura of upper-middle-class luxury; rather than the values of the average family—Mayes soon dropped the "togetherness" theme—the magazine reflected the aspirations of the upwardly mobile.

Interestingly, the *McCall's* of the late 1950s and early 1960s strongly resembled the *McCall's* of the 1920s, when its circulation first exceeded 2 million and it became a competitor to *Ladies' Home Journal*. As was the case in the later period, the 1920s issues of *McCall's* featured lavish cover illustrations, and both articles and advertisements spoke of and to the privileged. An article in the January 1924 issue featured Mary Pickford as the woman who "has earned more money by her own efforts than any other woman in the world." The month's dress patterns were touted as having come "to Fifth Avenue via Paris," and the text of a Chevrolet ad read in part, "every 2- or 3-car private garage in the country should have at least one Chevrolet for daily use, going to and from work or for milady's shopping." An advertisement for Lux soap in the September 1924 issue included endorsements of the product from Russian and Italian princesses and from the wife of violinist Fritz Kreisler, who used it to clean her rare Viennese porcelain collection. The following month an article took readers behind the scenes at Paris fashion houses, and in the January 1925 issue three of the short stories are set in New York, one is set in California during the gold rush, and another features an American who has inherited an English estate.

Articles on homemaking similarly reflected affluence. Cooking articles featured desserts such as cakes and meringues; an article on housecleaning in the October 1924 issue emphasized the use of electrical appliances; and the August 1924 issue included an article on making homemaking an efficient "business": "Just as you cannot do good work in a kitchen which lacks the necessary utensils and conveniences, so you cannot be efficient in the business management of your home without some place in it which corresponds to an office, and equipment with which to work properly."

While *McCall's* and *Ladies' Home Journal* competed fiercely at the end of the 1950s by trying to make themselves more attractive to readers and advertisers, *Good Housekeeping* responded by rededicating itself to the utilitarian needs of the middle-class housewife. In the pages of the advertising trade journals, *Good Housekeeping* claimed to be above the "fanfare or frenzy" of the race for first place; any success the magazine had, it announced, was the result of an "honest accumulation of those women who care most about what this magazine is best able to give them" (qtd. in Peterson 216). Mayes painted a bleak picture of *Good Housekeeping*'s fortunes at the end of the 1950s: "My position on *Good Housekeeping* was given by Richard Deems to Wade Nichols, who had been editor of *Redbook*. He proved not to be the happiest choice. From being the company's most prosperous magazine, *Good Housekeeping* under Nichols went deeply into the red" (291). Mayes's comments may have been colored by his firing from *Good Housekeeping*, and any dip in the magazine's success was temporary: by 1963 its circulation exceeded 5 million, which represented an increase of more than 50 percent since 1953, and it was drawing advertising revenues of more than $25 million annually. An editorial statement from the September 1957 *Good Housekeeping* (during Mayes's tenure as editor) not only articulates the philosophy that sustained the magazine into the 1960s but also describes a magazine's ideal involvement in the world of home and family:

> A magazine can be like a good friend, taking on actual personality in its communication between minds, and it seems unlikely that any magazine has ever had closer friendship with its readers than *Good Housekeeping*. Hundreds of thousands of letters, visits, and phone calls from readers every year attest this fact. Questions, personal or impersonal, germane to our contents or absolutely remote, pour in on us, and we take them all seriously and answer them to the

best of our ability. Advice on every subject from lumbago to love is requested. Information on everything from how to build a house to how to catch a mouse is cheerfully supplied. We share in our readers' minor triumphs; praise the snapshots of their new babies; read their poems; receive post cards from Yellowstone Park and Paris, France, where they have gone on vacation; hear what their husbands had to say about the barbeque recipe; read reports on the joy engendered by the new dishwasher; sort out and follow up and do something about complaints; help plan parties, wardrobes, weddings, itineraries, and budgets. We are profoundly and personally involved with American life.

While not all women's magazines could claim to be "profoundly and personally" involved in their readers' lives and hence in "American life," it is clear that between 1940 and 1960 a dozen or so magazines participated directly in creating images and expectations of American domesticity. As America emerged from the Depression and confronted the possibility of a world war, the women's magazines solidified their identity as American periodicals, whether seeking to introduce citizens to one another, as did the *Journal's* "How America Lives" series, recruiting women for volunteer war work, or providing warnings about black-market goods. Before television began to provide a visual rendition of the middle-class family, the magazines chronicled the movement to the suburbs, charted—in both advertisements and editorial content—developments in household technology and home design, and introduced readers to styles in both food and clothing. As the Cold War placed increasing emphasis on home and family as central to democracy itself, the magazines responded with a roster of experts to advise on improving the marital relationship, child care, health, home technology and decoration, and the quality of leisure activities. Even the social issues to which the magazines paid attention were in some senses part of the domestic, broadly defined: educational quality, teenage pregnancy, juvenile delinquency, women working outside the home.

Yet to view the magazines of this period as conspiring to prescribe a particular role for women, as feminist groups in the 1960s and 1970s alleged, is to ignore the publications' status as businesses operating within a complex political and social framework. The campaign by *McCall's* editor Wiese to create the "magazine of togetherness" in the mid-1950s originated as much in a desire to appeal to male as well as female readers as it did in a belief in the primacy of the nuclear family; similarly, Mayes's decision to drop this slogan a few years later resulted from his plan to eschew the cozy in favor of the glitzy to attract readers and advertisers rather than from a particular vision of American womanhood. Further, as published letters to the editors attest, many readers were quite selective about which of the magazines' messages they chose to accept or reject. But the *Newsweek* author who wrote about changes in the women's magazines in 1971, the year after feminist leaders had formally protested the editorial policies of *Ladies' Home Journal* and *Cosmopolitan*, assumed that such publications had powerful influence. Identifying as the seven leading magazines at the time *Family Circle, Cosmopolitan, Good Housekeeping, Ladies' Home Journal, McCall's, Redbook*, and *Woman's Day*, the article noted that "their influence, from the Good Housekeeping Seal of Approval to the sophisticated life-style exemplified by 'That Cosmopolitan Girl,' touches American women from the most remote town to the biggest metropolis" ("Liberating Magazines" 101). Apparently lost on *Newsweek* was the irony that the protesters had targeted two magazines with diametrically opposed ideals of womanhood: the venerable *Journal*, self-described as "the magazine women believe in" and offering the standard articles on parenting, cooking, fashion, and celebrities, and *Cosmopolitan*, which appealed to the young, independent, sexually liberated woman. Although the magazines underwent alterations—Betty Friedan became a columnist for *McCall's*, for example—the real news of the 1960s and beyond has been the proliferation of magazines for different ages, racial and ethnic groups, interests, social classes, and even geographical areas.

Such proliferation reflects, as much as anything, the market segmentation that influences the marketing of virtually all products—from toothpaste and frozen foods to clothing and automobiles—at the turn of the twenty-first century. While some of this segmentation affected women's magazines before the 1960s—as dramatic differences between, for example, *Harper's Bazaar* and *Good Housekeeping* attest—the largest magazines considered a diverse readership to benefit their domestic enterprise. If magazines sought to positively affect family life and hence national life as a whole, then it made sense for them to reach as diverse a readership—among homemakers—as possible. Lacking serious competition from other media, the magazines had widespread influence on home design, social behavior, attitudes toward politics, and fashions in clothing, food, and furniture, and the publications sought readers wishing to be informed about a way of life rather than those already identified by demographic markers. Such a stance was articulated by Barton W. Currie, a member of the *Ladies' Home Journal* editorial staff, in the February 1925 issue. Currie's essential message in "Like What You Like, But—" was that he and the other *Journal* staff members were aware that not all readers would like all of the contents of this or any other issue of the magazine, but the magazine's employees accepted this situation as an inevitable part of editing a mass-circulation magazine. This issue, Currie notes, would "probably be read by ten million individuals of both sexes and varying ages. Imagine, if you can, the infinity of differences in contacts and experiences of this huge family of readers." The editors knew that "large numbers will prefer Zane Grey to Booth Tarkington, that equally large numbers will prefer Tarkington to Grey." The biography of Brigham Young in the issue would "probably offend some Mormons and some non-Mormons," and "there are some who may not like the first of William Lyon Phelps' new series of lay sermons." Hundreds of thousands of members of the *Journal* "family" wrote to the magazine each year to express their likes and dislikes, Currie stated, but he concluded the article with a letter that suggests reader loyalty on the part of even those who might have disagreed with editorial decisions: "Dear Sir: My wife, Mrs. D. V. Sivitzer, has been taking *The Ladies' Home Journal* continuously for forty years. . . . Have you any older subscriber?" Currie responded, "None that we have record of." By the 1960s the concept of a family of 10 million readers who might have little in common except a monthly magazine had been replaced by attempts to target separate groups of readers with similar values, ages, income levels, and goals.

Even as such phenomena as *TV Guide,* shopping malls, and McDonald's restaurant franchises signaled the beginnings of mass culture in the 1950s, the women's magazines demonstrated the paradox that while the domestic world loomed large as an ideal in both personal and national life, its precise shape and definition were far from fixed but instead continued to undergo constant negotiation in a process in which the magazines were one set of voices among many. The world of Kelvinators and breezeways that DeLillo recreated in "Sputnik" surely existed, but, like Erica Deming's Jell-O molds, it was a fragile structure, vulnerable to assault by competing realities. *McCall's* sounded its cozy note of "togetherness" in 1954, and in June 1955 Adlai Stevenson advised the graduates of Smith College that their "job" was to support their husbands' aspirations: "keep him Western, . . . keep him purposeful, . . . keep him whole" (qtd. in Carter 86). The sense in Stevenson's remarks that without women's guidance, men were subject to fragmentation is emblematic of the fragility of domesticity itself, represented in the growing divorce rate, the increase in dual-career marriages, and a daily life taking place more and more outside the home, whether at a fast-food restaurant or through the television screen. In 1940 *Ladies' Home Journal*'s "How America Lives" series could take readers as "neighbors" into each others' homes, but by 1960 such a project would have seemed naive and nostalgic; the characters in television situation comedies and soap operas were as familiar as the people next door, and the core middle-class values the series espoused had been eclipsed by the lure of a burgeoning manufactured material culture. The May 1960 *McCall's* includes reviews of television programs as well as films, and several letters to the editor deplore television violence. The editors suggest that readers send for eleven booklets, three of them dealing with careers for women and one concerning women's legal status. Ads for everything from eyedrops and pain relievers to lawn furniture promise to relieve the stress and tension of modern life. If there had ever been a distinct line separating the domestic world from the rest of the culture, it was becoming less and less easy to locate.

July 1998

Between the 1950s, when, as a child, I read the women's magazines to which my mother subscribed, and the early 1990s, when I began doing research on women's magazines of the midcentury period, I seldom read them, nor do I routinely read them now. Because my projects constituted an inquiry into social history, I went full circle: as an adult scholar, I returned to the magazines that had informed my mother's generation and to which I was drawn then by emerging interests in cooking, fashion, and fiction. Like others who were to enter the academy, I grew to prefer *The New Yorker* and *Harper's* to *Good Housekeeping*, and I later read *Ms.* The persistently domestic part of my nature sought instruction from *Bon Appetit* rather than the recipes in *Ladies' Home Journal*, *Organic Gardening* rather than *Better Homes and Gardens*. But immediately after I had drafted the preceding chapters, I went to my local bookstore to look at current issues of women's magazines. What follows is by no means a thorough study of contemporary magazines for women but instead some observations on continuities and discontinuities.

One of the most notable developments—a continuation of the trend begun in the 1960s—is the extreme segmentation of the magazine market by age group. Magazines such as *Shape* and *Self* and many others are intended for the young woman and, as a number of critics have noted, promote an almost narcissistic preoccupation with the female body. But these magazines are not alone: *Glamour* and *Cosmopolitan* use cover models in extremely revealing outfits, and even *McCall's* cover presents both actress

Helen Hunt and Princess Diana displaying a good deal of cleavage. Magazines for more mature women, such as *Mirabella* and *Lear's*, consider the mind almost as important as the body, including thoughtful articles that are often quite well written. In addition to age, magazines for women are also diversified ethnically. *Essence*, begun in 1970, remains the leading magazine for African American women, but there are also periodicals for readers in other racial and ethnic groups, such as *Latina* and *Moderna*, some of them bilingual. There are magazines expressly for women who work outside the home and for those who work out in gyms. One of the most interesting developments is what might be called the "alternative" magazine—one that attempts to counter the values and images promoted by most women's magazines. *Ms.*, founded in 1972, was the first of these publications, and it became even more radical in 1990 when it stopped depending on advertising revenue. While *Ms.* is intended primarily for adult women, its alternative ranks have been joined by magazines for teenagers, including *Bluejean Magazine* and *Teen Voices*, the second of which carries an explicit statement of purpose on its masthead: "provides an intelligent alternative to glitzy, gossipy fashion-oriented publications that too often exploit the insecurities of their young audience."

But it was to the women's service magazines that I turned with the greatest interest, wondering how they had changed since the early 1960s, how they might be said to shape the domestic in midsummer 1998. The five leading magazines in this category are by now venerable periodicals: *Ladies' Home Journal, McCall's*, and *Good Housekeeping* have been in business for more than a century, and *Woman's Day* and *Family Circle* for more than sixty years. What is most immediately striking about these five today is how similar they are. All use a compact 10½-by-8-inch format, whereas some older magazines once measured as much as 14 by 11 inches; issues range in length between 138 and 180 pages, with *Family Circle* the shortest and *Good Housekeeping* the longest, and advertising occupies at least two-thirds of the page space. Newsstand prices range from $1.39 (*Family Circle*) to $2.49 (*Ladies' Home Journal*). All have sections on food, fashion, parenting, health, home decor, the family, and shopping for household goods. Articles about celebrities remain staples, as do hints on homemaking. The nuclear, middle-class family is still the norm, although foster and adopted children appear with some frequency, and *Good Housekeeping* features an article about three widowed fathers raising their children alone. All five not only offer advice but trumpet it on their covers: "Quick Fixes for Skin and Hair," "The No-Sweat Summer Diet," "10-minute Meals," "Easy-Living Backyard Projects," "45 Ways to Simplify Your Life."

Much, of course, has changed since the early 1960s. The editors in chief of all five magazines are women. And, although the magazines still focus most of their editorial content on home, family, and physical appearance, there are not-so-subtle suggestions that the woman who is cooking, planning the family Fourth of July celebration, and thinning her thighs is also holding down a nine-to-five job. *Woman's Day* offers "36 Great Ideas" for earning money at home, ranging from telecommuting to a catering business. *Good Housekeeping* presents its annual awards to women who hold government positions. *Ladies' Home Journal* offers advice on health insurance for the self-employed. The fact that everything must be accomplished quickly suggests that readers have little time to accomplish their homemaking chores; even the reading of the magazine should not take much time—articles are short, the style is clipped and breezy. Letters to the editor can be sent by E-mail, and each magazine invites visits to its Internet website. No canned condensed soups are used in the magazines' recipes; although shortcuts are still suggested, they are apt to be quick-cooking couscous or packaged shredded cabbage for cole slaw. The women pictured in the magazines—especially in advertisements—are sometimes over thirty, although this phenomenon is largely a function of the numerous ads for menopausal remedies and wrinkle-fighting creams for aging baby boomers. Nor are all women thin: *Ladies' Home Journal* offers a page of bathing suit styles for "plus-size" women.

Even more interesting, however, is what has not changed in the magazines over the past fifty years. Middle-class, heterosexual marriage remains the ideal. Not only is "Can This Marriage Be Saved?" still a feature of *Ladies' Home Journal* (now written by a woman but based on the files of a male "family therapist"), but the *Journal* expresses pride that it is the "most popular, most enduring magazine feature in the world" and offers, as in 1960, a book-length compilation of these articles. Apart from numerous indications that the woman of the late 1990s is very busy, her role in the home seems not to have changed since the 1950s: she remains the cook, the major parent, the household consumer. If she is an activist, it is largely on the community level. She does not mop her kitchen floor in her high heels anymore, but she still keeps it clean. Most surprising to me is the fact that she is still almost exclusively Caucasian. With the exception of a few Asian women in fashion layouts and a few African American women in advertisements—which serves to reinforce their status as helpers/servants—these magazines seem to be about and for white women, and the few exceptions, like the exceptions in the magazines of fifty years ago, somehow only underscore the concept of a culture that is not racially integrated. *McCall's* features the menu and recipes for a dinner party given by black restaurateur Barbara Smith at her home in Sag Harbor; photographs show a racially mixed and very upscale dinner party, as the location would suggest. The only black woman featured in *Woman's Day* is a community activist fighting crime in her marginal Philadelphia neighborhood. It seems likely that the very market segmentation that has produced magazines for African American and Latina women has, ironically, allowed these five magazines to continue to portray a world centered on the white, middle-class, suburban nuclear family.

In fact, if one were to seek the stereotypical temper of the 1950s in the late 1990s, these five magazines would serve the purpose quite well. Ignore the Internet references, the recipes using microwave ovens, and the glimpses of bare female flesh, and little has really changed. Cute dogs smile from the covers of *Woman's Day* and *Family Circle*. Everyone has a backyard in which to grill food and build window boxes. Children and their behavior and ailments are central to normal life, and marriage has certain problems that can be solved. The three oldest magazines invoke their own histories. *McCall's* places "since 1876" below its name on the cover, and a regular feature is "McCall's Recalls"—this month a replica of its July 1942 cover. *Ladies' Home Journal* announces that it is celebrating its 115th anniversary year. *Good Housekeeping* publishes an etiquette column by Peggy Post, the great-granddaughter-in-law of Emily Post, who wrote such a column for the magazine in the 1920s. *Family Circle* recalls the opening of the first Walt Disney theme park, Disneyland, in 1955, by featuring recipes from Disney World and continues the Disney theme by providing directions for making a Cinderella cake. If cultural historians have succeeded in establishing that postwar America's idealized domestic life was largely a fiction, it seems to be a fiction with remarkable continuing appeal.

Introduction

1. The magazine's original title was *Fruit, Garden and Home;* the current title was adopted in 1924. The January 1997 issue of *Better Homes and Gardens* (63–73) includes a brief retrospective of its first seventy-five years of publication.

Chapter 1

1. The *Delineator,* which began in the 1870s as a magazine devoted to fashion, was by the 1920s one of the five leading magazines for women, with a circulation of more than 2 million in the late 1920s and early 1930s. Theodore Dreiser served as its editor from 1907 to 1910, helping to attract some of America's finest fiction writers to its pages. *Pictorial Review* absorbed *Delineator* in 1937 (Peterson 165–66).

2. This complexity is underscored by the fact that *Good Housekeeping* published an article titled "I Say: Women Are *People* Too!" (September 1960) based on Friedan's research for *The Feminine Mystique* and that a prepublication excerpt from her book, titled "The Fraud of Femininity," appeared in *Ladies' Home Journal* (winter 1963). Further, "The Fourth Dimension," her study of women moving beyond the mystique to achieve more fulfilling lives, was excerpted in the *Journal* (June 1964). In short, the magazines did not shy away from publishing material that indicted the values that Friedan proposed they encouraged.

3. Meyerowitz here conflates the concepts of "popular" and "mass" culture, which Kammen is at pains to distinguish in *American Culture, American Tastes;* her point, however, would be relevant to either.

4. All text citations are to the 1989 Vintage edition rather than to the edition that Lhamon cites.

Chapter 2

1. One of the most committed visionaries to remark on the benefits of technology for the American housewife was Thomas A. Edison. In an interview published in the October 1912 issue of *Good Housekeeping,* Edison prophesied that electricity—particularly the vacuum cleaner—would utterly change the lives of women: "She will give less attention to the home, because the home will need less; she will be

rather a domestic engineer than a domestic laborer, with the greatest of all hand-maidens, electricity, at her service." While such remarks were not unlike the predictions made by others during the period, Edison surpassed his contemporaries—not to mention his own expertise—by suggesting that relief from such physical drudgery as sweeping floors would allow women to develop their brains, leading to physical changes that would make women more nearly equal to men: "The exercise of women's brains will build for them new fibers, new involutions, and new folds. . . . It is lack of those brain folds which has made her so illogical. Now, as they begin to come to her she will gain in logic." The benefit of women's improved brains, according to Edison, would not be their own fulfillment but rather would be the improvement of the race, as women gave birth to more intelligent children. The "Wizard of Menlo Park," as Edison was known, was fond of predicting the benefits of his inventions. In the February 1906 issue of *Woman's Home Companion*, the editors promised that Edison's article "The Scientific Solution of the Servant Girl Problem" would appear in a forthcoming issue. Edison would predict, according to the editors, that "all we'll have to do will be to press a button, and, lo and behold! the room will be swept, the dinner will be cooked and served, the table will be set or cleared, the dishes will be washed, and all without a hitch or a grumble."

2. Two other magazines established during this period did not survive into the 1940s. The *Delineator*, published by the Butterick pattern company, began in 1873 as a means of selling paper clothing patterns, but it soon became a general-purpose women's magazine with articles on parenting, home decor, personal appearance, and household management. At least two members of *Delineator*'s "home management" staff, Ann Batchelder and Grace L. Pennock, became staff members at *Ladies' Home Journal* following *Delineator*'s demise in 1937. *People's Home Journal*, published by F. M. Lupton in New York, began publication in 1886 and lasted until 1929. In the 1920s, the *Journal*'s slogan was "Devoted to the Best Traditions of the American Home," and in 1925 it claimed to have been "for forty years the home magazine of America." *Delineator* was particularly well known for the quality of the fiction it published, and *People's Home Journal* emphasized home design and decor.

3. For a penetrating analysis of women's fashion magazines at midcentury, see McCarthy.

4. Kerr also suggests that the anonymous marriage counselor is not simply the objective professional that his role would dictate. Toward the end of the piece he announces, "I have decided to take [Lolita] into my home as a ward" (71). Even if this gesture does not suggest a replication of Humbert's prurient interest in the young girl, it represents an intervention into the lives of his "clients."

5. Walker, *Very Serious*, esp. 95–99, 125–26, 154–56.

6. In the 1930s, two of America's foremost male humorous writers made women's fashion magazines the targets of their wit. In "Frou-Frou, or, The Future of Vertigo," published in the *New Yorker,* S. J. Perelman addressed what seems to him the absurdity of a regular feature in *Harper's Bazaar* titled "Why Don't You?" that suggested to readers that they do such things as "travel with a little raspberry-colored cashmere blanket to throw over yourself in hotels and trains" or "twist [a child's] pigtails around her ears like macaroons." This latter piece of advice sent Perelman to the magazine's masthead to look for the name of the Marquis de Sade. So compelling did Perelman find this feature that although he tried "tapering [himself] off on *Pictorial Review* and *Good Housekeeping,*" he found the *Bazaar* column "coiling around [him], its hot breath on [his] neck." E. B. White's 1934 book *Quo Vadimus* includes "Dusk in Fierce Pajamas," in which White recorded the fantasies induced by his reading of *Harper's Bazaar* and *Vogue.* The magazines caused him to contrast his own "unlovely" life to those presented in their pages, "in which every moment is a tiny pearl of good taste, and in which every acquaintance has the common decency to possess a good background." White imagined himself attending parties at extravagant homes, while in reality he was "down on [his] knees in front of an airbound radiator, trying to fix it by sticking pins in the vent."

7. Stein makes the further point that the mixture of "pleasure" and "instructive" visual images "trained the female viewer for the distinctive flow of messages delivered by the predominant cultural institution of the post-war era: television" (160).

8. This reputation for stodginess apparently developed in the early 1930s. The *Journal* during the 1920s featured striking cover art and lavishly illustrated articles and fiction by such authors as Zane Grey, Booth Tarkington, and Rose Wilder Lane. Fashion layouts emphasized the latest styles, and both home designs and advertisements for home decor and beauty products conveyed elegance and luxury.

9. George Horace Lorimer (1867–1937) served as editor of the *Saturday Evening Post* from 1899 until 1936, during which time he raised its circulation from 1,800 to 3,000,000.

10. The Goulds do not identify the product whose advertising they rejected, but a 1929 ad for Lysol disinfectant, which did appear in *Ladies' Home Journal,* promotes its use for "feminine hygiene," which suggests that Lysol was the product. The text of the ad uses language strikingly similar to advertisements for more recent feminine hygiene products: "True cleanliness comes only through attention to the little details of the toilette often neglected. Beautiful clothes and dainty cosmetics cannot simulate the charm of the woman who gives her body meticulous care."

11. Bok saw himself as an "executive" whose responsibility was to study "currents" and "movements" and then to select "those that were for the best interests of

the home." For "home," Bok claimed, was "something Edward Bok did understand.
. . . And at the home he aimed rather than at the woman in it" (168). Of course, by
"aiming" at the home, Bok focused on the site of most women's major responsibilities.

12. Although it is unclear how much the *Journal* series had to do with the change,
the maternal death rate had dropped considerably by 1941 (Gould and Gould 173).

13. *Essence*, the first mass-circulation magazine for African American women,
did not begin publication until 1970. *Ebony*, which started in 1944, was intended as
the black counterpart to such pictorial magazines as *Life* and *Look*.

Chapter 3

1. The WAVES (Women Accepted for Volunteer Emergency Service) was the
women's branch of the Navy, created in July 1942; the WAC (Women's Army Corps),
established in May 1943, differed from the WAVES in that its members were given
ranks, titles, and salaries equivalent to those of their male peers. More than 100,000
women had served in each of these organizations by war's end.

2. "If You Ask Me" was a popular feature in *Ladies' Home Journal* for most of the
1940s and in *McCall's* from 1949 until Roosevelt's death in 1962. By no means were
all of the questions readers addressed to her about political matters. In the July 1941
issue of the *Journal*, for example, she was asked to name six of her favorite contemporary authors (she listed Willa Cather, Elizabeth Goudge, David Grayson, Countee
Cullen, Harold Laski, and Archibald McLeish), whether she started her Christmas
shopping early (yes), whether she would rather be a nurse, a stenographer, or a
schoolteacher (teacher), and whether she expected ever to run for political office ("I
most certainly do not").

3. Buck (1892–1973), raised in China as the daughter of American missionaries,
won the Pulitzer Prize (for her novel *The Good Earth* [1931]) and the Nobel Prize
for Literature (1938). Thompson (1894–1961) wrote a monthly column for the *Journal* from 1937 until 1961. During the 1920s she was a foreign correspondent for the
Philadelphia Public Ledger and the *New York Evening Post*, and from 1936 to 1941
she wrote a column titled "On the Record" for the *New York Herald Tribune*.

4. See also Westbrook, "I Want a Girl." Here Westbrook proposes that the pinup
photographs of Hollywood actresses with which American servicemen decorated
their barracks, foxholes, and airplanes appealed less to sexual interests than to the
domestic lives back home that they fought to protect. By far the most popular image
was that of Betty Grable, who represented wives, girlfriends, and the virtues of dis-
cretion and common sense.

5. Bessie Wallis Warfield Simpson (1896–1986), an American divorcée, became Duchess of Windsor in 1937, when she married the former King Edward VIII of England, who had received the title Duke of Windsor when he abdicated the throne because of his love for Simpson.

6. The preface to the seventh edition of *The Boston Cooking School Cook Book* (1943) similarly refers to the war having shaped the edition. Noting that the new edition particularly emphasized vitamins, Wilma Lord Perkins noted that "a special impetus to this study has been given by the emphasis placed on it by national governments as part of the task of national defense" (n.p.).

7. In 1943 the FBI reported that arrests of juveniles for crimes had increased 17 percent over the previous year (Braverman 23).

8. Hoover (1895–1972) served as director of the Federal Bureau of Investigation from 1924 until his death. Wood (1875–1958) served as president of Stephens College in Columbia, Missouri, then a two-year college for women, from 1912 until 1947. Both Wood and Hoover were responding in part to the fact that the American armed services accepted women whose children were fourteen and older. Also, Hoover's emphasis on "decency" signaled the fact that one of the forms of "delinquency" about which he was concerned was teenage pregnancy. The editors' introduction provided an additional hint that such was the case, reporting that a recent "Companion Poll" showed that readers "endorsed by an overwhelming majority sex education in high schools as a weapon to combat juvenile delinquency."

9. Alsop was a physician at Barnard College of Columbia University, and McBride served as director of the Business and Professional Girls' Department of the central YWCA in Brooklyn, New York.

10. The fact remains that many employers were reluctant to hire black women, and following the war they were often the first female workers to lose their jobs.

11. Janeway (1913–) became well known in the 1970s as a feminist cultural analyst with her books *Man's World—Woman's Place* (1971), *Women: Their Changing Roles* (1973), and *Between Myth and Morning: Women Awakening* (1974). At the time that the Tillson profile was written, however, Janeway was a novelist.

12. Not all readers of women's magazines took kindly to the continual stream of advice about how to nurture the male ego. The author of a letter to the editor of *Redbook* in July 1945 observed that "almost every magazine I pick up has at least one article or paragraph concerning how to hold a man, how to attract a man, how to please a man, how to keep up his morale, and so on. . . . [P]lease won't some kindhearted man write some articles on how to hold a woman, how to please her and build up her morale?"

Chapter 4

1. As late as 1940, an article in *Ladies' Home Journal* described how a woman trained her two black live-in servants, but such references to household employees had become rare in women's magazines by that time. The article did not say where the family lived, but the practice of blacks serving as household help for white families persisted longest in the Deep South, where industrial jobs were scarce and a family of even modest means could afford at least a part-time servant.

2. Perhaps not coincidentally, the product advertisements that surround the text of the article offer just such assurances of quality. A full-page ad for Swift's Brookfield butter testifies that it is made of "sorted, graded cream" and shipped in "spotless Swift refrigerator cars." Northern bathroom tissue claims to use the kind of paper recommended by "health commissioners in 45 states" so that families can avoid the "menacing disorders" caused by inferior paper.

3. Concern about so-called race suicide was by no means new, although it had renewed force as impending war bolstered nationalism and highlighted ethnic identity. As early as 1906, Charlotte Perkins Gilman, writing in the February 1906 *Woman's Home Companion*, had attempted to debunk the concept, positing that "the maintenance and improvement of a civilized race depends far more on quality than on quantity." She distinguished human beings from other organisms: "Your best breeder is the microbe; the lowest organisms lay the most eggs. The higher the type, the more it develops individual effort as a means of maintenance, rather than an endless repetition of individual inadequacy. The gain of our race comes more from being intelligent than from being born; it is better to have six children who live, than to have twelve and lose six; and better to have one who lives nobly and serves society than six who merely do not die."

4. In 1956 *Better Homes and Gardens* published a series of articles designed to describe how American families lived at a series of income levels, beginning with $5,000 a year. Unlike the *Journal* series, *Better Homes* provided the families it profiled with fictitious names, but the articles were similar in their focus on family closeness and the material quality of everyday life. The couple living on $5,000 a year had dreamed of owning a home since their marriage in 1944, but the costs of raising five children prevented that dream from being realized; to those who might say the family had too many children, "Jack" responded that "each is a billion dollars worth of love." In contrast, the family living on $16,000 a year, featured two months later, was described as "realizing [their] dreams of the early postwar years," which the article defined as ownership of an "attractive and well equipped" ranch-style house and two children.

5. *McCall's* had undertaken a similar if more limited effort to display America's

ethnic diversity in the 1920s. A series of cover portraits drawn by Neysa McMein depicted "Types of American Beauty," including Spanish-American, Chinese-American, Italian-American, and Australian-American women.

6. The smiling chef image, named "Rastus" by the Cream of Wheat Company (later absorbed by Nabisco), was based on a 1925 photograph of a black waiter who was persuaded to pose for the camera for five dollars (Kern-Foxworth 45–46).

7. Such an advertisement could be seen as something of an improvement over those in the 1920s that proposed Aunt Jemima as an actual person, complete with a plantation-slavery past and a family. Whereas by the 1940s and 1950s she was more or less an emblem, an ad for Aunt Jemima pancake mix in the February 1925 *Ladies' Home Journal* spoke of her fame among plantation owners and reported that "long after her master's death, she finally consented to sell her recipe to the millers who now make Aunt Jemima Pancake Flour." Further, the *Journal* reader could "own" Jemima and her family by ordering rag dolls representing her; her husband, Uncle Mose; and their children, Wade and Diana.

8. Consumers' loyalty to particular brands of household products had been important to manufacturers for decades, but with the rise of the self-service market by midcentury, it became especially important for the makers of products purchased there. Recognition of this importance is embodied in advertisements such as the one in the July 1953 issue of *Ladies' Home Journal* paid for by the Brand Names Foundation, identified in the ad as "a non-profit educational foundation." The ad pictures a woman reaching for a jar on a market shelf, and the text maintains that the trusted brand name has taken the place of the salesclerk, encouraging the reader to "name your brand—and better your brand of living!"

9. While the vast majority of letters to the editors of women's magazines were, not surprisingly, written by women, male readers sometimes wrote to address issues of concern to them, and the subjects of their letters suggest stereotypical gender differences. Of the eighty-six letters printed in the May 1960 issue of *McCall's*, ten were written by men. Two of them remarked on the excerpts the magazine had published from the memoirs of Anthony Eden, who had served as Great Britain's prime minister in the mid-1950s, and three reacted with considerable anger to an article on the dangers of guns in the home. One writer, who identified himself as a member of the National Rifle Association, called the article "uninformed, stupid, idiotic and downright imbecile"; a second informed the editor that he had forbidden his wife to renew her subscription to *McCall's* or even bring a copy of the magazine home; and the third stated that he had burned the "dirty magazine."

10. Philip Wylie's book *Generation of Vipers* (1942) accused women of being too attentive to and protective of their children, rendering their sons, in particular, weak and passive.

Chapter 5

1. Such advice was not entirely new, although the *Good Housekeeping* story has distinct Cold War overtones that were not present when an editor of *McCall's* wrote in the October 1924 issue in praise of a housewife who used meal planning as an occasion for imaginary travel. In "And the Greatest of These Is Imagination," Sarah Field Splint stated that "a lively imagination is the homemaker's greatest blessing," and she quoted the imaginative "Frances" as saying, "Tea is never just tea to me. . . . It's China, and when I drink it I'm in the Orient, going lickety-split in a 'rickshaw through the narrow crooked streets of a city." Not only does Frances have the devotion of her husband and three children, but, Splint noted, "her age I know to be thirty-seven but she doesn't look a day over thirty."

2. The book titles, especially the first, seem to reflect the author's awareness of such recently published books as Ashley Montagu's *The Natural Superiority of Women*, which I will discuss below.

3. While cultural historians such as Ehrenreich and English tend to view such corporate affiliations as evidence that professional home economists sold out to commercial interests, Carolyn M. Goldstein argues that the relationship was far more complex, pointing to the fact that Mrs. Christine Frederick, whose *Selling Mrs. Consumer* has often been used as an example of the movement from education to exploitation, was neither a graduate of a college of home economics nor a member of the American Home Economics Association. Goldstein notes that Anna Burdick, of the Federal Bureau of Vocational Education, was dismayed by Frederick's book, saying, "I get quite wrought up over having women exploit their own kind. . . . Is Christine playing to the Gallery? Is she interested in Education or Exploitation?" (274–75). It is doubtful, of course, that the average reader of women's magazines had any awareness of such professional controversies, and the authority of the home economist made her an effective link between manufacturer and consumer.

4. Betty MacDonald was the pseudonym of Anne Elizabeth Campbell Bard (1908–1958), whose 1945 semiautobiographical best-seller *The Egg and I* depicted humorously the struggles of a young housewife on a chicken ranch in the Northwest.

5. Levenstein reports that as many as one-third of those rejected for military service on medical grounds suffered from conditions thought to be caused by poor nutrition, prompting the head of Selective Service to remark, "We are physically in a condition of which nationally we should be thoroughly ashamed" (65).

6. The advertisement that occupies the rest of the page on which Wylie's article appears addresses directly the anxieties of war. In large print at the top of the ad for Lysol disinfectant is the promise that the product offers "What to do—in air raids—in first aid—with incendiary bombs," if the reader equips herself with the

product's booklet "War-time Manual for Housewives." When the article and the ad are read together, the ad provides a context for Wylie's taking to task the woman who merely worries about what might befall her children.

7. *Journal* editor Gould recalled that Spock was among the magazine's more difficult regular contributors: "Handsome Benjamin Spock—the nation's pediatric daddy—as emotional as [Paul] de Kruif and even more intent on reforming the world, was forever deserting his little charges to say his intense say about civil rights, peace, and later Vietnam. We were constantly trying to herd him back to the nursery, where he was superb—though not always persuasive in other matters. Bleeding if a line of his copy was cut, always fearing editorial distortion of his tender ideas, he was as difficult to dandle on the editorial knee as a baby who needs to go to the bathroom instanter. But for mothers he had written 'The Bible.' It is, I believe, America's all-time best seller. We had been lucky to get him for the *Journal*. We spoon-fed him compliments, when he was not on the soapbox, and guarded him like Fort Knox" (Gould and Gould 297).

The editorial "spoon-feeding" must have succeeded, because in his autobiography Spock remembered the relationship with Gould differently. Recalling his support for presidential candidate Adlai Stevenson in 1956 because he felt Dwight Eisenhower was insincere in his statements of support for federal aid to education, Spock wrote, "I was writing a monthly column for the *Ladies' Home Journal* at the time, and I was so upset by [letters from women angry about his attitude toward Eisenhower] that I asked the editor, Mr. Gould, if it would be appropriate for me to explain this view some place in the *Ladies' Home Journal*. He was very amiable, as always, and said I could use the letters-to-the-editor column" (Spock and Morgan 159–60).

8. Distinctions between food for men and food for women persisted into the 1950s. An article in the July 1954 *Ladies' Home Journal*, for example, proposed separate menus for entertaining groups of men and women. Men were to have beef sandwiches, corn on the cob, apple pie, and coffee, while women were offered jellied chicken broth, shrimp, a green salad, ice cream in melon rings, and iced tea.

9. The American Meat Institute's advertising campaign had begun as a means of combating a drop in meat consumption during the 1930s, when, in addition to changing eating habits caused by the Depression, many Americans regarded meat as fattening and not particularly nutritious. When the federal government's Food and Nutrition Board established the Committee on Food Habits in 1941 to both study and attempt to improve American eating patterns, the committee (composed largely of social scientists) was chagrined to learn that such food industry advertising was far more effective in altering eating habits than were any government nutritional charts and guidelines (Levenstein 64–75).

10. The popularity of appliance-linked cookbooks began in the late 1920s with the availability of electric refrigerators; by 1937, more than 2 million American households had replaced their iceboxes, and twenty years later, 80 percent of homes had refrigerators. In 1927 General Electric published *Electric Refrigerator Recipes and Menus*, and in 1930 the Kelvinator Company issued *The Kelvinator Book of Recipes*. In *Fashionable Food*, Sylvia Lovegren notes that such books, combined with the magazines' enthusiasm for the new appliances, influenced menus by making it relatively easy for homemakers to prepare gelatine salads and frozen desserts. (9–13).

11. Competitive cookery found its way into magazine fiction as well, usually as an element in male-female relationships. Robert Zacks's story "Mama's Boy," in the October 1948 *Woman's Home Companion*, is a variation on the adage that the way to a man's heart is through his stomach. A twenty-four-year-old man living with his mother, an excellent cook, is reluctant to commit to marriage to his girlfriend until his mother, unknown to him, cooks a meal for the girlfriend to serve to him. The trick is discovered when Joe tastes the chicken stuffing and declares, "I'd know Mom's cooking anywhere." The reader was left to wonder how Joe's fiancée would compete with her mother-in-law's cooking. Another story from the January 1954 *Ladies' Home Journal* seems to refer directly to the Pillsbury Bake-Off. The heroine, who has won "an annual nationwide baking contest" with her enriched devil's food cake, is visited by the devil, who trades her a mink coat for a slice of the cake. But when the devil offers her husband anything he wants in exchange for her, the husband refuses, and at the end of the story the reader learns that the couple had met shortly after she baked a prizewinning angel food cake.

12. Smith also published *The Complete Book of Absolutely Perfect Baby and Child Care*, the title of which referred directly to Spock's *Common Sense Book of Baby and Child Care*.

Chapter 6

1. The full text of the poem reads as follows:

> In space, the lonely missile spins its way,
> Beyond the earth's soft-breathing atmosphere,
> Beyond the note of song, the wind's wild play,
> The cumulus, the rain's recurrent tear;
> Throughout the sky of orbits hung by One
> Who saw His handiwork and called it good,
> There moves this metal deed which man has done.
> I tremble in the name of Brotherhood.

For I remember how another night,
A new star pierced the heavens from above,
Not in the name of power or of might,
But in the name of His eternal love.
May satellite and star be reconciled
And bring us nearer to the waiting Child.

2. The number of women in the workforce who had school-age children increased from 26 percent in 1948 to 39 percent in 1960. At the same time, fewer than 7 percent of married women were childless in the 1950s, and the birthrate during the decade was the highest since 1910, an average of 3.5 children per mother (Gatlin 30, 61).

3. A study of coverage in mass-circulation magazines (including *Good Housekeeping* and *Ladies' Home Journal*) of women and paid employment shows that the number of such articles actually declined between 1950 and 1977 (Robinson). However, the study counted only articles dealing with issues such as salary equity, career preparation, and workplace discrimination, whereas equally telling are articles— some of them humorous or satiric—expressing confusion or dissatisfaction about traditional gender roles.

4. A close reading of McGinley's work calls her reputation as a defender of traditional women's roles into question. Her poem, "Occupation: Housewife," depicts a bored, unfulfilled middle-aged woman and concludes with the following lines:

She often says she might have been a painter
Or maybe writer, but she married young.
She diets. And with Contract she delays
The encroaching desolation of her days.

5. *Woman's Day* began publication in 1937, originating as a thirty-two-page magazine sold in A&P stores; Safeway launched *Family Circle* in 1932. By 1952 each magazine had more than two hundred pages per issue, and four other "supermarket magazines," some of them regional, had joined these two: *Everywoman's, Better Living, Western Family,* and *American Family.*

6. The other three—*Good Housekeeping, Ladies' Home Journal,* and *McCall's*— are going strong at the turn of the twenty-first century.

Bibliography

Abrahamson, David. *Magazine-Made America: The Cultural Transformation of the Postwar Periodical*. Crosshill, NJ: Hampton Press, 1996.

Agnew, Jean-Christophe. "Coming Up for Air: Consumer Culture in Historical Perspective." *Intellectual History Newsletter* 12 (1990): 3–21.

Alsop, Gulielma Fell, and Mary F. McBride. *Arms and the Girl: A Guide to Personal Adjustment in War Work and War Marriage*. New York: Vanguard, 1943.

———. *She's Off to Work: A Guide to Successful Earning and Living*. New York: Vanguard, 1941.

Anthony, Susan B., II. *Out of the Kitchen and Into the War: Women's Winning Role in the Nation's Drama*. New York: Stephen Daye, 1943.

Arfmann, Florence. *The Time Readers' Book of Recipes*. New York: Dutton, 1949.

Bailey, Beth L. *From Front Porch to Back Seat: Courtship in Twentieth-Century America*. Baltimore: Johns Hopkins University Press, 1988.

Baldwin, Faith. "Writing for the Women's Magazines." *The Writer's Book*. Ed. Helen Hull. New York: Harper and Brothers, 1950. 75–83.

Beard, Charles A., and Mary Ritter Beard. *The Rise of American Civilization*. Vol. 3 of *America in Midpassage*. New York: Macmillan, 1939.

Beauvoir, Simone de. *The Second Sex*. Trans. H. M. Parshley. 1952. New York: Vintage, 1989.

Beecher, Catharine. *Treatise on Domestic Economy for the Use of Young Ladies at Home and at School*. Rev. ed. New York: Harper's, 1868.

Beecher, Catharine, and Harriet Beecher Stowe. *The American Woman's Home; or, Principles of Domestic Science*. New York: Ford; Chicago: Stoddard, 1869.

Bentley, Amy. *Eating for Victory: Food Rationing and the Politics of Domesticity*. Urbana: University of Illinois Press, 1998.

Berch, Bettina. *The Endless Day: The Political Economy of Women and Work*. New York: Harcourt Brace Jovanovich, 1982.

The Betty Furness Westinghouse Cook Book. New York: Simon and Schuster, 1954.

Blood, Kathryn. *Negro Women War Workers*. Women's Bureau Bulletin 205. Washington, DC: U.S. Department of Labor, 1945.

Blum, John Morton. *V Was for Victory: Politics and American Culture during World War II*. New York: Harcourt Brace Jovanovich, 1976.

Bok, Edward. "The American Home, the Joyous Adventure." *American Home* January 1929: 287.

238   Bibliography

——. *The Americanization of Edward Bok: The Autobiography of a Dutch Boy Fifty Years After*. New York: Scribner's, 1923.

Bracken, Peg. *The I Hate to Cook Book*. New York: Harcourt, Brace, 1960.

Braverman, Jordan. *To Hasten the Homecoming: How Americans Fought World War II through the Media*. Lanham, MD: Madison Books, 1996.

Breines, Wini. *Young, White, and Miserable: Growing Up Female in the Fifties*. Boston: Beacon, 1992.

Bremner, Robert H., and Gary W. Reichard, eds. *Reshaping America: Society and Institutions, 1945–1960*. Columbus: Ohio State University Press, 1982.

Campbell, D'Ann. *Women at War with America: Private Lives in a Patriotic Era*. Cambridge: Harvard University Press, 1984.

Cancian, Francesca M., and Steven L. Gordon. "Changing Emotion Norms in Marriage: Love and Anger in U.S. Women's Magazines since 1900." *Gender and Society* 2 (1988): 308–42.

Carnegie, Mrs. Dale. *How to Help Your Husband Get Ahead*. New York: Greystone, 1953.

Carter, Paul A. *Another Part of the Fifties*. New York: Columbia University Press, 1983.

Chafe, William H. *The Paradox of Change: American Women in the Twentieth Century*. New York: Oxford University Press, 1991.

——. *The Unfinished Journey: America since World War II*. 2nd ed. New York: Oxford University Press, 1991.

Child, Lydia Maria. *The American Frugal Housewife*. Boston: Marsh and Capen, Carter and Hendee, 1829.

Cohn, David L. *Love in America: An Informal Study of Manners and Morals in American Marriage*. New York: Simon and Schuster, 1943.

Coontz, Stephanie. *The Way We Never Were: American Families and the Nostalgia Trap*. New York: Basic Books, 1992.

Cowan, Ruth Schwartz. "Two Washes in the Morning and a Bridge Party at Night: The American Housewife between the Wars." *Women's Studies* 3 (1976): 147–71.

Cravens, Hamilton. "The Case of the Manufactured Morons: Science and Social Policy in Two Eras, 1934–1966." *Technical Knowledge in American Culture: Science, Technology, and Medicine Since the Early 1800s*. Ed. Hamilton Cravens, Alan I. Marcus, and David H. Katzman. Tuscaloosa: University of Alabama Press, 1996. 151–68.

Damon-Moore, Helen. *Magazines for the Millions: Gender and Commerce in the* Ladies' Home Journal *and the* Saturday Evening Post, *1880–1910*. Albany: State University of New York Press, 1994.

DeLillo, Don. "Sputnik." *New Yorker* 8 September 1997: 76–78.

Diamond, Edwin. "The Unladylike Battle of the Women's Magazines." *New York* 20 May 1974: 43–46.

Dickstein, Morris. "Depression Culture: The Dream of Mobility." *Radical Revisions: Rereading 1930s Culture.* Ed. Bill Mullen and Sherry Linkon. Urbana: University of Illinois Press, 1996. 225–41.

Didion, Joan. "Marriage a la Mode." *National Review* 13 August 1960: 90–91.

Douglas, Susan J. *Where the Girls Are: Growing Up Female with the Mass Media.* New York: Random House, 1994.

Ehrenreich, Barbara, and Deirdre English. *For Her Own Good: 150 Years of the Experts' Advice to Women.* Garden City, NY: Doubleday, 1979.

Elder, Donald, ed. *The Good Housekeeping Treasury.* New York: Simon and Schuster, 1960.

Ferguson, Marjorie. *Forever Feminine: Women's Magazines and the Cult of Femininity.* London: Heinemann, 1983.

"Food-Store Magazines Hit the Big Time." *Business Week* 9 February 1952: 108, 110.

Fox, Bonnie J. "Selling the Mechanized Household: Seventy Years of Ads in *Ladies' Home Journal.*" *Gender and Society* 4 (1990): 25–40.

Franzwa, Helen H. "Pronatalism in Women's Magazine Fiction." *Pronatalism: The Myth of Mom and Apple Pie.* Ed. Ellen Peck and Judith Senderowitz. New York: Crowell, 1974. 68–77.

Frederick, Christine. *Selling Mrs. Consumer.* New York: Business Bourse, 1929.

Friedan, Betty. *The Feminine Mystique.* New York: Norton, 1963.

Garvey, Ellen Gruber. *The Adman in the Parlor: Magazines and the Gendering of Consumer Culture, 1880s to 1910s.* New York: Oxford University Press, 1996.

Gatlin, Rochelle. *American Women since 1945.* Jackson: University Press of Mississippi, 1987.

Gerstle, Gary. "The Working Class Goes to War." *The War in American Culture: Society and Consciousness during World War II.* Ed. Lewis A. Erenberg and Susan E. Hirsch. Chicago: University of Chicago Press, 1996. 105–27.

Goldstein, Carolyn M. "Part of the Package: Home Economics in the Consumer Products Industries." *Rethinking Home Economics: Women and the History of a Profession.* Ed. Sarah Stage and Virginia B. Vincenti. Ithaca: Cornell University Press, 1997. 271–96.

Goodwin, Doris Kearns. *No Ordinary Time: Franklin and Eleanor Roosevelt: The Home Front in World War II.* New York: Simon and Schuster, 1994.

Gould, Bruce, and Beatrice Blackmar Gould. *American Story.* New York: Harper and Row, 1968.

Graebner, William. *The Age of Doubt: American Thought and Culture in the 1940s.* Boston: Twayne, 1991.

Griffith, Ann. "The Magazines Women Read." *American Mercury* 68 (March 1949): 273–80.

Halsey, Margaret. *This Demi-Paradise: A Westchester Diary.* New York: Simon and Schuster, 1960.

Hartmann, Susan M. *The Home Front and Beyond: American Women in the 1940s.* Boston: Twayne, 1982.

———. "Prescriptions for Penelope: Literature on Women's Obligations to Returning World War II Veterans." *Women's Studies* 5 (1978): 223–39.

———. "Women's Employment and the Domestic Ideal in the Early Cold War Years." *Not June Cleaver: Women and Gender in Postwar America, 1945–1960.* Ed. Joanne Meyerowitz. Philadelphia: Temple University Press, 1994. 84–100.

Hess, John L., and Karen Hess. *The Taste of America.* 3rd ed. Columbia: University of South Carolina Press, 1989.

Hollingworth, Leta S. "Social Devices for Impelling Women to Bear and Raise Children." 1916. Reprinted in *Pronatalism: The Myth of Mom and Apple Pie.* Ed. Ellen Peck and Judith Senderowitz. New York: Crowell, 1974. 19–28.

Honey, Maureen. "Recruiting Women for War Work: OWI and the Magazine Industry during World War II." *Journal of American Culture* 3 (1980): 47–52.

Horowitz, Daniel. *Betty Friedan and the Making of* The Feminine Mystique: *The American Left, The Cold War, and Modern Feminism.* Amherst: University of Massachusetts Press, 1998.

———. "Rethinking Betty Friedan and *The Feminine Mystique:* Labor Union Radicalism and Feminism in Cold War America." *American Quarterly* 48 (March 1996): 1–42.

Hoy, Suellen. *Chasing Dirt: The American Pursuit of Cleanliness.* New York: Oxford University Press, 1995.

Humphreys, Nancy K. *American Women's Magazines: An Annotated Historical Guide.* New York: Garland, 1989.

Jackson, Kenneth T. *Crabgrass Frontier: The Suburbanization of the United States.* New York: Oxford University Press, 1985.

Jackson, Shirley. *Life among the Savages.* New York: Farrar, Straus, and Young, 1953.

Kammen, Michael. *American Culture, American Tastes: Social Change and the Twentieth Century.* New York: Knopf, 1999.

Kern-Foxworth, Marilyn. *Aunt Jemima, Uncle Ben, and Rastus: Blacks in Advertising Yesterday, Today, and Tomorrow.* Westport, CT: Greenwood, 1994.

Kerr, Jean. "Can This Romance Be Saved?" *Esquire* January 1960: 70.

———. *Please Don't Eat the Daisies.* Garden City, NY: Doubleday, 1957.

Kozol, Wendy. *Life's America: Family and Nation in Postwar Photojournalism.* Philadelphia: Temple University Press, 1994.

Laski, Marghanita. "What Every Woman Knows by Now." *Atlantic Monthly* May 1950: 90.

Lears, Jackson. *Fables of Abundance: A Cultural History of Advertising in America.* New York: Basic Books, 1994.

Leff, Mark H. "The Politics of Sacrifice on the American Home Front in World War II." *Journal of American History* 77: 1296–1318.

Levenstein, Harvey. *Paradox of Plenty: A Social History of Eating in Modern America.* New York: Oxford University Press, 1993.

Lhamon, W. T., Jr. *Deliberate Speed: The Origins of a Cultural Style in the American 1950s.* Washington, DC: Smithsonian Institution Press, 1998.

"Liberating Magazines." *Newsweek* 8 February 1971: 101–02.

Litoff, Judy Barrett, and David C. Smith, eds. *American Women in a World at War.* Wilmington, DE: Scholarly Resources, 1997.

Lovegren, Sylvia. *Fashionable Food: Seven Decades of Food Fads.* New York: Macmillan, 1995.

Lundberg, Ferdinand, and Marynia F. Farnham. *Modern Woman: The Lost Sex.* New York: Harper, 1947.

MacDonald, Betty. *The Egg and I.* Philadelphia: Lippincott, 1945.

Magid, Nora L. "The Heart, the Mind, the Pickled Okra: Women's Magazines in the Sixties." *North American Review* (Winter 1970): 20–29.

Marchand, Roland. *Advertising the American Dream: Making Way for Modernity, 1920–1940.* Berkeley: University of California Press, 1985.

———. "Visions of Classlessness, Quests for Dominion: American Popular Culture, 1945–1960." *Reshaping America: Society and Institutions, 1945–1960.* Ed. Robert H. Bremner and Gary W. Reichard. Columbus: Ohio State University Press, 1982. 163–90.

Marling, Karal Ann. *As Seen on TV: The Visual Culture of Everyday Life in the 1950s.* Cambridge: Harvard University Press, 1994.

Mathews, Glenna. *"Just a Housewife": The Rise and Fall of Domesticity in America.* New York: Oxford University Press, 1987.

Matthaei, Julie E. *An Economic History of Women in America: Women's Work, the Sexual Division of Labor, and the Development of Capitalism.* New York: Schocken, 1982.

May, Elaine Tyler. *Homeward Bound: American Families in the Cold War Era.* New York: Basic Books, 1988.

May, Lary, ed. *Recasting America: Culture and Politics in the Age of Cold War*. Chicago: University of Chicago Press, 1989.

Mayes, Herbert R. *The Magazine Maze: A Prejudiced Perspective*. Garden City, NY: Doubleday, 1980.

McCarthy, Mary. "Up the Ladder from *Charm* to *Vogue*." *Reporter* 18 July 1950: 36–40; 1 August 1950: 32–35.

McCracken, Ellen. *Decoding Women's Magazines: From* Mademoiselle *to* Ms. New York: St. Martin's, 1993.

McDowell, Margaret B. "The Children's Feature: A Guide to the Editors' Perceptions of Adult Readers of Women's Magazines." *Midwest Quarterly* 19 (1977): 36–50.

McGinley, Phyllis. *Stones from a Glass House*. New York: Viking, 1946.

Mendelson, Anne. *Stand Facing the Stove: The Story of the Women Who Gave America* The Joy of Cooking. New York: Henry Holt, 1996.

Merish, Lori. "Sentimental Consumption: Harriet Beecher Stowe and the Aesthetics of Middle-Class Ownership." *American Literary History* 8 (Spring 1996): 1–33.

Meyerowitz, Joanne, ed. *Not June Cleaver: Women and Gender in Postwar America, 1945–1960*. Philadelphia: Temple University Press, 1994.

Michel, Sonya. "American Women and the Discourse of the Democratic Family in World War II." *Behind the Lines: Gender and the Two World Wars*. Ed. Margaret Randolph Higgonet et al. New Haven: Yale University Press, 1987. 154–67.

Modell, John. *Into One's Own: From Youth to Adulthood in the United States, 1920–1975*. Berkeley: University of California Press, 1989.

Montagu, Ashley. *The Natural Superiority of Women*. Rev. ed. New York: Macmillan, 1974.

Munsey, Frank. "Advertising in Some of Its Phases." *Munsey's Magazine* October 1898–March 1899: 476–86.

Nabokov, Vladimir. *Lolita*. 1955. New York: Vintage, 1989.

Nadel, Alan. *Containment Culture: American Narratives, Postmodernism, and the Atomic Age*. Durham: Duke University Press, 1995.

Peck, Ellen. *The Baby Trap*. New York: Pinnacle Books, 1971.

Pepper, Beverly. *The Glamour Magazine after Five Cookbook*. Garden City, NY: Doubleday, 1952.

Perelman, S. J. "Frou-Frou, or, The Future of Vertigo." *The Most of S. J. Perelman*. New York: Simon and Schuster, 1958. 53–55.

Perkins, Wilma Lord. *The Boston Cooking School Cook Book*. 7th ed. Boston: Little, Brown, 1943.

Peterson, Theodore. *Magazines in the Twentieth Century.* Urbana: University of Illinois Press, 1964.

Popenoe, Paul. "Is There a Scarcity of Good Husbands?" *New York Times Magazine* 29 December 1935: 14.

Robinson, Gertrude Joch. "The Media and Social Change: Thirty Years of Magazine Coverage of Women and Work (1950–1977)." *Atlantis* 8 (Spring 1983): 87–111.

Rombauer, Irma S. *The Joy of Cooking: A Compilation of Reliable Recipes with an Occasional Culinary Chat.* Indianapolis: Bobbs-Merrill, 1943.

Rothman, Sheila M. *Woman's Proper Place: A History of Changing Ideals and Practices, 1870 to the Present.* New York: Basic Books, 1978.

Savan, Leslie. "The Trad Trade." *Village Voice,* 7 March 1989. Reprinted in *The Sponsored Life: Ads, TV, and American Culture.* Philadelphia: Temple University Press, 1994. 198–200.

Sayre, Nora. *Previous Convictions: A Journey through the 1950s.* New Brunswick: Rutgers University Press, 1995.

Scanlon, Jennifer. *Inarticulate Longings:* The Ladies Home Journal, *Gender, and the Promises of Consumer Culture.* New York: Routledge, 1995.

Schwartz, Ruth Cowan. *More Work for Mother: The Ironies of Household Technology from the Open Hearth to the Microwave.* New York: Basic Books, 1982.

Schweitzer, Gertrude. "The Women's Magazines Come of Age." *Writer* 64 (October 1951): 326.

Shapiro, Laura. *Perfection Salad: Women and Cooking at the Turn of the Century.* New York: Farrar, Straus, and Giroux, 1986.

Sibley, Sheila. "Accent on Love." *Writer* 68 (February 1955): 45.

Smith, Elinor Goulding. *The Complete Book of Absolutely Perfect Baby and Child Care.* New York: Harcourt, Brace, 1957.

——. *The Complete Book of Absolutely Perfect Housekeeping.* New York: Harcourt, Brace, 1956.

Spock, Benjamin. *The Common Sense Book of Baby and Child Care.* New York: Duell, Sloan and Pearce, 1946.

Spock, Benjamin, and Mary Morgan. *Spock on Spock: A Memoir of Growing Up with the Century.* New York: Pantheon, 1989.

Stein, Sally. "The Graphic Ordering of Desire: Modernization at a Middle-Class Women's Magazine, 1919–1939." *The Contest of Meaning: Critical Histories of Photography.* Ed. Richard Bolton. Cambridge: MIT Press, 1989. 146–61.

Steinberg, Salme Harja. *Reformer in the Marketplace: Edward W. Bok and the Ladies' Home Journal.* Baton Rouge: Louisiana State University Press, 1979.

Steinem, Gloria. "Sex, Lies, and Advertising." *Moving beyond Words*. New York: Simon and Schuster, 1994. 130–68.

Strasser, Susan. *Never Done: A History of American Housework*. New York: Pantheon, 1982.

———. *Satisfaction Guaranteed: The Making of the American Mass Market*. Washington, DC: Smithsonian Institution Press, 1989.

Taber, Gladys. *Stillmeadow Cook Book*. New York: Harper and Row, 1947.

Tebbel, John, and Mary Ellen Zuckerman. *The Magazine in America, 1741–1990*. New York: Oxford University Press, 1991.

Tobias, Sheila, and Lisa Anderson. "What Really Happened to Rosie the Riveter? Demobilization and the Female Labor Force, 1944–1947." *Women's America: Refocusing the Past*. Ed. Linda K. Kerber and Jane DeHart Mathews. New York: Oxford University Press, 1982. 354–73.

Tuttle, William M., Jr. *"Daddy's Gone to War": The Second World War in the Lives of America's Children*. New York: Oxford University Press, 1993.

Valverde, Mariana. "The Class Struggles of the Cosmo Girl and the Ms. Woman." *Heresies* 5 (1985): 78–82.

van Zuilen, A. J. *The Life Cycle of Magazines: A Historical Study of the Decline and Fall of the General Interest Mass Audience Magazine in the United States during the Period 1946–1972*. Uithoorn, the Netherlands: Graduate Press, 1977.

Walker, Nancy A. "Humor and Gender Roles: The 'Funny' Feminism of the Post–World War II Suburbs." *American Quarterly* 37 (1985): 98–113.

———. *A Very Serious Thing: Women's Humor and American Culture*. Minneapolis: University of Minnesota Press, 1988.

———, ed. *Women's Magazines 1940–1960: Gender Roles and the Popular Press*. Boston: Bedford, 1998.

Westbrook, Robert B. "Fighting for the American Family: Private Interests and Political Obligation in World War II." *The Power of Culture: Critical Essays in American History*. Ed. Richard Wightman Fox and T. J. Jackson Lears. Chicago: University of Chicago Press, 1993. 195–221.

———. "'I Want a Girl, Just Like the Girl That Married Harry James': American Women and the Problem of Political Obligation in World War II." *American Quarterly* 42 (1990): 587–614.

Whitaker, Craig. *Architecture and the American Dream*. New York: Potter, 1996.

White, E. B. "Dusk in Fierce Pajamas." *A Subtreasury of American Humor*. Ed. E. B. White and Katharine S. White. New York: Random House, 1941. 271–74.

Wilkinson, Virginia Snow. "From Housewife to Shipfitter." *The World War Two Era:*

Perspectives on All Fronts from Harper's Magazine. Ed. Katharine Whittemore. New York: Franklin Square Press, 1994. 141–48.

Williams, Ivor. "The Pious Pornographers." *Playboy* October 1957: 25–26, 62–64, 70–74.

Wolseley, Roland E. *The Magazine World: An Introduction to Magazine Journalism.* New York: Prentice-Hall, 1951.

Wylie, Philip. *Generation of Vipers.* New York: Rinehart, 1942.

Zuckerman, Mary Ellen. *Sources on the History of Women's Magazines, 1792–1960: An Annotated Bibliography.* New York: Greenwood, 1991.